Car Hacks and Mods
For Dummies®

D1027065

Standalone ECU Features

	Apexi Power FC	Autronic SMC/SM2	AEM EMS	Electromotive TEC1/TEC2	EMS Dual Sport I	Haltech E6H/E6K/ E6M/E6H	Hawk EC21	Link Plug-In/ Wire-In	Motec M4 Clubman, Motec M48 Clubman	Motec M4 Pro, Motec M48 Pro, Motec M8 Pro	Motec M800	Wolf 3D v3.0
Plug-and-play setup	Yes	No	Yes	No	No	No	No	Yes and No	No	No	No	No
CPU	NEC 78P334 @ 16 MHz	Intel 16-bit @ 16 MHz	Motorola 16/32 bit hybrid	Motorola 16-bit	Motorola 16-bit	Motorola 68HC11E2 @ 8 MHz (E6S); 68HC11K4 @ 16 MHz (others)	8 MHz	Unknown	Motorola 32-bit @ 33 MHz	Motorola 32-bit @ 33 MHz	Motorola 32-bit @ 66 MHz (not confirmed)	16 MHz
Max Cylinders	6	16	10	12	16	12	128	6 (plug-in); 12 (plug-in)	12	12	12	12
Fuel Maps	20	32			26	17 or 22	128	8	40	40	40	16
Ignition Maps	20	32			26	17 or 22	128	8	40	40	40	16
Load Points per Map	20	16			3 + 16 Curve Modifiers	32	16	16	21	21	21	8
Total Fuel Points	400	512			78 (excluding curve modifiers)	544 or 704	2048	128	840	840	840	128
Total Ignition Points	400	512			78 (excluding curve modifiers)	544 or 704	2048	128	840	840	840	128
Injector Outputs	6	8	10		8	4 or 8 (E6S); 8 (others)	2	6 (plug-in); 8 (plug-in)	4 (M4 Clubman); 8 (M48 Clubman)	4 (M4 & M8 Pro); 8 (M48 Pro)	8 (unused outputs can be used as general purpose)	4
Ignition Outputs	6	4	16 general outputs		4	4	4	4	4 (M4 Clubman); 2 (M48 Clubman)	4 (M4 & M8 Pro); 2 (M48 Pro)	6 (unused outputs can be used as general purpose)	4

(continued)

Car Hacks and Mods For Dummies®

Cheat Sheet

Standalone ECU Features (continued)

	Apexi Power FC	Autronic SMC/SM2	AEM EMS	Electromotive TEC1/TEC2	EMS Dual Sport I	Haltech E6K/E6M/E6H	Hawk EC21	Link Plug-In/Wire-In	Motec M4 Clubman, Motec M48 Clubman	Motec M4 Pro, Motec M48 Pro, Motec M8 Pro	Motec M800	Wolf 3D v3.0
Auxiliary Inputs	0	1 (SMC); 3 (SM2)	7		1	2	0	2 (wire-in only)	2	2	4	Unknown
Auxiliary Outputs	0	Up to 5 (SMC); 9 (SM2)	16		4	6 (E6K); 2 (others)	2	4 (wire-in only)	Max 3 (depending on number of cylinders)	Max 3 (depending on number of cylinders)	8	2
O2 Sensor	Yes (OEM)	Yes (wideband in SMC)	Optional (wideband)	Yes	Optional (wideband)	Yes (wideband)	Yes	Yes (wideband with wire-in)	Yes (narrowband)	Yes (wideband)	Yes (dual wideband)	Yes (narrow-band)
Closed Loop Operation	Yes	Yes	Yes	Yes	No	Yes	Yes	Yes	Yes	Yes	Yes	No
Datalogging	No	Yes	Yes		Yes (to laptop)	Yes	No	Optional	Optional	Yes	Yes	Optional
Boost Control	Yes Z (optional)	Yes	Yes		Yes	Yes	No	Yes	Yes	Yes	Yes	Yes
Traction/Launch Control	No	SM2 only	Yes (launch)		No	Yes	No	No	Optional	Optional (M4 Pro & M48 Pro); Yes (M8 Pro)	Yes	No
Nitrous Management	No	SM2 only	Yes		Yes	Yes	No	No	Yes	Yes	Yes	No
VTEC Control	No	Indirect (RPM/load operated output)			Yes	Yes	No	Wire-in only	Indirect (RPM operated output)	Indirect (RPM operated output)	Indirect (RPM operated output)	No
Anti-Lag	No	Yes	Yes		Yes	Yes	No	No	No	Yes	Yes	No
Flat-Shift	No	Yes	Yes		No	E6K/E6H/E6M only	No	No	No	Yes	Yes	Yes
PC Programming	Yes (DOS)	Yes (Windows)	Yes (Windows)	Yes	Yes (Windows)	Yes (DOS)	Yes (DOS)	Minimal: Download maps via comms program	Yes (DOS)	Yes (DOS)	Yes (DOS)	Yes (Windows)
Handset Programming	Requires optional controller	No			Yes; Included	No	No	No	No	No	No	No

Copyright © 2004 Wiley Publishing, Inc.
All rights reserved.
Item 7142-7.
For more information about Wiley Publishing, call 1-800-762-2974.

For Dummies: Bestselling Book Series for Beginners

Car Hacks & Mods

FOR

DUMMIES®

Car Hacks & Mods FOR DUMMIES®

by David Vespremi

Wiley Publishing, Inc.

Car Hacks & Mods For Dummies®

Published by
Wiley Publishing, Inc.
111 River Street
Hoboken, NJ 07030-5774

Published by Wiley Publishing, Inc., Indianapolis, Indiana

Published simultaneously in Canada

WILEY

About the Author

David Vespremi is an automotive expert and has appeared on national television programs and automotive print media for his unique insights into cutting edge import car technology.

An attorney by trade, David has spent the past few years living and breathing car modifications, and working closely with top engineers and tuners in the hub of California's import car scene. A track driving instructor with various car clubs at Thunderhill Raceway in Northern California, David enjoys modding and driving his JDM Toyota MR2 Turbo (featured numerous times in *Sport Compact Car* magazine) and (having grown up on his share of Volkswagen Golfs, Jettas and GTIs) has recently acquired an E30 BMW that he has been tinkering with to get back in touch with his Euro roots.

David lives in Menlo Park, California, with his wife Hadley.

For more on *Car Hacks & Mods For Dummies*, visit www.carhacks andmods.com. David can be reached at author@carhacksand mods.com.

Dedication

I would like to dedicate this book to my parents, for their unequivocal and boundless support of my enthusiasm for all things car related, even if none of us have any idea how I became so fascinated with cars. I would also like to thank my wife Hadley, for being patient and devoted through the course of this book. There is, however, one person that captures the spirit of this book, and that is my sister Sarah, a critical co-editor and contributor to this project. Couldn't have done it without you — thanks to the best sister ever!

Author's Acknowledgments

There are books dealing with cars, various aspects of their upkeep and ownership, and then there are car books. This project, which represents a comprehensive and current reference, for touching on nearly all performance aspects of late model cars, required a fair bit of technical expertise and guidance. The list of those that helped along the way is far too long to recount here, but a few contributors to this project merit special acknowledgement:

Sarah Vespremi. No single person has spent more painstaking hours on this project than Sarah, and if she didn't know every last technical nuance of automotive performance going into this project, she does now. Really. Ask her anything.

Terry Heick. Terry has been a wealth of information, not to mention character/flavor in writing this book. He truly deserves special recognition for his role.

Yoshi Deherrera. I have Yoshi to thank for his expert guidance, for being a good friend, and for his vision of this book as a viable project.

Pete Kang, Tyler Orr, Bryan Moore, Eric Hsu, Mike Kojima, Bill Davis, Troy Truglio, Eric Lapka, Richard Lamb, and all of the other tech gurus that helped contribute their wisdom and guidance over the years.

Cover photography by Stephen Westhafer.

Finally, I would like to thank Melody Layne, Pat O'Brien, and Jason Marcusson at Wiley for believing in this project from the very beginning and ensuring that it is a success.

Publisher's Acknowledgments

We're proud of this book; please send us your comments through our online registration form located at www.dummies.com/register/.

Some of the people who helped bring this book to market include the following:

Acquisitions, Editorial, and Media Development

Project Editor: Pat O'Brien

Acquisitions Editor: Melody Layne

Copy Editor: Jean Rogers

Technical Editor: Per Schroeder

Editorial Manager: Kevin Kirschner

Media Development Supervisor: Richard Graves

Editorial Assistant: Amanda Foxworth

Cartoons: Rich Tennant (www.the5thwave.com)

Production

Project Coordinator: Nancee Reeves

Layout and Graphics: Karl Brandt, Andrea Dahl, Denny Hager, Joyce Haughey, Michael Kruzil, Shelley Norris, Barry Offringa, Heather Ryan, Rashell Smith

Proofreaders: David Faust, John Greenough, Brian H. Walls, TECHBOOKS Production Services

Indexer: TECHBOOKS Production Services

Publishing and Editorial for Technology Dummies

  Richard Swadley, Vice President and Executive Group Publisher

  Andy Cummings, Vice President and Publisher

  Mary Bednarek, Executive Acquisitions Director

  Mary C. Corder, Editorial Director

Publishing for Consumer Dummies

  Diane Graves Steele, Vice President and Publisher

  Joyce Pepple, Acquisitions Director

Composition Services

  Gerry Fahey, Vice President of Production Services

  Debbie Stailey, Director of Composition Services

Contents at a Glance

Table of Contents

Foreword

Cars are literally the vehicles by which we see the world, and by which the world sees us. Second in value only to the homes in which we live, cars are the reflection of who we are when we are in transit — out in the world commuting to work or having fun on the weekend. They are also the closet bond most people ever form with a machine. We think a movement, and the car translates that thought, that impulse, into action. The car becomes an extension of ourselves.

Few things are as often mutually desired and accessible as an automobile. With that possession comes opportunity, as some folks see it, to do something different. Something cool. As cars become more and more alike with each passing model year, the drive for owners to individualize them grows increasingly stronger. We want to feel something towards our cars — and anonymity isn't conducive to generating powerful emotions.

For some, that means making horsepower, or building the ultimate handling machine, while others opt for cosmetic upgrades. An ambitious few genuinely attempt all improvements in all areas. If every car is a blank canvas, there are a lot of blank canvases out there and a lot of visionaries that will commit some degree of their time, money and energy into expressing themselves through that canvas.

There is also a multi-billion dollar aftermarket literally overflowing with parts and accessories that provide the pallet for working the canvas. But getting results that improve upon what you have rather than detract from it is no easy endeavor. It is with these costly pitfalls — and glorious potential — in mind that this book was born.

Though outright performance can be objectively measured, verified and quantified, the overall success of a project cannot. Money is often wasted on ill-conceived or poorly executed modifications. So many cars are impressive on paper, but in application are underwhelming. Still others are so one-dimensional that their owners are left disillusioned after the novelty of their one-trick pony wears off (and therein lies the rub: a focused "one-trick pony" is often the perfect, uncompromised project — although few people are content with a car that only does one thing well). Planning and honest appraisal then is key — and that planning cannot come without knowledge, perspective, and the resources this book provides.

This book will not go into detail discussing compressor maps, valve overlap, or rod ratios on stroker engines. There is plenty of room left for further research. Rather, it is intended as a general guide for the novice and tuning veteran alike — the entire industry, as we could fit it, in a nutshell. This is the reference guide that we, the "experts," wish we had when we started, and the book that the headstrong don't think they need today — but will someday when their intentions don't necessarily match their results. Some things are eternal.

Drive safely, and happy modding!

Terrell E. Heick III

Editor-in-Chief, FreshAlloy.com

Automotive Freelance Writer

Introduction

*W*elcome to *Car Hacks & Mods For Dummies!* This book covers
everything you need to increase the performance of your car for
faster acceleration, shorter stopping, improved handling, and increased
overall performance. It's my pleasure to introduce you to the world of car
hacks and mods — an important part of my life for the past 15 years and
one in which I have been immersed nearly every waking hour of every day.

The hacks and modifications that you can make to your car range from
accessible and inexpensive to as technically demanding and costly as you
want. It's very easy to find ways to improve the car you drive. Most people
(Americans especially) spend so much time in their cars that these improvements can often be profoundly rewarding.

Even if this book is your first conscious exploration of how to go about
improving the appearance or performance of your car, you've probably
thought about what you would have done differently had you participated
in the design and engineering meetings when your car was created. This
book frames those thoughts and guides you through implementing the
changes that you want to make to your car.

This book identifies areas of car dynamics and performance that you might not
have realized were issues until after you had the opportunity to understand the
how's, why's, and what's of the way car enthusiasts go about tuning and tweak-
ing their cars (for example, making a humble economy sedan perform more like
a high-performance sports car, and making a sports car perform at a whole new
level). This book also provides useful modification tips that allow car owners to
begin exploring popular weekend automotive performance pastimes, including
autocross, drag racing, road course driving, drifting, and rally racing — many
of which can help make you a safer and more confident driver on the road.

Modifying cars for higher performance is a multibillion-dollar industry in the
United States. Upgrades are available for most late model cars and SUVs that
fit any budget and any set of requirements. Americans spend more time behind
the wheels of their cars than any other nationality. To most Americans, their
automobiles are their costliest and most valued possessions, second only to
their homes.

As cars become more sophisticated, more reliable, and better built, drivers
become more attached to them. During the week, people rely on their cars
for safe transportation to and from work, for running errands, for taking the
kids to soccer practice, and so on. On the weekends, drivers take their cars
out for the joy of driving or for a fun-filled getaway from their workaday lives.

So cars become an extension of their drivers. Discretionary spending on cars is at an all-time high. Americans are keeping cars longer while finding new ways to fall in love all over again with the cars they already own.

Sprucing up a car you already own is a terrific way to give an existing car a second lease on life and make a new car purchase (and the depreciation that accompanies it) much less attractive. Or perhaps you want your new car to be a little bit better or different from any other car in your neighborhood. Still another reason to modify your car is because you have a particular area or areas of your car that you want to improve so your car will be perfect.

Whether you want a little more power for merging on the freeway on-ramp every morning, or you want less slipping and squealing around the corners on your favorite twisty road, this book helps you make your car everything you want and more.

As you read this book, you'll pick up some useful technical insights along the way, and you'll have a terrific time finding out how to make your car better suit your driving style and your personal flair.

About This Book

Many of the concepts that I discuss in this book are related and naturally flow together. Reading about one particular modification path may encourage you to read further about other areas of modification. This book is nonetheless a reference manual designed to guide you to useful information on specific areas of car modification. Feel free to skip ahead and jump around from chapter to chapter. There's no test at the end of this book, so have fun with it!

Although many of the concepts discussed in this book apply to most cars, this book most directly speaks to the owner of a late model "sport compact" car such as a Honda Civic or a Ford Focus. But this book is also useful if you own a truck or SUV. Although the manufacturers used to illustrate performance products may differ, the core technology and engineering concepts apply universally.

How This Book Is Organized

This book is divided into nine parts, each part containing chapters that address a different aspect of modifying your car. The areas include appearance, acceleration, braking, handling, safety, and diagnostics. While this book is not intended to be an instruction manual, I do indicate the relative ease or difficulty of installation for many of the products discussed in each of these areas.

Part 1: Owning a Performance Car

The term *performance car* is not as literal as it sounds, and it can mean many things. While you might be tempted to scoff at the little economy car with pretensions of being a performance car, innovations in the performance aftermarket industry allow this benign platform to match conventional performance cars. Even the owner of a Ferrari F40, a benchmark if ever there was one, may have modified it for even better performance than a stock F40.

But there's no free lunch. Performance often goes hand-in-hand with compromise. This can mean the expense and time needed to purchase and install the shiny new go-fast part, or the compromise can be that improving one aspect of a car's performance means that another aspect has to suffer. For example, the suspension part that allows the car to corner faster and more confidently may also make the ride rougher. Likewise, an exhaust system that looks and sounds great on a car, and maybe even adds some power, might become obnoxious on longer trips or draw the unwanted attention of local police.

Owning a performance car may mean different things to different types of drivers. This part of the book explores what it is that drivers are really after when they choose to modify their cars, how they set realistic expectations, and how to know whether they will be happy with the finished modification.

Part 11: Safety

You shouldn't be surprised that safety comes first. Though it's tempting to dive headlong into the horsepower modifications, it's essential to increase the car's safety as its performance increases.

This part covers the safety upgrades to help ensure that, as the car becomes leaner, meaner, and a whole lot faster, driver and passenger safety is part of the plan. This part places equal emphasis on active safety upgrades, such as handling, and passive safety modifications, such as roll bars.

Part 111: Rims and Rubber

Changing the wheels and tires is one of the first upgrades most people make to their otherwise stock cars. Wheels can make or break the look of a car. Wheel and tire selection also has a profound impact on a car's performance. Considerations such as rotating and unsprung mass, as well as grip and breakaway characteristics, all come into play with rims and rubber.

Part IV: Stylin'

This section emphasizes what ensures that your car looks its best. Read this part before you order a full set of underbody neons or a monster aluminum wing that could double as a park bench. Fashion is fickle in the car world. A sense of what is appropriate when improving a car's looks and aerodynamics can keep you off the Web sites that mock poorly executed automotive dress-up attempts. (The Honda with a plywood body kit holds a special place in my heart.) This part also covers detailing to keep your car looking its best whether it is your daily driver or weekend cruiser.

Part V: Slowing Down

An often-quoted racing adage is that you have to go slow to go fast. This part discusses the importance of being able to safely, quickly, and predictably scrub off speed, whether on the track or on the freeway. Races are won and lost in the braking zones, and beautiful cars are crumpled and lives lost for lack of attention to brakes. Brakes are actually equal parts performance modification and active safety. The moral of this part: Never add power to your car without thinking about the implications to stopping ability.

Part VI: Corner Carver

Some modifiers live for the corners. This part guides you through making your car handle with the best. Cornering is where a Subaru WRX station wagon can be set up to pass a Porsche 911 on a twisty road. In motor sports, corners are the great equalizers. Whether you have 900 horsepower under the hood or 90, balancing the car and taking corners at speed is where the gods of G-forces and adhesion don't play favorites. This section covers everything from simple spring and shock upgrades to full racing coilover suspensions and corner balancing.

Part VII: Let's Go!

Absolute power corrupts absolutely. The most sought-after goal of automotive performance is extra power with minimum hassle and expense. Whether you want to eke out a few extra horsepower or triple your car's original output, this part walks you through the fundamentals of adding power.

Part VIII: Faster Thinking

This part goes straight to your car's brain, the ECU (Engine Control Unit). You can optimize your car's engine performance, fuel mileage, and even emissions by hacking your car's computer with electronic controllers, standalone engine management systems, and remaps. As cars depend more on ECUs to control nearly all aspects of performance, extracting additional performance from your car often becomes less about what you have under your hood and more about what is going on in your car's brain.

Part IX: The Part of Tens

Whether it's online resources you're after, or you simply want to avoid common mistakes, the Part of Tens is here to help. In this part, I show you were to find resources to debunk common myths about modifying cars, as well as areas to consider in your car hacking and modding adventures.

Icons Used in This Book

This icon points you to useful tips and insights to keep you on the right track when hacking or modding your car.

This icon is often used to explain technical concepts or provide background on the how's or why's behind the modification being discussed. This icon is excellent for those wanting to understand a bit more in depth the functional or engineering context around which a modification is being presented.

Car hacking and modding can have dire consequences if done incorrectly. This warning icon helps steer you away from common pitfalls, blunders, and misconceptions.

These icons identify key information that you should keep at the top of your brain.

Part I

Owning a Performance Car

"Somebody order a birthday cake in the shape of an aluminum VTEC engine block?"

In this part . . .

In this part, I explain the warranty and legal issues involved in modifying your car. This part also guides you through the considerations you need to make to decide whether modifying your car will get you the results that you're after.

Chapter 1

Cool Car Basics

- -

In This Chapter

▶ Keeping mods legal

▶ Keeping the warranty intact

▶ Setting realistic expectations

▶ Making your car cool

▶ Planning it smart

- -

*B*y virtue of holding this book in your hands, it is clear that the concept of improving a car's performance intrigues you. Perhaps a friend planted the idea of doing a little something to your car to make it look and/or perform better, and ever since, the idea has bounced around in your head from time to time. Perhaps your car is starting to feel a little worn and tired compared to the newer models you're seeing on the road or in your neighbor's driveway, and you're wondering whether it's worth the time and expense to try to improve upon what you already have. Of course, it could just be that you have noticed a lot more souped-up imports on the road and wonder why the whole country seems to have gone crazy over *The Fast and the Furious*.

Regardless of what brought you to this particular subject, this chapter will guide you through the core issues at the heart of car modification and allow you to plan ahead so that you will know what to expect going in — the good, the bad, and the ugly — and improve the odds that you'll be satisfied with the changes you make to your car.

Keeping It Legal and Keeping the Warranty Intact

Two pervasive myths of hacking or modding your car are that

✔ Modifying your car automatically cancels your warranty.

✔ Modifying your car is illegal.

Just as these blanket statements cannot be relied on as gospel — after all, changing the windshield wiper blades can't cause the transmission to break — neither can you assume that both the law and your warranty allow you to do whatever you want to your car.

The purpose of this section is not to provide a legal dissertation, but to offer an introduction to the regulatory bodies and commercial entities that have an interest in what you do to make your car different from the way it was when you drove it back from the dealership with that new-car smell still wafting through the cabin.

Federal regulations

Broadly speaking, two regulatory agencies oversee the automotive industry on a federal level:

- ✔ EPA (Environmental Protection Agency)
- ✔ DOT (Department of Transportation)

The regulatory power of the EPA and DOT is primarily concerned with setting and enforcing the regulations dealing with the type of safety and emission equipment that need to be present in cars in order for them to be sold in the United States. If you are the CEO of an automobile manufacturer or parts supplier, plan on looking closely at the guidelines set by these agencies.

As a private consumer, with few exceptions (like federal prohibitions against running leaded race gas on public roadways), you are unlikely to have direct contact with the federal government.

There is one instance in which the federal government takes a very active interest in your private vehicle, and this is where individuals either themselves, or through a broker, bring gray market cars into the U.S. for road use. A *gray market* car may be a model that was never officially sold in the U.S., but has become desirable enough to compel people to either skirt the law in order to bring them in, or to go through an expensive and time-consuming certification process involving crash testing and retrofitting emissions and safety equipment. The Porsche 959 and Nissan Skyline GT-R are examples of cars that were both so coveted by enthusiasts that companies and individuals certified some of these for legitimate gray market use. Other cars that have been available as variants outside of the U.S. (for example, high-spec and special performance editions) needed changes made to their equipment, such as glass, bumpers, turn signals, lighting, emissions equipment, and safety equipment, in order to be brought up to the same standards as their U.S. counterparts. If you are interested in either importing a gray market car or purchasing one that has already been brought in as a gray market import, have an attorney check to ensure that everything that needs to have been addressed to make the car legal for road use has been covered, including the accuracy of any and all documents submitted to both state and federal regulatory bodies. Fraud and perjury are serious crimes, and people have ended up with stiff fines and even jail time (and the cars were crushed) for gray market car deals gone bad.

Local regulations

As an individual, you are most likely to be concerned with regulatory agencies at the state and local level. While the federal government has many vehicle standards, when the car is on the road, the regulations are enforced almost exclusively by state or local government. Drivers in the U.S. encounter state-level involvement of vehicle registrations and/or safety inspections. Each state sets its own standards on how closely, and how often, they will scrutinize a car before issuing a license plate for the car or reviewing the vehicle's registration. These regulations may be enforced differently depending on which county your car is registered in within the state. In California, for example, some counties require emissions testing every two years, while others require only that the vehicle pass emissions when it is first registered and do not require further testing, unless the car has been cited by law enforcement as a suspected polluter.

State regulatory agencies

Before embarking on your modification regimen, it can be helpful to familiarize yourself with your local vehicle code. As the old saying goes, forewarned is forearmed.

Motor vehicle code

The state regulatory agencies generally set forth their requirements in the motor vehicle code for each state. Many people are familiar with the VC initials followed by a series of numbers on the ticket for a traffic citation (for example, exceeding the posted speed limit). The same book of codes that dictates how fast you may drive on the highways of your state, or whether you can make a right turn against a red light, also lists requirements that vehicles must meet within that state's jurisdiction. This includes everything from how low or high your car may sit, how loud the exhaust may be, to what type of lighting is or isn't acceptable. Because driving on public roadways is "a privilege, not a right," these are the concessions that you as a driver must agree to abide by in order to exercise your privilege to use your car on public roadways.

Before beginning any modifications to your car, including those seemingly noble and uncontroversial modifications designed to improve its safety, acquaint yourself with the vehicle code regulations in your state:

✔ Your local Department of Motor Vehicles (DMV) or Bureau of Motor Vehicles (BMV) can steer you toward listings of applicable codes.

✔ Many public libraries keep current vehicle codes on file.

Private roads (including the local racetrack and drag strip) are generally exempt from vehicle code regulations. These regulations are not in force at those venues.

Because vehicle code regulations vary greatly from state to state, this book does not assume that the particular modifications it describes are legal in your jurisdiction. When in doubt about the legality of the modifications you are considering (this includes the fuzzy dice hanging from your mirror — seriously), check your local vehicle code. Also note that assurances from the manufacturer that the parts are legal for emissions in all 50 states, for example, does not mean that they are legal everywhere for noise. Similarly, just because you bought your parts from a local car dealer for your brand of car and had them installed there does not mean that the parts meet vehicle code requirements in your jurisdiction. Note that the ARB (Air Resources Board) regulations concerning emissions may be listed separately and are also subject to enforcement in your home state.

Air pollution

The state corollary for the EPA is your local ARB. The primary concern of the ARB is to regulate the levels and types of allowable automobile emissions in your state. Some areas require stringent testing and monitoring of vehicle emissions, others require little or no such testing. These restrictions can be limited to problem metropolitan areas or may be statewide. Before tampering with emissions equipment, check the requirements of your local ARB.

Local ordinances

Local ordinances at the county or city level (even your homeowners association may have ordinances) may set specific requirements.

Generally, if you have met the requirements of the state vehicle code, then you are operating within the letter of the law. However, if your car with wild graphics and flaming hot pink paint is considered an eyesore by your neighbors, expect that there will be repercussions for parking it prominently outside. If the neighbors complain about tacky pink flamingo lawn ornaments, they will most certainly complain about a tacky pink car.

Warranty requirements

When it comes to new car warranties, automotive owners and enthusiasts have a very important lobbying body on their side, namely SEMA (the Specialty Equipment Market Association). SEMA represents the aftermarket manufacturers, wholesalers, retailers, and distributors in North America. Because this association of aftermarket parts suppliers has a vested interest in the continued sale of aftermarket parts, it has helped to keep new car manufacturers in check by successfully lobbying for legislation that prevents new car dealership service providers from denying warranty coverage, for example in a seized motor, because you chose to use those snazzy aftermarket carbon fiber windshield wipers instead of the OEM (Original Equipment Manufacturer) parts sold through their parts/service departments.

Magnuson-Moss Warranty Act

The relevant legislation here, the Magnuson-Moss Warranty - Federal Trade Commission Improvement Act of 1975, protects consumers from being wrongfully denied warranty coverage by new car dealers.

The Magnuson-Moss Warranty Act states, in part, in Title 15, United States Code, Section 2302, subdivision (c):

> No warrantor of a consumer product may condition his written or implied warranty of such product on the consumer's using, in connection with such product, any article or service (other than article or service provided without charge under the terms of the warranty) which is identified by brand, trade, or corporate name; except that the prohibition of this subsection may be waived by the [Federal Trade] Commission if —
>
> (1) the warrantor satisfies the Commission that the warranted product will function properly only if the article or service so identified is used in connection with the warranted product, and
>
> (2) the Commission finds that such a waiver is in the public interest. The Commission shall identify in the Federal Register, and permit public comment on, all applications for waiver of the prohibition of this subsection, and shall publish in the Federal Register its disposition of any such application, including the reasons therefore.

Under this federal statute, a manufacturer who issues a warranty on your motor vehicle is prohibited from requiring you to use a service or maintenance item, unless such item is provided, free of charge, under your warranty or unless the Federal Trade Commission (FTC) waives this prohibition against the manufacturer.

Further, under the act, aftermarket equipment that improves performance does not automatically void a vehicle manufacturer's original warranty, unless the warranty clearly states the addition of aftermarket equipment automatically voids your vehicle's warranty, or if it can be proven that the aftermarket device is the direct cause of the failure.

Specifically, the rules and regulations adopted by the FTC to govern the interpretation and enforcement of the Magnuson-Moss Warranty Act are set forth in the Code of Federal Regulations, Title 16 - Commercial Practices, Chapter I - Federal Trade Commission, Subchapter G - Rules, Regulations, Statements and Interpretations under the Magnuson-Moss Warranty Act, Part 700 - Interpretations under the Magnuson-Moss Warranty Act. Contained within these rules and regulations is Section 700.10, which states:

> No warrantor may condition the continued validity of a warranty on the use of only authorized repair service and/or authorized replacement parts for non-warranty service and maintenance. For example, provisions such as, **"This warranty is void if service is performed by anyone other than an authorized 'ABC' dealer and all replacement parts must be genuine 'ABC' parts," and the like, are prohibited where the service or parts are not covered by the warranty.** These provisions violate the Act in two ways. First, they violate the section 102(c) ban against tying arrangements. Second, such provisions are deceptive under section 110 of the Act, because a warrantor cannot, as a matter of law, avoid liability under a written warranty where a defect is unrelated to the use by a consumer of "unauthorized" articles or service. **This does not preclude a warrantor from expressly excluding liability for defects or damage caused by such "unauthorized" articles or service; nor does it preclude the warrantor from denying liability where the warrantor can demonstrate that the defect or damage was so caused.**

Under the Magnuson-Moss Act, a dealer must prove, not just vocalize, that aftermarket equipment caused the need for repairs before it can deny warranty coverage. If the dealer cannot prove such a claim — or it proffers a questionable explanation — it is your legal right to demand compliance with the warranty. The Federal Trade Commission administers the Magnuson-Moss Act and monitors compliance with warranty law.

That being said, if you choose to modify your car, and suddenly the fancy new electronic control boxes that you added to your car make it run rough, not start when cold, or buck like a bronco, the dealer can and will charge a diagnostic fee to find out what is wrong with your car. If it turns out that your modifications are the cause of the problem, the dealer has every right not only to charge you for the diagnosis and repair, but to also void the portion of the warranty that has been compromised by the use of those aftermarket parts.

Likewise, a dealer may refuse to service your car if it is adorned with after-market parts to the extent that its technicians cannot reasonably be expected to diagnose what is wrong with your car. As an example, all cars manufactured after 1994 are equipped with OBDII (On Board Diagnostics II) ports that dealers use to read engine diagnostic codes for everything from an engine vacuum leak to a malfunctioning emissions system. If your chosen modification has compromised the dealer service center's ability to scan for these codes (aftermarket ECUs generally do not support OBDII), then there is a strong probability that the dealer service center will

- ✔ Deny warranty coverage
- ✔ Refuse to service the car
- ✔ Note with your factory field representative for your region/district that your car has been "modified"

Your car's manufacturer notes are your car's "permanent record." Above all else, avoid compromising these notes. This is nearly always connected with your vehicles' VIN (Vehicle Identification Number) and will

- ✔ Ensure that your car will not have its warranty honored at any dealer service center in your area.
- ✔ Dramatically reduce the resale and/or trade-in value of your car.

Event participation

Some recent controversy surrounds car manufacturers' monitoring of SCCA (Sports Car Club of America) and NHRA (National Hot Rod Association) events and noting license plates and VINs as a justification for denying warranty coverage and either voiding out the warranty, or placing it on "restricted" status.

The legality of these tactics by automobile manufacturers, in particular where the car is marketed with SCCA membership or literature or advertised in race-modified form, is questionable. To protect yourself, be aware of this trend and take the appropriate precautions in listing critical identifying information when participating in regional autocrosses, tracks days, and drag races.

If you believe that your warranty has been wrongly canceled or placed on restriction either because of modifications made to your car, or because of your membership in, affiliation with, or participating in sanctioned club events or gatherings, consult with an attorney and use SEMA as a resource to fight the denial of coverage.

When it comes to legality and warranty concerns, I advise you to neither proceed based solely on slick advertising and marketing by parts manufacturers
and resellers, nor allow yourself to be cowed into paranoia. Information is
power, and knowing your rights and obligations is the foundation to any
thoughtfully modified car.

Setting Realistic Expectations

You've probably heard this argument before: Why would you even consider
fixing up your car when it will always be slower than *fill-in-the-blank* faster car?
Sometimes this argument makes sense, but often it doesn't.

For many people, owning the humble car that over many years is built to be
faster, leaner, and meaner is a convenient way to avoid the crippling down
payment on the expensive high-performance car by spreading out the overall
cost of modifications over a longer period of time, as budget and time allow.
Rather than suck up an $800 or $900 monthly car payment, stratospheric insurance and servicing costs, and the image of just having given in to a mid-life
crisis, many choose instead to lavish a little extra attention and money into
their current automobile of choice. In addition, because this existing car has
generally already seen its share of use, the extra attention can give it a second
lease on life and maintain whatever practicality was part of that car's original
appeal.

Why'd you do it?

As the owner of a highly modified import car, I am
often asked, with the enormous amount of money
and attention I have invested in my chosen automobile of humble origins, why I didn't instead
choose to just buy a true exotic and get the peace
of mind that comes from owning a car that was
engineered from the beginning to go fast? I would
have spent the same or less money with a lot
less time or hassle, had the benefit of a new car
warranty, and gained some prestige and badge
appeal along the way.

My answer is that I know myself all too well —
I am never content with "good enough." After a
while, absurdly fast no longer feels fast enough
to me (yes, horsepower is addictive). I could win
the lottery and be given the keys to a $120,000
Porsche 911 Turbo and be content with it — for
about a week. Then one restless night I would
walk into the garage with a glint in my eye and
wonder how much better the car would perform
with 100 pounds stripped out of it, or with a few
psi more boost from the turbos, or with stickier
tires and stiffer sway bars. . . .

A friend's Subaru WRX station wagon has been used many times to carry four of us plus a trunk full of supplies from Home Depot away from a stoplight, leaving a very frustrated Porsche driver in its wake. I am a big fan of Porsches, but I am an even bigger fan of making one's car a unique reflection of oneself, and a capable, well-balanced machine as well. This WRX certainly fits the bill. It is practical, reasonably affordable, reliable, and was modified within the letter of the law. In short, it is a good use of a very capable platform endowed with the ability to perform to amazing potential with minimal compromises to its usability or reliability.

However, the less flattering counterpoint is the unglamorous, unfast car that will never be fast, will never live up to expectations, and will never make sense to anyone, including its owner, regardless of how much time or money is thrown into it. All across this country, collecting dust on jack stands and with half empty cans of house paint and boxes of Christmas tree ornaments stacked on top, are the "forgotten cars." These less-than-glamorous projects that never quite worked out, many of which the owners still make monthly payments on, greatly outnumber the successfully executed modified cars that are seen rolling down the road with style and stellar performance. With enough patience, time, money, and planning/skill, anything can be accomplished. There have been minivans that ran nine-second quarter miles at the drag strip and Toyota MR2s that have lapped Ferraris on racetracks, but for every one of these examples, there are dozens if not hundreds of examples that fell well short of what their owners had hoped to achieve.

Generally, knowing what others have achieved with cars of the same make, model, and year as that which you are planning to modify is a good starting point for deciding how far, or whether at all, to begin making changes (particularly expensive ones).

One useful tool in keeping expectations in check is to list on paper, as objectively as possible, the merits of the car to be modified:

- ✔ If it's an older car, what would it take to bring it back to a state of health so that it would take well to the modifications?

- ✔ What kinds of modifications are readily available, and how much do they cost relative to the *substantiated* gains that others have seen them provide?

- ✔ How might these changes impact the usability, legality, and reliability of the car?

- ✔ Would the modifications be easily reversible should the car need to be serviced, sold, or traded?

- ✔ Is the car leased or owned?

After tallying these points, you can make an informed decision on your car's fate, including the following possible outcomes:

✔ Further explore modifying your current car, if the pros outweigh the cons, and you either

  • Hope to make your current car cooler than anything you can buy.

  • Want to fix up your current car to your level of satisfaction for less money than you can buy a car that will make you happy.

✔ If the tally of relevant considerations just does not balance out, it might be wise to write the idea off and either

  • Get the car that will truly make you happy when you can afford it.

  • Be happy with what you already have.

Making It Cool

You can't please everyone, but the main question at hand is what makes a car "cool," and when is it appropriate to mod a car in an effort to turn it into something arguably better than its humble origins would have indicated it ever could become.

Pretty much everyone wants a cool car, although what constitutes "cool" can vary greatly. Housewives like cool cars. Businessmen like cool cars. Kindergarten teachers like cool cars. That creepy-looking guy in the house with the blinds always drawn likes cool cars.

Given that no two people will agree on what is cool, the question can be logically framed only as whether either

✔ A car will appeal to one's peer group.

✔ A car will meet one's own vision of "cool."

The short answer is to modify a car with two distinct goals in mind:

✔ Modify a car to suit yourself.

✔ Remain true to the car's unique lineage, lines, or image, while putting a personal twist on the whole package.

To illustrate the need to make your car suit you, those who have seen the 1972 film *Harold and Maude*, starring Ruth Gordon and Bud Cort, will recall Harold, a morose and introspective young man, transforming his expensive Jaguar sports car into a hearse. This is a prime example of building a car to suit his unique vision of what he would like to drive, making something that suits his personality and values, and would not otherwise be available to him or anyone else. To Harold (and many others who admired his unique vision), the Jaguar he modified became inherently "cool" by virtue of how unusual, striking, and yet appropriate the car was to him as an individual, while remaining true to the car's classic British lines.

All things being equal, a properly modified classic 1960s Mustang with period pieces (from the time it was new) is inherently more "cool" than a 1960s Mustang seen in an owner's club somewhere in Frankfurt, Germany, that has been adorned with the latest European tuning parts. Likewise, a Nissan 240SX that has been converted mechanically to its more-powerful Japanese equivalent model Silvia and adorned with the correct JDM (Japanese Domestic Market) performance parts not normally seen on U.S. model cars is inherently more cool than the same 240SX adorned with Dodge Viper-style striped decals running the length of the car, a fiberglass hood scoop borrowed from a Camaro, and a set of over-sized chrome rims that, while flashy, have no particular connection to the 240SX. This is not to say that any one particular trend (for instance, the JDM craze in the United States) is right, whereas the other fashions in car adornment are wrong. However, the industry is fickle, and the big-mouthed bumpers and aggressive front ends that were all the rage two years ago might be the butt of jokes today. You're less likely to be left a fashion victim when your car follows in some logical way its heritage, while employing a personal spin that differentiates it from the crowd and still preserves its overall aesthetic.

Not All Platforms Are Created Equal

If there has been a point to the *Monster Garage* television series on Discovery Channel, it is that, given enough time, money, and talent, anything can become pretty much, well, anything — from an RX-7 sand rail to a Formula 1 road stripe painter. However, just because something *can* be done doesn't always mean it *should.*

Modifying a car means learning to frame your expectations of what your car can and cannot reasonably be expected to do. Every car, to a greater or lesser extent, is over-engineered from the factory to perform better than it actually does when it is released for public consumption. This detuning is done for a number of reasons, including the manufacturer's desire to

- Minimize exposure to warranty claims
- Keep insurance rates down (and thereby sell more cars)
- Comply with emissions requirements

   Manufacturers in the U.S. have target emissions requirements to meet for all models they have for sale in the U.S. Performance levels are often adjusted to attain these figures.

The million-dollar question is whether your own car is over-engineered by 2 percent, 20 percent, or 200 percent.

As an example, Toyota's MKIV Supra Turbo (1993–1997 models in the U.S.) can readily obtain nearly three times its stock engine horsepower rating before the engine requires additional internal fortification to keep its longevity from being severely compromised. By contrast, other makes and models will begin suffering catastrophic internal failure with a mere fraction of their stock power level added back in.

However, it isn't always about the amount of power a car can take when you're deciding whether to take the plunge into modifying for performance. Oftentimes, a car's motor will be more than willing, but the chassis can become overwhelmed with significantly increased power demands. Likewise, for the aspiring Michael Schumacher, Honda's popular Civic platform may respond well to additional power and have an enviable level of aftermarket support, but its front-wheel drive configuration makes it less desirable, in the eyes of many track enthusiasts, relative to the handling dynamics afforded by a rear-wheel drive car that can more easily be steered with the throttle.

On the flipside, sometimes a car will have all the right ingredients, but it simply doesn't have a high volume of aftermarket support, never really having caught on as a popular platform for upgrading. Here, the car gains points for uniqueness when someone finally appreciates its true potential and shows the world what the car can do, but generally the cost in sourcing and fabricating components is financially and logistically prohibitive.

When in doubt, it is helpful to look into enthusiast clubs for the particular make and model of car you are seeking to modify. Many enthusiast discussion forums and message boards exist on the Internet and can provide a wealth of information by owners and would-be owners of the car you are considering modifying. By seeing what others have or haven't been able to achieve with the particular car, you can better assess whether your car is even a viable candidate for its intended path.

Chapter 2

Planning It Smart

*P*ick the right tool for the job. On a micro level, this adage applies to all of the tools you need to meet your performance goals. On a macro level, it also means that your car should be the right tool for how you intend to apply it. If you want to create an autocross dominator, a Lincoln Continental may not be the best starting point. If your goal is drag racing, unless you are trying to make a statement, leave that Hummer at home. Of course, there are even less drastic examples, and more subtle shades of gray when identifying both an appropriate starting point and your intended outcome. This chapter helps address the evaluation process that precedes any successful car modification plan.

Choosing a Car

The choice may not be a choice at all, but a default "to mod or not to mod" decision based on what vehicle you already own. However, if you're shopping for a new car, or you can afford to buy a car just to mod, the process is perhaps more critical because you want to choose a car that's appropriate for a particular use or set of uses.

Part of choosing a car to modify — whether or not it is one that you already own — is identifying its uses and assigning percentages. The percentages don't have to add up to 100 percent — the goal of this exercise is just to realistically identify the type of use your car generally sees. For example, if I own a car and

I have aspirations of using it as a weekend track car, I might assign percentages as follows:

- Commuting to work: 100 percent

  Because this car is the only car available to me for getting to work, I assigned a value of 100 percent — if my car fails to take me to work, I won't be able to get to work that day.

- Weekend track use: 50 percent

  I anticipate using this car every other weekend for track use (alternate weekends I'll go to the track in my friend's car), so I assign 50 percent.

- Running errands: 30 percent

  Because my wife and I generally split running errands on the weekends between our two cars, and her car is the larger of the two, my car is used on average maybe three out of ten times, hence the assignment of 30 percent.

- Client meetings/business: 15 percent

- My spouse's use: 25 percent

This exercise helps me prioritize whether I have chosen an appropriate car for the purpose for which I intend to use it. Now, assume that the car I am contemplating using is a 1999 BMW M3 with 25,000 miles. Realistically, I can expect it to take me to and from work, run errands, bring clients to and from business meetings and lunches, and still hold up to the rigors of steady track use. I might want to keep my modifications to a minimum because the car is fairly stout even in stock condition. I also would likely want to make sure that the modifications to the car don't change how presentable it is for business clients or void its warranty. My consumables costs (primarily brakes and tires) might be on the high side, but the car should do well in its intended roles as outlined with little fuss.

On the other hand, say that the car I have in mind is a 1986 Volkswagen Golf with 145,000 miles. Arguably, the car is already fairly marginal for its intended role taking me to work every day, and even more so as an appropriate vehicle for transporting business clients. It would require a larger financial outlay relative to its value to make it a track-appropriate car, and the rigors of track use every other weekend would most certainly compromise its daily functionality. I wouldn't have a warranty to worry about, and my consumables costs might be a bit lower than for the late model BMW, but clearly the VW would require a substantial investment to make it serve its intended functions. Even then, the specter of losing my job if the car failed to take me to work would make this an unwise choice for further modification in its intended role.

Planning ahead is a critical and often overlooked aspect of car modification. Some people can keep different cars for each of the different roles those cars play in their lives: something for running errands, something for work, and something for just having fun. Most people have one car in their households that must do each of these tasks with minimal impact on its other roles. For example, if the BMW M3, which is well-suited for many of the roles in my life, were to have the percentages shifted around a bit — for example, if nearly every day (100 percent of the time) I needed the car for taking clients around, and I only went to the track one in ten weekends (10 percent) — it would be foolish of me to install a roll bar and gut the car's interior to make it better suited for track usage.

This may seem obvious, but it is alarming how many novices (myself included!) have made profoundly misguided decisions about how they intend to use their cars, and what does or does not constitute an appropriate modification, until after the fact. Going through the exercise of assigning percentages to the intended use of the car beforehand can save you a lot of grief, money, and labor that could otherwise have easily been avoided with a bit of planning.

Defining the Scope of the Project

Related but separate from the issue of deciding whether a car is appropriate for its intended purpose(s) is deciding how far you are willing to go to meet your goals, and which areas you want the car to excel in versus those areas in which it need only be passable.

Set realistic expectations for the scope of the project, and then set a realistic time frame and budget for accomplishing those goals. Of course, in your heart of hearts, you would like the wonder car that does everything well and always looks perfect, but for most people, it is a matter of picking the categories in which it is most important for the car to excel, and then setting a timeline and a budget for meeting those objectives. Trying to do it all is the most certain way to either disillusionment or disappointment.

All too often, when talking to a first-time modder, I hear enthusiasm without a lot of direction. For example, typical first-time modder Joe Schmoe has a 1993 Honda Prelude, and I ask what his plans are for his car. The first answer, of course, is generally, "I want to make it fast!" How fast is usually defined as faster than a buddy's car who drives X, Y, or Z. Or perhaps a quarter-mile time is what Joe is after, "Fast enough to hit 12s!" Fair enough. There is nothing wrong with wanting a fast car, and building a car for speed is one of the oldest American pastimes since the hot rodding days. "But I also want it to handle," the Prelude owner says next. So now I'm thinking that Joe is going to need to do a bit of planning to balance out the time and money he will spend working on the motor with an equal if not greater amount of care in choosing his suspension components, wheels, and tires. Then Joe adds, "Oh, and it's got to look good, because I want it to be a show car, too." So now Joe has a very fast Prelude that handles well and still looks pristine for car shows — meaning that it will need a flawless trick paint job, some tasteful body mods, and a pristine engine bay. "But it's also my daily driver, so it's got to have a bumping sound system." Okay, so this very fast car that handles great and looks pristine is also going to take its proud owner to and from work or school year round, all while weighed down with a huge stereo system. Of course, the end result is going to be a very compromised car that can hope to do well in none of the categories to which it aspires, even with barrels upon barrels of cash thrown at it.

The problem with Joe's Prelude is that, while it could have done any one of these things very well, and could arguably have excelled in two or even three of the categories, trying to do it all ensures that it will fail in everything the owner set out to do with it. If the goal was to go fast, then a tremendous amount of money spent on engine mods would be the call of the day, and even the suspension would best be set up to provide consistent launches on this front-wheel drive platform. Certainly, extra body kit components, a fancy paint job, and heavy subwoofers would do this car no favors at the drag strip. On the other hand, if it was to be used at shows, that same body kit and paint job, not to mention the gleaming engine compartment, would soon become compromised as the car began to be used for driving all over town to and from work or school. In fact, even the act of building the motor for all-out straight-line speed down the quarter mile, if not done with careful attention to the car's power curve, could very well ensure that its cornering abilities, even compared to a stock Prelude, suffered greatly. This is without factoring in the added weight of the stereo and body kit add-ons, or the level of paranoia with which the owner would have to drive to avoid chips on the paint job or cracks in the fiberglass aero components.

Compromises

Here you are faced with the issue of defining what it is that you say you want as opposed to what it is that you are actually willing to put up with to have it. How many of us have fantasized about owning a Ferrari? And yet the image you may conjure up of ripping down a twisty section of road on Monaco has about as much to do with Ferrari ownership as does driving the Rubicon trail for most of the SUVs you see at the local strip mall. When you factor in about $5,000 in routine maintenance appointments, $400 for tires, and crawling in bumper-to-bumper traffic with no safe place to park when you finally arrive, the reality of what it must be like for regular folk to own and drive a Ferrari every day sinks in — and the next time you find yourself drooling over one on the freeway, you might even feel a tinge of superiority — especially when you see an elite Italian exotic disabled at the side of the road or on the back of a flatbed while you drive past in a dependable little Japanese econo-car.

The allure of advertisements for flashy new products in magazines is no different. That straight-through exhaust would look great on the back of a Lexus IS300 — and it even adds 15 horsepower at the wheels! Of course, the Lexus that had previously been a quiet and sophisticated driving experience now drones and buzzes endlessly like a high school kid's pizza delivery car, police seem to be following the car wherever it's driven, and the local dealership charges a small fortune to replace a catalytic converter that failed prematurely. And the 15 horsepower gain? That was a peak reading at the very top of the rpm range just before redline. Elsewhere, the car's horsepower levels are the same as stock or just a hair above — certainly not enough to feel — and the torque, which was enjoyable in the midrange, is now greatly diminished.

The reality behind car mods designed to extract additional performance from your car is that every part, no matter how well engineered, is based on an inherent compromise. In the preceding example, while the shiny new exhaust looked great and made higher peak horsepower, drivability suffered as a result of excess noise, the midrange torque that matters most for around-town driving was diminished, the car drew unwanted attention from local law enforcement for a probable noise violation, and a factory part failed as either the direct or indirect result of the installation of the new exhaust.

The same spring and shock absorber package that allows for greater control in corners and better road feel will nearly always compromise ride quality. The turbo kit that provides all the extra power you could ever want will generally cost a small fortune to both buy and install, will have a number of hidden costs in the form of needing an upgraded clutch, fuel system, a set of gauges, engine management, and tuning, and will become a real headache for emissions testing purposes. Furthermore, the car's engine warranty will become a distant memory and routine maintenance will need to be followed religiously to prevent engine wear. The roll bar that enhances safety will render the back seat all but useless and may be more dangerous for street use than if it had never been installed. The list goes on and on. When buying a new performance product, understand that most every product on the market is designed to make your car do certain things better, but at the expense of letting certain other areas fall by the wayside.

In addition, performance products generally hurt the resale value of your car, even as they add to your enjoyment of it, because not all buyers would get the same satisfaction out of the modifications that you might. Even if they did, they would strongly suspect that the car has lived a hard life by virtue of the fact that is has been modified — whether or not this is the case. Lastly, replacement parts for damaged or failed performance items can be hard to locate. Certainly, these items are not as easy to come by as those from your local dealership's parts department, and the more rare and desirable the part, the more of a headache it will be to replace if it is ever damaged or worn.

Car mods can dramatically improve an aspect of your car's performance, but can also

- ✔ Sacrifice another aspect of performance.
- ✔ Hurt your car's resale value.
- ✔ Be expensive or difficult to repair or replace.

Contingency Plan/Exit Strategy

Murphy's Law, "Anything that can go wrong, will go wrong," is never more appropriate than when modifying a car.

You will sleep better knowing that you are not about to get in too far over your head. Above all else, look ahead:

✔ Either hold off on modifying your car, or stick to the most affordable and easily reversible modifications, if you may

    • Start school in the foreseeable future

    • Go into active military service

    • Move to another country

✔ Limit the scope of your project to constrain the costs for both

    • Performing the modifications (both in terms of time and money)

    • Undoing the modifications

✔ Before you start the project, figure out the time and money required to wrap up loose ends if you call it off. (For example, do you have the cash for a stock engine rebuild if your new turbo system causes you to blow a piston or two?)

Murphy's Law in action

Some years back, I bought a premapped engine management system for my car, a $1,300 unit that I could just barely afford — but in my mind, it was worth the premium price because it was premapped and would not require expensive Dyno tuning, at $150 to $200 an hour, to set up (see Part VII of this book for a discussion on Dyno tuning). Well, it turns out the unit I purchased was premapped as advertised, but the mapping was for a Japanese version of the car running 95 octane fuel, and at the time, I had access to only 92 octane pump gas here in California. It would have been dangerous to run my car on such an aggressive tune. Further, even in Japan, the preloaded maps are only regarded as good enough to get the car running so that it could immediately be driven to the Dyno for a proper tune. After spending another $1,200 for a full two days on the Dyno, I now had a $2,500 engine management solution. And then four months later, California gas stations stopped selling 92 octane and 91 octane become the highest available grade of pump gas. Back to the Dyno I went. . . .

This sounds bad, and yet I count myself lucky. I can only imagine how bad things could have been had I run the car on the more aggressive Japanese starter tune and blown the motor in the process. Barely able to afford the $1,300 controller, and strapped past my limits at $2,500, I would have been completely ruined facing a complete engine rebuild on my brand new motor.

Delays

Parts fail to arrive on time, and you find yourself renting a car to get to work while you wait for the package to ship. When it does, the parts you ordered for your U.S. version Mitsubishi Evo 8 turn out to be for a Japanese version Evo 7 and don't fit. A local fabricator says he'll bail you out and make the necessary changes, but he disappears and closes down shop for a week while he's at the races. When you get the part back, it still doesn't fit, and now it can't be returned. You place another order for what you believe to be the correct part, paying an arm and leg for expedited shipping, but the part you need is on back order. When it finally ships, they send it cargo freight from Japan instead of the international priority shipping you had paid for. You've now had the rental car for over two weeks. . . .

If there is one overriding theme that rings true for every level of car modification — regardless of the car make or model — it is to plan for and expect dramatic delays, parts not fitting, and the need to spend a great deal of money, sometimes many times the original amount anticipated, to make things work as planned. Delays, botched orders, faulty parts, and unexpected twists and turns are all part of the scenic journey that is modifying a car. In the end, you have no one but yourself to blame because this was, after all, elective surgery (the car would have been just fine without the latest and greatest performance regimen that you have laid out for it). With a bit of foresight, at the end of the project, you can sit back and have a laugh over the trials and tribulations. However, it is always easier to laugh it off when the stakes have been kept manageable to the best extent possible, and the risks to your own personal sanity and wellbeing are kept in close check.

As a contingency plan, at the very least have the following when modifying a car:

- ✔ Extra time to get the project done

- ✔ Extra cash reserves

- ✔ Good friends nearby who are willing to lend a hand or just moral support when needed

- ✔ An alternate mode of transportation

- ✔ Access to online resources (message boards and forums) to check for answers and leads — even at 2:00 a.m.

- ✔ A cell phone for the inevitable frantic phone calls from the side of the road or in front of the closed shop that was supposed to have your car/parts/service finished

- ✔ A bottle of aspirin and a sense of humor — you'll need both

So long, farewell

Sooner or later, you'll probably want to sell your car. The modifications that you add to your car will serve as a red flag to potential buyers, whether they buy from you or the dealer with whom you will be trading in the car, that the car has been abused or otherwise tampered with.

Ironically, most modified cars likely have been more meticulously maintained than the leased cars that are treated like disposable cars. An enthusiast bonds with his or her car and would never forget to fill up with premium gas or miss an oil change. The same can't be said of someone who figures that the car he or she is driving today needs to stay intact only so long as the lease is in effect.

Reselling your car

To preserve the value of your car, keep the stock parts. For better or worse, stock cars have a higher value on the open market. Even tuners shopping for their next hot ride generally prefer to fix up a stock vehicle to their liking, and not buy something that has already been enhanced.

Label the stock parts and document them with Polaroids or digital pictures so that you (or your mechanic) know where they are and how they go back together.

Reselling your parts

There is an enormous secondary market for automotive performance parts. Online auctions like eBay and enthusiast boards offer free or inexpensive classified listings.

Recouping losses on an unfinished project is easier if you can return the car to stock condition and sell its hot rod goodies separately.

Part II
Safety

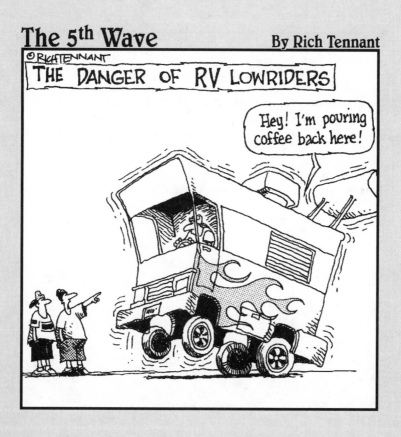

In this part . . .

This part explains important active and passive safety modifications designed to improve the car's ability to both avoid and withstand accidents. Because many performance modifications elsewhere in this book are designed to make the car travel at higher speeds, it is important to consider the relative safety of the car before increasing its performance envelope.

Chapter 3

Balanced Performance

The two distinct classes of safety that are engineered into every car are active and passive safety. Both are included by auto manufacturers in the designs of new cars. Both are subject to modification and improvement.

Active safety is a car's ability to avoid an accident/collision. This includes its ability to brake, turn, and accelerate, or some combination thereof, in an emergency avoidance maneuver. After all, the safest collision is the one that is avoided entirely.

Passive safety refers to a car's ability to protect its occupants during a collision. This refers to the car's ability to channel life-threatening impact forces away from both the driver and passengers and to preserve its structural integrity so as to avoid causing harm to the car's occupants.

A smart modder thinks about both active and passive safety as a critical part of the modding regimen.

The Concept of Active Safety

Active safety has an inherent appeal to car modders in that making a car perform at higher overall limits is generally making that car safer. As an example, a 5,000 pound SUV with knobby tires and a high center of gravity may do well at protecting its occupants when a collision occurs by the simple virtue of its mass relative to any other car it might encounter on the road, but its likelihood of putting its occupants' lives at risk during normal driving is significantly higher than a well-balanced, nimble sports car.

At the speeds that most automobiles travel on U.S. highways (generally 65 to 75 mph), an SUV that is engineered to be capable of reaching speeds of 85 to 110 mph is always much closer to the outer limits of its performance envelope, as opposed to an exotic sports car that is engineered to remain stable and usable at speeds exceeding 200 mph. Likewise, the same SUV will break traction under far lower cornering loads when swerving, will provide the driver with less control and feedback during avoidance maneuvers, and will stop at nearly double the braking distance of a well-equipped sports car.

All things being equal, the car that stops shorter, remains stable at higher speeds (even in inclement weather), and exhibits more predictable break-away characteristics at its limits when driven responsibly will do a better job of keeping its driver and occupants safe than the car that takes more space to stop, breaks away more suddenly and less predictably as its grip runs out, and is generally operating closer to its mechanical limits at the speeds that most traffic moves on the freeway.

There is an important caveat here: For the better performing car to truly be safer, it needs to be driven responsibly; when its limits are increased, it must be done with minimal compromise to the car's ability to communicate with the driver and perform seamlessly at its operating parameters. All too often, you hear or read of unfortunate accidents that have resulted from when a misguided performance enthusiast equips his or her car with a stiffer suspension and stickier tires believing these to be ideal from an active safety standpoint, only to learn the hard way that the car which once exhibited mild and controllable understeer characteristics (with plenty of warning before the tires reached their limit) now corners at higher limits under ideal conditions, but on public roads is easily caught off balance by normal road imperfections, transitions from understeer to sudden oversteer with little provocation, and exhibits a razor-thin envelope between having grip and suddenly having no grip at all. The performance envelope of the car did in fact move up dramatically — and for a skilled driver on a smooth racetrack, the car would provide noticeably lower lap times — but the car has gone from benign and safe in the hands of even a novice driver to a nerve-racking and challenging creation that would give even Michael Schumacher white knuckles on a public road.

Generally speaking, higher performance is better for active safety but, taken to extremes, high performance in less-than-optimal conditions in the hands of an unskilled driver can often be an accident waiting to happen — especially when those limits are first explored on a public road.

Building a Balanced Car

Building a balanced car involves understanding several key concepts:

✔ **Performance envelope:** Loosely speaking, what is the car capable of? How far can it be pushed in any aspect (acceleration, braking, handling)?

✔ **Handling attitude:** Refers to whether, when the car's limits have been reached, it tends to break away at the front first and run wide (understeer — most factory cars do this by design), break away at the rear first and rotate in the direction the car is turning (oversteer — difficult for novice drivers to correct as it requires carefully modulating the throttle to correct rather than lifting the accelerator or, worse yet, jumping on the brakes), or whether the car breaks away at all four corners relatively equally (neutral handling — ideal on the track, but not well-suited to novice drivers on public roads).

✔ **Breakaway characteristics:** How much warning does the car provide before it reaches its outermost performance limits? How much warning does the driver have before the tires lose grip in a corner? How much warning does the car give before it locks up its tires under braking? Is the braking force well proportioned relative to both the front and rear of the car, or does one end of the car lock up its tires well before the other? How well does the car transition from extreme lateral load on one side to the other — like when a child runs out in the street and the car needs to swerve to the left or right and then quickly back again without losing its composure?

✔ **Weight distribution:** Where is the weight located in the car, and how does this affect the car's ability to cope with steering, braking, and handling inputs? Optimally, the weight should be spread out uniformly both front-to-back and side-to-side (accounting for the driver's weight) and as low below the car's beltline as possible. Weight at the extreme ends of the car, ahead of the front axle and behind the rear axle, should also be kept to a minimum.

✔ **Overall balance:** Do the critical performance aspects of the car all increase by roughly the same amount after modification, or is something out of proportion to the rest? How does the car itself take to the level of modifications used? For instance, if I add 900 horsepower to a Geo Metro by installing an enormous engine under the hood but leave the remainder of the car untouched, what does this do to the overall balance of the Metro? Short answer: The Metro, which was far from a strong handling or braking car to begin with, is now twisting and straining its chassis under the added power, is hopelessly nose-heavy, and has even worse stopping and cornering characteristics than it had before. It might be able to accelerate out of harm's way, when merging on the freeway for example, but that assumes that the tires don't pop, the welds holding the car together don't come apart, and the car neither needs to steer nor brake at any point in the merging maneuver.

So how does the average car owner go about ensuring that modifications made to the car help, rather than hinder, its active safety? The answer is fairly straightforward:

1. **Take the time to learn about vehicle dynamics, both as they apply to cars generally (as outlined in the preceding list) and as they apply to your specific car.**

   The best and smartest way to go about exploring vehicle dynamics is by signing up for a performance driving school in your area. Skip Barber runs a terrific series of classes all over the country (www.skipbarber.com). Here, the instructors teach you how to identify how your car behaves at its limits by simulating everything from an emergency lane change to a panic stop. It is only after exploring both your limits as a driver and your car's limits that you can identify what feels safe and predictable to you (because this varies from person to person) and what aspects of your car need the most attention when modding. Ideally, after the modding regimen has been carried out, or better yet, in stages along the way, either go back to the driving school for a refresher, or sign up for a local SCCA (www.scca.org) autocross or track day. This will help identify whether the changes you are making to the car are in fact increasing its active safety.

2. **When possible, buy adjustable.**

   Avoiding an accident comes down to having the reflexive response to make the car do what you need it to do to get out of harm's way without the time for thought. Under these circumstances, the car is truly an extension of the driver. There is no time to set the car up, plan the maneuver, and execute. The car must do exactly what the driver's inputs tell it to do in a manner that feels intuitive to the driver. The more adjustability that is built into your car, the more likely it is that you will be able to dial your car's performance in to set your car up to perform in a way that feels predicable, safe, and intuitive to you. The following components are generally available in both adjustable and non-adjustable designs:

   - **Sway bars:** Help set the car's cornering attitude.

   - **Sway bar end links:** Used in conjunction with sway bars to further dial in cornering attitude.

   - **Shocks:** Adjustable for rebound and/or compression dampening.

   - **Camber plates:** For alignment settings going beyond those available from the factory.

   - **Springs and coilovers:** Available with either progressive (varies upon compression) or linear (static) spring rates. A good coilover should allow you to set the ride height of your car to help give you more communicative handling. A new set of springs can change the ride height of your car, but are not adjustable.

- **Brake proportioning valve:** Only needed if the brake lock-up point is deemed to be an issue, but a huge benefit if this is indeed an issue in your particular car.

- **Boost controller:** Limits or adds boost on forced-induction cars. Generally, less boost under cornering helps prevent power-on oversteer/understeer.

3. **Understand how environmental- and maintenance-related factors can dramatically change your car's personality when it is asked to react in an emergency.**

   A classic example involves the owners of Toyota's mid-engined MR2 that have gone spinning backwards off the road when heavy items are placed in the rear trunk (bags of gardening soil or concrete mix for home improvement projects are often cited as culprits).

In the MR2, for example, the car's weight distribution changes dramatically when weight is added behind the engine and can catch the unwary driver off guard. It's no wonder that Toyota eliminated the rear trunk from the current model MR2 Spyder. However, even a conventional front-engine sedan with four passengers will handle very differently with the added 350 to 600 additional pounds versus a car with just the driver. A car with one or more under-inflated tires will behave very differently than a car with properly inflated tires, regardless of how carefully the suspension and brakes have been dialed in. The same is true for a car that is even slightly out of alignment, or one riding on cold tires or brake pads (especially performance brake pads or tire compounds that need to be brought up to operating temperature before they are ready to perform their best). Each of these cars will feel 100 percent fine in normal use — but push them a bit, as in an emergency braking and/or cornering maneuver, and they will react very differently from what the driver is expecting, catching the driver off guard when he or she most needs the car to follow his or her inputs. Worn or damaged tires, suspension, brakes, and/or driveline components will only further compromise your car's ability to bail you out of a bad situation.

Of course, building a balanced car serves not only as the foundation for heightening active safety, but also serves as the basis for increasing performance, making your car faster and more enjoyable. It's not as much about the brand names of the hardware it takes to get the job done as it is about understanding how your car behaves at the limit, and how the behavior changes as the limit increases. Working within the context of balance and active safety is the cornerstone of a successfully modified car, and if no other part of this book changes the way you think about your car or your plans to improve it, keep this chapter close to heart. The auto manufacturers spend countless hours planning and designing how your stock automobile reacts on the aggregate in a wide range of operating conditions and with a wide range of drivers.

You improve on what they have given you and make the car fit your needs and style better than a stock car — just as a well-tailored suit should always fit better than one pulled off the rack — but do it right, because the consequences of building an unpredictable car far outweigh the benefits of simply "improving" its performance.

Chapter 4

Safety Gear

. . . .

In This Chapter

▶ Grasping the concept of passive safety

▶ Installing roll bars and cages

▶ Taking your seat

▶ Strapping in with harnesses

. . . .

*I*t may not bling, blink, or zoom, but automotive safety is an integral part of any balanced car's build-up. Enhancing the passive safety of your car could save your life.

There is an entire industry full of gear and equipment designed to increase the passive safety of your car; that is, increase the survivability of an accident. But unlike performance modifications, where the wrong part may simply slow you down, a poorly chosen or incorrectly installed safety product can have far worse results. This is not a loud-mouthed label on a mattress but an honest reality every driver must face now, or at some (possibly inconvenient) point in the future.

So what exactly do we mean by "safe"?

Passive Safety Essentials

With passive safety, the accident is a foregone conclusion, and the impact has occurred or is unfolding. Active safety has failed, the driver being unable to maneuver the car out of harm's way. As the impact occurs, the vehicle must simultaneously

✔ Maintain the structural integrity of the car's cabin (to prevent crush injuries)

✔ Restrain the driver and passengers until both the car and its occupants stop moving

✔ Channel the energy of the impact away from the driver and passengers

Passive safety can be tricky to implement or enhance. Consumers can't work with crash test dummies, monitoring equipment, and dozens of tests to determine the ideal solution under the most likely of circumstances. Passive safety upgrades are a one-shot deal; if done wrong, injuries can be more severe than if the car had been left in stock condition.

Even without the resources of a major auto manufacturer, you can draw from a collective mind-share: motor sports. If your goals include competing at the drag strip at an NHRA (National Hot Rod Association) event, or on road courses for SCCA (Sports Car Club of America) or other events, follow the guidelines of those sanctioning bodies to make your car legal for either amateur or professional competitive use and safer.

For current autocross, drag racing, and road race safety regulations, check directly with the sanctioning bodies for firsthand information. Quality secondary resources include the car clubs that often sponsor such events and the regulations listed by hosting racetracks. On the Web, consider

✔ www.nhra.org

✔ www.scca.org

✔ www.imsaracing.net

A couple of rules usually apply when assessing passive safety:

✔ Usually, it's illegal to alter safety equipment on a street-driven car. That includes permanently disabling airbags.

✔ If your car ever has a collision, there's more to do than count fingers and toes and then sweep up some glass. Though the car may move under its own power and "feel fine," there are a few things that may not be so obvious that you should check before resuming business as usual:

    • Have your factory seatbelts checked. They may look fine, but the belt material stretches on impact. If the material has stretched, it may not work properly again. *Better safe than sorry* definitely applies here, an axiom that can be freely imposed on automotive safety at large.

- Ensure that the crumple zones aren't compromised, and that the car's overall structure is sound.

A botched repair may look fine cosmetically, and the car may even drive normally, but it could cost you your life in a serious collision. When in doubt, consult with a third party body shop that you trust and make sure that your car's structure is sound.

Generally, street cars are designed to react predictably to one hard hit in the course of their lives. You can't ensure that the car will deform and absorb impact energy, as it was designed to, the second time around. If your car can't be brought within factory alignment specifications, or requires the use of "crash bolts" (suspension-mounting hardware that allows for alignment settings outside of the factory specifications), then there's a good chance that your car will not respond appropriately in its next accident.

- Having your airbags checked by a qualified technician, even if they didn't deploy in the collision, is a good idea. Many manufacturers recommend checking the airbags every ten years to insure that the connectors, circuitry, and triggers are functioning correctly.

A collision of any kind (on either the track or the street) is a violent event, with often incomprehensibly damaging forces exerted on driver and car. The calculated containment and channeling of these forces can make the difference between walking away with scrapes and bruises, or being airlifted away with worse.

Roll Bars and Roll Cages

Roll bars and roll cages are common modifications among performance cars, particularly cars that are regularly used at weekend drag and track events. Such enhancements to your vehicle's structure make it safer on the track and often improve cornering by reducing chassis flex, even if they add weight.

Materials

Structural bars and cages are enhancements that protect the structural integrity of the passenger compartment. There are many ways to provide this enhancement, with various amounts of intrusion into the passenger compartment, and various levels of safety provided.

Unsafe at any speed

Cosmetic, non-functional "roll bars" and "roll cages" (known as style bars or monkey bars) are common among the show car crowd. Many sanctioning bodies require fully functional roll bars or roll cages when capable of certain levels of performance. Basically, as your car gets faster, the safety requirements get more involved. Many show cars display cage-mounted chrome fire extinguishers and race-style harnesses for more image boosting. As a result of this trend, a truly dangerous phenomenon has cropped up: cars that are modified, improperly, for a race-ready look with

✔ "Style bars" that are more likely to injure or kill their occupants than a completely stock car. For example, the bars in the adjacent figure don't have any diagonal bracing, so they may simply fold over.

✔ Fire extinguishers that can't put out more than a cigarette, yet are mounted where they can contact a passenger's head

✔ "Aero" or "Body" kits, made of various materials that do not deform in safe, predictable ways, and/or require the removal of factory bumper bars that are designed to channel impact energy into the appropriate crumple zones of your car's chassis

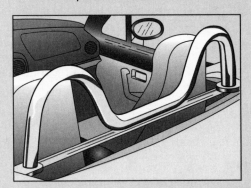

Structural bars

Roll bars (as shown in Figure 4-1) and roll cages usually are made from either

✔ DOM steel

DOM steel is

- Less expensive
- Easier to find
- Easier to weld

✔ Chromoly steel

Chromoly steel is more expensive, but it has a better strength-to-weight ratio than DOM steel, so it's the cost-no-object choice. Compared to DOM, Chromoly is

- Lighter
- Stronger
- Smaller (it leaves more space in your interior)

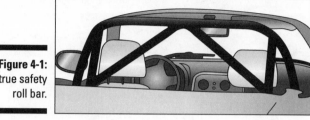

Figure 4-1:
A true safety
roll bar.

Padding

All roll bars and roll cages should be appropriately padded everywhere the driver's or passenger's head or limbs can come into contact with the bar in a collision.

Roll bars and roll cages can fracture a skull or break bones. Thoughtful padding is essential. When it's time to wrap your cage or bar, be sure to choose the appropriate padding. Not all padding squishes, bends, and burns the same.

- High-density padding is preferred if a helmet will be worn inside the vehicle.
- Looser density padding can be used if the car will be driven on the street without a helmet.

Never wrap padding in any vinyl or other plastic material that can release noxious fumes or blinding smoke if the interior of the car catches on fire.

Padding is essential anywhere that your (or your passengers') head or extremities could potentially come into contact with the roll cage or bar in a violent collision or rollover.

You can figure out where you need to pad by sitting in the driver's seat and reaching out your arms and legs in every direction. Wherever your head, arms and legs can touch the cage, you need to pad.

Secure padding with zip ties. Be sure to orient the zip tie closure away from the driver and passengers because these are sharp and can puncture the skin.

Design

Several categories of functional roll bars and cages can be installed in your car.

A true roll bar is a structural and safety hoop behind the driver and passenger seats, as shown in Figure 4-2, that can support the weight of the vehicle in a rollover. The roll bar usually connects to the chassis at four points (two on the floor, two to the rear deck or firewall (depending on your exact application).

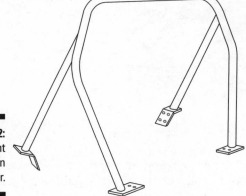

Figure 4-2:
A four-point
bolt-in
roll bar.

Some roll bars have integrated harness bars for the installation of a race harness and/or in-car video equipment.

Roll bars are required for convertibles at many racetracks, even at the beginner driving school level.

Roll bars are available for many cars and trucks. A typical roll bar costs approximately $200 to $300 (US dollars) and requires up to six hours to install. Expect to

- Add up to 50 pounds of weight
- Lose the use of your back seat (unless your car doesn't have a back seat)

Stay away from *style bars*. Far away. These bars are non-functional junk designed to *look* like roll bars. Style bars may be prettier and less expensive than real roll bars, but they aren't designed to support the weight of the car and can't prevent critical chassis points from buckling on impact. In an impact, they may break or buckle, turning into projectiles inside the car that can cause severe injury to you or your passengers. Remember, street-driven cars typically carry passengers who are very much your responsibility, legally and morally. This responsibility isn't fully satisfied simply by driving safely. Collisions happen, and when they do, the passive safety of your car becomes critical. Plan ahead when considering modifications like these.

Roll cage

A roll cage protects against side and front intrusion in a crash, while increasing the stiffness of the chassis for better cornering. The typical roll cage requires time to install correctly and can make entry and exit from the vehicle more difficult. Depending on which chassis and cabin reinforcement you choose, a variety of bars and bends will now occupy not insignificant space in your car. They will typically run parallel to the doors, behind the driver, and up beneath the roof. It is akin to wrestling a ladder every time you get in and out of the car.

Yes, it's cool, but the novelty can and will wear off quickly. For this reason, honest reflection is necessary when it comes time to choose the best reinforcing product for your car.

If your car is to be used as a daily driver, stay away from NASCAR or fixed-beam style side-impact bars, as shown in Figure 4-3. Opt for either swing-out or removable bars in the door beams, as shown in Figure 4-4.

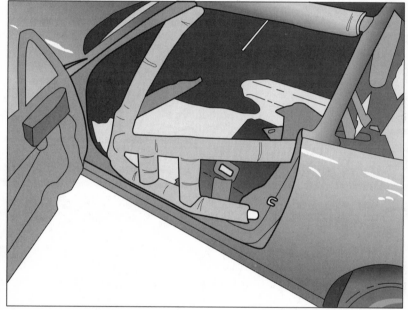

Figure 4-3:
A cage with NASCAR style side-impact bars.

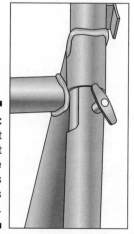

Figure 4-4:
Swing-out side-impact bars — the pin locks the bars in place.

Usually, a roll cage connects to the car's chassis at six, eight, or ten points, as shown in Figure 4-5 and Figure 4-6. Reinforcements run down the A-pillars (the "pillars" in your car's frame or unibody that run along the sides of the windshield) to the floor, as shown in Figure 4-7.

Roll cages add more stiffness and safety than a roll bar by "closing the box" of your car's passenger compartment, but further compromise the car's comfort. Most roll cages add 75–125 pounds to the car. Extensive padding is required with a roll cage, and this padding should never be wrapped in any vinyl or plastic material.

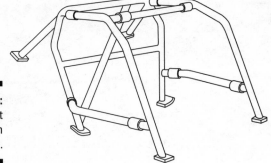

Figure 4-5:
A six-point bolt-in roll cage.

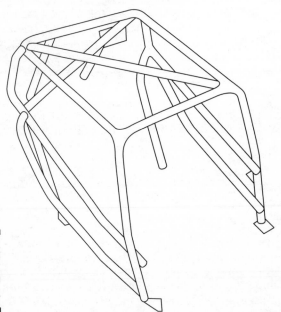

Figure 4-6:
An eight-point bolt-in roll cage.

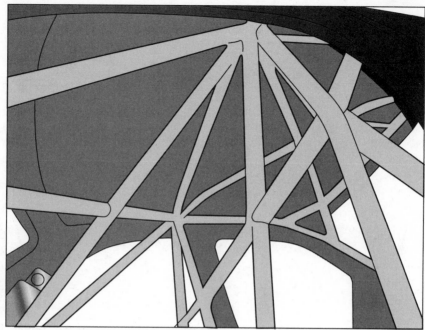

Figure 4-7:
A ten-point
bolt-in roll
cage
(yikes!).

Roll cages are designed for a helmeted driver wearing a competition harness. On the street, with a standard seatbelt and without a helmet, the roll cage may be life threatening in a collision, even if properly padded. A standard seatbelt allows much more forward and lateral movement than a competition seat and harness, so the driver's head and extremities can make contact with the cage in an accident. Without a helmet, even a padded cage can crack a skull like a coconut.

Roll cages are available for many cars and trucks. A typical roll cage costs from $650 to $1,200 and can require six hours or longer to install.

Harness bar

Used either with a roll bar/roll cage or on its own, a harness bar's sole function is as an attachment for a race harness restraint system. Figure 4-8 shows a harness bar.

Harness bars can be installed without a cage or roll bar, but they lock you in an upright position with your head as the highest point of the car's interior. If you have a car with a back seat, and you intend to maintain the use of your back seat, but would like to use a harness for weekend track events, then the harness bar is your best option because it is easily removable when not in use. On the other hand, if you have a two-seater or can live without the use of your back seat, a roll bar or roll cage with an integrated harness bar is a much better solution, from both a structural and safety standpoint.

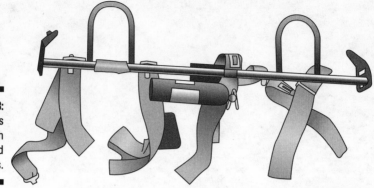

Figure 4-8:
A harness
bar with
attached
belts.

Harness bars are available from many vendors for most cars. They are about the same price as a simple roll bar at around $200 to $300.

Installation

Roll bars, harness bars, and roll cages are installed with a couple of methods, depending on

- ✔ The bar or cage design
- ✔ The rules of your competition sanctioning body

Bolt-in

Bolt-in roll bars and roll cages are removable, though the evidence of installation is visible with careful inspection. They can be installed with hand tools.

In addition to the visible structure, bolt-in installation requires

- ✔ *Backing plates* at all mounting points
- ✔ *AN-grade bolts* (consult with the roll bar/roll cage manufacturer and your race sanctioning body for current, exact standards)

Bolt-in roll bars are stronger in today's *unibody* cars (also called *unit body*; most modern cars are designed without the use of traditional frame rails). Welding can weaken the metal of a car's unibody.

Welding

Welded roll bars and roll cages are permanently connected to a car's unibody.

Welding usually requires that you first remove all of the car's interior trim to avoid damage from stray sparks.

Seats and Braces

While they can make a striking visual impact, specialized seats can also enhance your car's performance and safety in competition.

Factory seats

In everyday driving, *factory seats* (the standard seats that were installed in your car when it was manufactured) have a couple of major benefits:

✔ **Comfort:** Factory seats are generally more comfortable, and adjustable to suit most drivers. Many luxury cars have seats with leather upholstery, seat heaters, and built-in speakers.

✔ **Safety:** Many factory seats have

- Side impact airbags

- Inertia reel seatbelts, which automatically lock the seatbelt during an accident.

- Some cars have *pretensioners* that actually tighten the seat belt during an accident.

 It is illegal in most jurisdictions to disable or modify airbag equipment on a street-driven car.

Factory seats have a downside for performance:

✔ Factory seats weigh as much as 180 pounds a pair when equipped with lots of gadgets and comfy upholstery.

✔ Competition harnesses usually won't work with factory seats.

✔ Hinges in the factory seat can break.

 A seatback that breaks at the hinge in a crash is an almost certain recipe for paralysis or spinal injury.

✔ Factory seats often lack side support to keep the driver in place.

 A driver who is securely positioned usually is better focused than a driver bracing a knee against the center console and an arm against the door to keep from sliding around.

Competition seats

Race seats from such companies as Recaro, Sparco, Bride, Momo, and Corbeau are available to replace most factory seats. Exactly how comfortable and use-able seats like these are for a daily-driven vehicle depends on your body type, personal preference, and the particular model seat you choose. Pure shell-style, non-reclining bucket seats might not be your best bet for a street-driven car, but function and performance can coexist. Recaro produces seats for fac-tory equipment for OEMs (Original Equipment Manufacturer) from Wolfsburg to Tokyo, as well as some of the finest race seats ever constructed.

Design

Racing seats are less adjustable than factory seats, but they significantly increase support, they can weigh as little as six or eight pounds each, and they can withstand much more impact force than factory-installed seats.

Aftermarket seats are any seats other than those installed as factory equipment. They are available with or without adjustable recliners, in many guises, and with many functions. Non-adjustable shell-type seats are lighter and stronger than adjustable seats, and compatible with five-point harnesses and a seat-back brace to secure the seat to a roll bar or cage. They lack the comfort and utility of a factory seat, and are considered an extreme modification with the sole purpose of racing your car.

Construction of aftermarket seats varies, depending on manufacturer and intended use:

✔ Rigid-shell seats (as shown in Figure 4-9) made of such materials as fiber-glass, aluminum, carbon fiber, carbon/Kevlar, or some similar material

✔ Tubular steel framing similar to factory seat construction

All reclining seats (as shown in Figure 4-10 and Figure 4-11) use a tubular frame.

Figure 4-9:
A typical rigid-shell seat, with slots for a five-point harness.

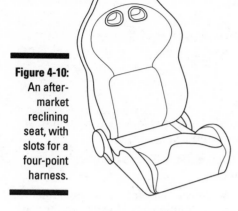

Figure 4-10:
An after-market reclining seat, with slots for a four-point harness.

Figure 4-11:
An after-market reclining seat is lighter than a standard factory seat.

Performance

Racing shell–type seats securely situate the driver under hard cornering. Their reduced padding allows for more direct communication between car and driver.

A race driver once told me that a good guideline (though not entirely accurate) is that for every inch that the driver moves laterally in his or her seat, the rear of the car will step out by a foot before the driver feels the slip and can adjust for it. A heavily cushioned factory seat designed to smooth out the rough roads and potholes encountered during mundane driving excursions may not be well suited for the driver looking for as much input from the car as he or she can get.

Shopping

Typical shell-type seats cost from $250 to $1,500 each, depending on

✔ Design

✔ Construction method

✔ Weight

✔ Certification by either

- FIA (*Fédération Internationale de l'Automobile,* which is French for International Federation of Automobiles)

- TUV (*Technischer Überwachungsverein,* which is German for Technical Inspection Association)

Neither sanctioning body's approval is necessary for a safe, high-quality seat, but a manufacturer that goes through the expense and red tape of submitting a seat for approval with these organizations definitely has done its homework.

Safe installation of aftermarket seats often requires use of model-specific sliders. Sliders are what connect the seat to the car, and allow the seat to slide forward and rearward in the cabin. A major consideration for many, especially those long-limbed folks, is helmet clearance. Different seat and slider combinations yield unique headroom. For this reason, some dedicated (and tall) racers forego sliders altogether, and simply bolt the seats straight into the floor pan (with appropriate hardware). Even shorter drivers often use this approach to lower the center of gravity of the car.

When you're shopping for a racing seat, make sure that (if the car will be driven on public roadways) the stock seatbelt latch carries over to the new seat (many have a mounting spot specifically designated for this purpose). Most seats can be installed in under two hours with basic hand tools, using the factory mounting holes where available.

Racing seats usually are made to hold you closely and securely. When you buy a seat, make sure it fits you around the shoulders, waist, and (ahem) hips.

Braces

Bolt-in seatback braces, as shown in Figure 4-12, are available from companies like Autopower and Ioport Racing for shell-type racing seats, and these braces cost less than $100. A seatback brace restricts the movement of the seat back by securing it to the primary roll hoop or harness bar of the roll cage. Before you buy a seatback brace, confirm that

- ✔ Your primary sanctioning organization requires a seatback brace
- ✔ Your racing seat can use this extra brace

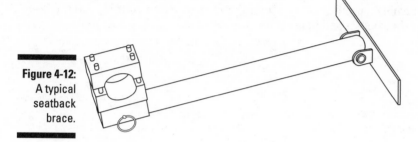

Figure 4-12:
A typical
seatback
brace.

Harnesses

A competition harness helps keep the driver in place both while driving and in a collision. It is both

- ✔ An active safety feature for greater control
- ✔ A passive safety feature that improves the driver's odds of surviving a serious collision or rollover

Straps

Harnesses can be found with varying widths of webbing in four configurations:

- ✔ Three straps (as shown in Figure 4-13)

  Usually, you should avoid three-strap or Y design harnesses. These

  - Put a lot of force on a single mounting point
  - Do a poor job of preventing the occupants from "submarining" under the lap belt (sliding forward under the harness).

- ✔ Four straps (as shown in Figure 4-14 and Figure 4-15)

✔ Five straps (as shown in Figure 4-16)

Straps that connect to the floor (like the "fifth" strap that connects between your legs) aren't supposed to restrain you by catching you directly. They keep the lap belt on your hips in an accident so you are less likely to slide forward under the harness.

✔ Six straps (as shown in Figure 4-17)

The straps in a six-strap harnesses don't pass between your legs, if you're squeamish about that. The "extra" straps run from your hips to the floor to keep the lap belt in position on your hips.

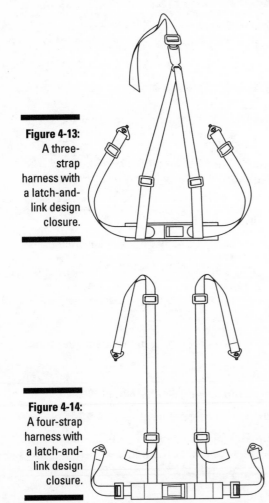

Figure 4-13:
A three-strap harness with a latch-and-link design closure.

Figure 4-14:
A four-strap harness with a latch-and-link design closure.

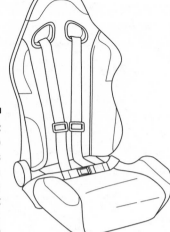

Figure 4-15:
A four-strap harness installed on a reclining aftermarket seat.

Each has more restraint than the standard three-point passenger car inertia reel seatbelt.

Serious racing restraint systems typically don't use a latch like a standard street car. Instead, they usually use either

- Cam lock design
- A latch-and-link design

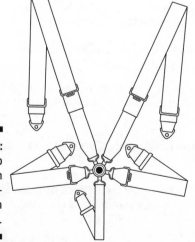

Figure 4-16:
A five-strap harness with a latch-and-link design closure.

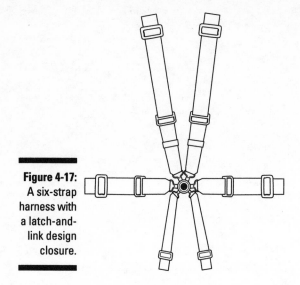

Figure 4-17:
A six-strap
harness with
a latch-and-
link design
closure.

Installation styles depend on whether the shoulder straps are to be mounted to

✔ A roll bar, roll cage, or harness bar

✔ Mounting plates that are secured to the chassis

Latches

Two-harness types are often accepted by race sanctioning bodies. They've generally proven themselves to hold more force than traditional seatbelt buckles. Both of these function equally well in an accident:

✔ Cam lock latches (shown in Figure 4-18) are easier to operate quickly, but they're more expensive and tend to jam with dirt accumulation.

✔ Latch and link designs take more time to operate, but are preferred by rally drivers in the dirt, and other off-road applications. They are also considerably less expensive.

Usually, a five- or six-strap unit is the best choice if you have a racing seat with harness slots.

When shopping for a competition harness, get a cam lock or latch-and-link design instead of the traditional buckle-type connectors (as used in street driven cars).

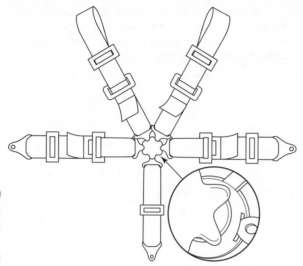

Figure 4-18:
A cam lock
latch design.

Installation

Installing a competition harness is straightforward, and even easier if a cage, roll bar, or harness bar already is installed in the car. Plan on spending up to two hours installing each harness.

If the harness will be used without a cage or roll bar, use care in ensuring that the shoulder straps sit at an appropriate angle to the driver's seated position; compressed vertebrae and herniated discs can result if the harness exerts downward force on the spine in a collision.

Don't use competition harnesses on the street.

- ✔ **Harnesses severely restrict mobility.** Forget about turning to look over your shoulder to change lanes or back out of the garage, much less reaching out at a toll booth or a drive-thru window.

- ✔ **Highway rescue personnel may have trouble getting you out.** An EMT at a highway wreck may not

  - Be prepared to cut you out of a competition harness
  - Know how to open the latch

- ✔ **Competition harnesses are extremely uncomfortable.** They must be tightened at all points, almost to the point that circulation is cut off. Wearing a harness loosely or leaving straps unfastened may put you at more risk for harm than using the factory seatbelts.

If a harness has been used in a collision, its webbing is compromised. (Harnesses have expiration dates — avoid buying a harness past its expiration date.) Also be wary of sun faded or dirty harnesses. Both UV and dirt can degrade the integrity of the webbing.

Part III
Rims and Rubber

In this part . . .

This part explains the importance of choosing the correct wheels and tires for your application. Different tire types and ratings are explained, as are wheel designs and construction methods.

Chapter 5

Tires

ires are the only contact point between your car and the road, so when you're tire shopping, think beyond the basic questions: Will they fit? How many miles will I get out of them? How much do they cost?

Tires, perhaps more than any other part of the car, help define how the car behaves and feels, how it takes corners, how quickly it can stop, how it transitions from one direction to another, how planted the car feels in different road and weather conditions, how much warning the driver has when approaching the car's limits of grip, and how hard the car launches under full acceleration. Without danger of overstatement, it is safe to say that tires are among the most critical items on your car.

Knowing When to Say When

According to the law in most U.S. states, tires must be replaced when they have reached a tread depth of ²⁄₃₂ of an inch. While the "penny test" has been the tried and true way of measuring tread depth, tire manufacturers have made it even easier for consumers by including tread wear bars on tires to help show when they are due for replacement.

The wear bar test is simply a matter of looking for a narrow section of rubber (the tread bar) bridging the tread on your tire, going horizontally across the entire width of the tire. This bar was inserted at a depth of ²⁄₃₂ of an inch when your tire was manufactured. If the wear indicator is at the same height as the tread it bridges, your tires are done and should be replaced. If you drive primarily in wet or snowy conditions, you would be well served by replacing your tires well before they wear down to ²⁄₃₂ of an inch. Tire replacement at ⁴⁄₃₂ of an inch, or even ⁵⁄₃₂ of an inch, may be a good idea depending on seasonal road conditions.

The penny test involves placing a penny into the tread grooves on a tire, as illustrated in Figure 5-1. If part of Lincoln's head is not covered by tire tread, then there is less than $\frac{2}{32}$ of an inch of tread remaining, and the tires are due for immediate replacement. You can measure for $\frac{4}{32}$ of an inch similarly using a quarter and George Washington's head, and you can measure for $\frac{6}{32}$ of an inch with a penny and the Lincoln Memorial monument on the back. For those of you outside the U.S. who don't have access to U.S. coinage, you will have to use a ruler with 32nd-inch demarcations.

Figure 5-1:
The penny test — this tire fails.

Reading a Tire Sidewall

When shopping for tires, you need to know what the numbers and letters on your sidewall mean in order to select the appropriate replacement tire.

Tires usually follow a pattern that I can illustrate by dissecting "Bridgestone Potenza RE040 205/50VR15 85V" like an earthworm in formaldehyde:

- **Brand:** Bridgestone

  This is the company that manufactured the tire.

- **Series:** Potenza

  Tire manufacturers often create a series of tires with somewhat similar handling and performance characteristics. For example, Bridgestone uses the *Potenza* name on many tires that may appeal to drivers who want a performance tire, and the *Turanza* name on many tires that are intended for less aggressive driving (or drivers with a less aggressive self-image).

- **Model:** RE040

  This is a pretty specific identification of the general performance characteristics of this tire, regardless of its size.

  Tires in the Potenza *series* vary greatly in performance, but tires of the RE040 *model* have virtually identical

- Construction
- Tread compound
- Design
- Ride

✔ **Width:** 205

This number is the width of the tire in millimeters. This is the most important number to describe a tire's *contact patch*.

For example, a 215-width, 17-inch tire may look great, but all things being equal, a 245-width, 15-inch tire will out-corner it every time, because the contact patch is wider.

✔ **Aspect ratio:** 50

This is the *height* of the sidewall from the rim to the tread, expressed as a *percentage* of the tread width.

For example, if the tire is 205 mm wide, and its aspect ratio is 50, then the sidewall is about 102.5 mm tall (50 percent of 205 mm).

Sidewall height is important for a number of reasons:

- As you move up to larger wheels, or down to smaller ones, a corresponding change needs to happen in the sidewall height of the tire in order for the rolling diameter of the wheel and tire combination to be as close to stock as possible. This will ensure the accuracy of your speedometer and prevent unwanted alignment changes.

- The sidewall height affects the turn-in feel (the responsiveness you feel at the steering wheel) and the ride quality.

    Lower aspect ratio (shorter sidewall) provides better turn-in response than a higher aspect ratio, but at the expense of less break-away warning and a more jarring ride — in extreme cases, even exposing the wheels to potential bending and breaking damage from potholes and other surface irregularities.

✔ **Speed rating:** VR (V-rated radial)

In this case, V identifies a speed rating above 149 mph.

It's almost impossible to find a public road in the U.S. where you can legally drive faster than any tire's rated speed, but speed ratings are a very important safety consideration when shopping for tires for

- Motor sports
- Countries that allow high speeds on public roads

Table 5-1 lists speed ratings.

The *R* means the tire is a *radial*. Virtually every new tire is a radial, unless you have a special tire for a classic car or a racing car.

Table 5-1	Speed Rating Designations
Speed Designation	*Maximum Speed Rating*
N	87 mph
P	93 mph
Q	99 mph
R	106 mph
S	112 mph
T	118 mph
U	124 mph
H	130 mph
V	149 mph
W	168 mph
Y	186 mph
Z	149+ mph

✔ **Load rating:** 85V

In this case, 85 means the tire is rated for 1,135 pounds (see Table 5-2). Multiply this by the number of tires on the car, and you get a maximum safe loaded vehicle weight of 4,540 pounds (including people, luggage, a full tank of gas, and all the loose change under the seats).

The last *V* repeats the V speed rating, listed in Table 5-1.

Table 5-2	Load Rating Designations		
Load Index	*Load Carrying Capacity (Per Tire)*	*Load Index*	*Load Carrying Capacity (Per Tire)*
71	761	77	908
72	783	78	937
73	805	79	963
74	827	80	992
75	853	81	1019
76	882	82	1047

Load Index	Load Carrying Capacity (Per Tire)	Load Index	Load Carrying Capacity (Per Tire)
83	1074	97	1609
84	1102	98	1653
85	1135	99	1709
86	1168	100	1764
87	1201	101	1819
88	1235	102	1874
89	1279	103	1929
90	1323	104	1984
91	1356	105	2039
92	1389	106	2094
93	1433	107	2149
94	1477	108	2205
95	1521	109	2271
96	1565	110	2337

If your tire isn't described by these two tables, then consult the tire manufacturer or a tire specialist, such as Tire Rack or Wheel Works, for further information.

Tire Shopping

Major tire retailers have tires for your car at almost any price and for almost any use. A smart buyer considers these factors when it's time to purchase:

- ✔ Weather extremes
- ✔ Driving style
- ✔ Ride and noise
- ✔ Tread life
- ✔ Styling
- ✔ Puncture resistance
- ✔ Price

Even if you aren't modifying your car, its current tires aren't always best for you:

- ✔ Car manufacturers want low costs and high profits. They may use an inexpensive tire or the brand that gives the biggest discount.

- ✔ Car manufacturers want cars to be easy to sell. They usually want tires that are smooth and quiet on a test drive, even if the tires don't grip so well.

- ✔ Car manufacturers don't want complaints. They want tires that last a long time, and do little to offend Joe or Jane Car-Buyer.

Some cars ship from the factory with tires that aren't intended for snow. If you have one of these cars, winter tires (preferably on a separate set of rims) might be a good idea. How good an idea depends mainly on such factors as

- ✔ How often you encounter snow

- ✔ How deep the snow is

- ✔ Whether you have another car to drive in snowy weather

- ✔ Whether you can just stay home when there's too much snow to drive on high-performance tires

Don't get sentimental toward tires — when it's time for them to go, let them go. They are not T-shirts, they are critical automotive components. It doesn't matter how expensive or cool they were when you bought them. Tires are expendable, and need to be treated as such. When they become sub par, replace them with the best new tires for your needs, even if your old tires still have legal tread.

Don't ignore the warning signs of a worn tire, or put off replacement to a more convenient time. This can't be stated strongly enough. The price you pay for saving money on a replacement set of tires may be your car or your well-being.

Tire Selection

Tire technology marches forward with time. The cutting-edge tire that shipped on a 1989 Corvette isn't cutting-edge by today's standards.

The simple process for selecting a tire is

1. Consider each tire's unique characteristics carefully — and you can't do that without doing your homework.

2. Decide which characteristics that a tire might possess are most important to you.

3. Take into account factors such as speed ratings and tire sizing.

It can be that simple, or far more complex:

- ✔ A smart tire buyer will need to consider a slew of traits that each tire possesses, from cost to wear rating, what tire is available in what size, breakaway communication, and more. Talk to friends (and foes) and see what kind of tires they have, and how they like them. Maybe even ask for a test drive.

  Breakaway characteristics refers to a tire's ability to let you know when grip is turning to slip. This kind of information inspires confidence and allows the driver to always maintain complete control.

- ✔ Don't assume that because Tire Company X makes one brilliant tire, their entire line will be equally brilliant. No matter how similar the nomenclature, do not assume the Johnson Racing SuperSticky 5000 is "close enough" to the SuperSticky 6000.

How tires work

There are several variables that determine a tire's performance. Considering these variables may help you determine what you expect out of your tires, and thus help you pick the most appropriate tires for your application. You need to consider

- ✔ Forces on tires
- ✔ Compound
- ✔ Tread pattern
- ✔ Sidewall height and stiffness

Air pressure is part of the tire's strength. A tire without full air pressure is at risk of a big blowout, and will not feel or perform as it should. Check your tires' air pressure every other time you stop for gas for normal driving, and before *every* competition.

Forces on tires

Generally, a tire's grip must be shared three ways:

 ✔ Transferring power to the ground

 ✔ Providing grip against lateral forces when cornering

 ✔ Stopping grip, when braking

Because the car rides on four tires, the car always rides on what are referred to as four *contact patches.*

When the car is at rest, its entire weight is resting on these four points; a 4000-pound car with approximately 50/50 weight distribution is putting down 1000 pounds of static weight at each corner. When the car is under way at speed on a straight road, these numbers decrease as aerodynamics operate to lift the car from its tires. Depending on the design of the car's body, including spoilers, wings, diffusers, splitters, and air channels which are designed to either combat lift through vacuum or create down force through wind resistance, the car will put down varying amounts of pressure front to rear at speed, but will generally match the amount of pressure holding the car to the road from side to side.

 ✔ When accelerating, weight shifts rearward, reducing the weight on the front tires.

   This is why pure drag racing cars are built with rear-wheel drive — so that the massive amount of power doesn't lift the drive wheels right off the ground, effectively stopping the acceleration.

 ✔ When braking is applied, weight shifts *forward,* reducing the weight on the rear tires.

   This is why most street cars have more powerful brakes on the front wheels — they bear the brunt of the car's weight under heavy braking.

 ✔ When cornering, weight transfers to the tires on the *outside* of the turn.

   Things get more complicated as the car is, for example, both braking and turning at the same time, or accelerating and turning, in which case the car's weight will shift around as dynamic forces transfer the car's weight from tire to tire.

Compound

What the rubber in the tire is made of (the *tread compound*) determines how *grippy* the tire is. This grip depends on such conditions as

 ✔ Road surface

 ✔ Operating temperature range

 ✔ Tread depth

Street tires can be characterized by

- ✔ Working consistently across a wide range of temperatures
- ✔ Retaining their grip through month after month of *heat cycles* (rising to normal operating temperature while driving, then cooling back down while parked)

Generally, the grippier the tire, the faster it wears.

Tire manufacturers list tread wear ratings on the tire's sidewall. There isn't an industry standard for measuring tread wear, so these numbers are really only useful for comparing tires from the same manufacturer.

The Department of Transportation (DOT) requires tread wear ratings on all road-approved tires sold in the U.S., with the exception of winter and light truck tires. This tread wear rating, known as the Uniform Tire Quality Grade (UTQG) is expressed on the tire's sidewall as a number above or below 100. For tires of the same brand, a 125 tread-wear-rated tire should last 1.25 times as long as a tire with a 100 tread-wear rating.

Manufacturers do their *own* testing for UTQG numbers. There's no independent body checking in on the manufacturers at this time, so you should rely on a UTQG number strictly for the purposes of evaluating tires of the same brand:

- ✔ While a GripCzar tire rated at 300 should last about ten times as long as a 30-rated GripCzar tire, the difference between a GripCzar 30 and a NeverSlip 30 may be significant — and it's anyone's guess.
- ✔ Things get even murkier with house brand tires sold by large retail chains. Any tire can be sourced from any manufacturer, so the UTQG numbers can be even harder to decipher.
- ✔ If you aren't sure, look for independent third-party tests or consumer reviews like those found at `www.tirerack.com` or published by *Consumer Reports* magazine.

Tread pattern

The tire tread pattern is the series of grooves, rain channels, and tread blocks that allow the tire to grip the road surface and channel water or snow to prevent hydroplaning. (Hydroplaning occurs when the tire is unable to channel enough water from under the contact patch, forcing the car to lift up and skim across the water and so lose traction with the road.)

A tread design that is more like a treadless racing slick resists

- ✔ *Chunking* (literally ripping off tread blocks)
- ✔ *Squirming* (tread blocks twisting under load)

Of course, if everyone drove around on slicks all the time, the roadways would turn into giant pinball machines during the first rain or snowfall. But you can check these aspects of a tread design:

✔ Deeper water channels and smaller tread blocks can move more water from under the contact patch. But these helpful smaller tread blocks with deeper channels also squirm a lot under aggressive maneuvering, so keep the universal idea of *compromise* in mind here.

✔ Shallow water channels and larger tread blocks provide

  • More direct cornering response

  • More grip

  • Less chunking

High-performance street tires often have a center water channel, with smaller channels whisking water away from the center.

✔ Deeper water channels and a more complex tread pattern provide

  • More squirminess when cornering

  • Less grip and a louder ride on dry roads

  • Superior grip and more confidence on a wet road

Sidewall height and stiffness

Sidewall *height* and *stiffness* affect responsiveness and ride.

A tire with a lower, stiffer sidewall usually responds to your steering inputs faster than a tire with a taller or less rigid sidewall. The downsides to a tire with a lower or stiffer sidewall are

✔ More ride harshness

✔ More vulnerability to rim damage

✔ Less warning of breakaway

A tire with a stiffer *carcass* (a tire's internal structure and reinforcements) usually weighs more than a tire with less internal reinforcement belting. A heavier tire has slightly slower suspension and acceleration response than a lighter tire of the same size.

The difference between sidewalls may depend on how you use your tires:

✔ A stiffer sidewall helps in cornering.

✔ A softer sidewall is preferred for speed.

Street tires

A street tire is a compromise of handling characteristics against wear, noise, weather conditions, temperature variations, and puncture resistance.

Off-road truck and SUV tires aside, street tires for passenger cars can further be broken down into several different types. Please refer to Table 5-3 for a quick comparison.

Table 5-3	**Comparing Different Kinds of Tires**
Type of Tire	*Designed For*
Winter/Snow	Street driving in wet, snowy, or icy conditions
Touring	Minimum noise, a cushy ride, and long wear, but no performance
All Season Performance	Spirited driving all year round
Summer High Performance	Optimized for performance on dry roads
Ultra-High Performance	Similar to Summer Performance with more grip and lower tread wear
Dual Purpose	A track or auto-cross tire that can be driven to and from the event

Summer performance tires and *ultra-high performance* tires are essentially the same, but they are offered in different sizes. Ultra-high performance tires are generally offered in larger sizes.

Disregarding the collision between the permanence of book publishing, and the fast-moving evolution of the performance tire, as of the press date, the following summer performance tires offer good value for their performance level:

- Toyo T1-S (see Figure 5-2)
- Falken Azenis (see Figure 5-3)
- Yokohama Advan A048 (see Figure 5-4)

Figure 5-2:
The Toyo
T1-S tire.

Figure 5-3:
The Falken
Azenis.

Figure 5-4:
The
Yokahama
Advan A048.

Maybe you shouldn't spend the big bucks on an ultra-high performance tire:

✔ A dual-purpose or competition tire outperforms an ultra-high performance tire on the track.

At a track or an autocross, it *hurts* to demolish a $1,000 set of prestige street tires in a few hours trying to keep up with someone on a better track tire.

✔ A summer performance tire nearly matches an ultra-high performance tire on the street for less money.

On the street, you're a menace to yourself and others if you drive hard enough to justify upgrading from a well-engineered summer performance tire to an ultra-high performance tire. If you care whether you can drive 83 mph or 89 mph through a highway curve posted at 35 mph, something is very wrong with your street driving habits. And a dual-purpose DOT (Department of Transportation) legal race/street tire probably can make it at 95 mph!

Other types of tires are available, and may fit your needs better than summer performance tires:

- ✔ **Winter snow/ice tires:** A deep, open tread pattern resists snow clogging. A soft tread compound provides more grip on icy surfaces.

  If you drive your performance car in snowy months, mount snow tires on the stock wheels for winter and use upgraded aftermarket wheels for performance tires in other months. Winter tires are available in most original-equipment sizes.

- ✔ **All-season tires:** These aren't for performance driving. They're compromised for very long tread life and all extremes of weather.

  Manufacturers offer mud and snow rated all-season "performance" tires. These outperform the average Touring tire, but are by no means comparable to summer performance or ultra-high performance tires.

- ✔ **Touring tires:** These aren't for performance driving. They're compromised for a very quiet and gentle ride.

There are a couple of reasons to consider ultra-high performance tires:

- ✔ They may be the only tires with the larger diameter and low aspect ratio you want for your car.

- ✔ They deliver the most grip and best handling response of any street tire.

Your best tire and wheel decisions may depend on your wallet and your storage space:

- ✔ The ideal solution is *two* sets of wheels and tires you can swap at a moment's notice:

  - On the street, your everyday wear can be whatever tickles your fancy, whether you want stock wheels with reasonably priced performance rubber or oversized bling-bling spinner rims with wide whitewall tires.

  - For the track or autocross, you want a dedicated competition performance tire on lightweight wheels.

- ✔ If you're limited to one set of wheels and tires, and you want a performance feel for street driving, track days, or autocrosses, your best bet is almost always a *dual purpose tire,* not a high-dollar prestige street tire.

When you attend your first performance driving school, stick with street tires for the first few track visits. Street tires tend to be more gradual and forgiving at the limit, which makes learning your car's limits easier (while putting less stress on your suspension components and chassis). Begin the switch to race tires when

- ✔ You're comfortable driving your car at 80 percent or 90 percent of its potential.

- ✔ You're turning consistent lap times at the track on your street tires.

- ✔ You have adjusted your car's suspension to suit your driving style.

  After switching to competition tires, you may need to readjust your suspension if your car's behavior changes.

Race tires

Unlike on the street, race tires are less about brand appeal and more about finding something that you are comfortable driving consistently at the limit.

Race tires have some quirks:

- ✔ A race tire becomes hard and unpredictable after a number of *heat cycles* (heating up through use, then cooling down again). This number of cycles varies from tire to tire.

- ✔ Race tires need to be slowly brought up to an optimal temperature before they perform their best. This can take a few turns or an entire lap, depending on the length of the circuit, the weather, and other factors.

  Autocross and gymkhana drivers have even less opportunity to bring the tires up to temperature because their runs are shorter than track drivers.

- ✔ A race tire has a very narrow warning envelope at its limits. It demands a more skilled driver to feel out where those limits are.

- ✔ Race tires are needed in both grooved and slick or shaved versions, depending on whether there is moisture on the track.

  Race tires can flat-spot (get shaved flat in one spot, from skidding) when the brakes lock up or when the car spins/slides. A flat-spotted tire is like a square wheel, which is both an oxymoron and the end of your day (unless you have a replacement).

  This isn't same kind of flat-spotting that appears when a car is parked for an extended period and the tires become out of round. A parking flat spot, unlike one caused by friction, is generally temporary and disappears after the car has been driven a few miles.

Using racing tires meant for the track on public roads might be tempting, but don't do it. Why?

✔ Non-DOT racing tires are illegal on public roads in the U.S.

✔ Racing tires puncture easily.

✔ Racing slicks are hazardous to your health in a sudden rain.

✔ Racing tires will blast your paint job with gravel and other debris.

A car on slicks accelerates and corners on a dry race track in ways that street tires can't approach. Even a dual-purpose DOT-legal street/race tire pales in comparison to a true race slick.

To get the most out of race slicks, your car needs to undergo some preparation in order to handle all that extra grip. Race slicks (see Figure 5-5 for an example) will work your suspension to its limits. The car leans, the chassis twists, and the body groans under the strain. The sway bar end link mounting tabs, if not reinforced, may bend or break. Without mudguards (or careful application of masking tape) slicks will kick up enough gravel to sandblast the rocker panels under cornering. Perhaps most disastrous, cars can suffer engine oil starvation under the extreme cornering.

Figure 5-5:
A racing
slick.

A well-baffled oil pan and oil pressure gauge, with a warning light, are essential if you're running on racing slicks. Increased cornering forces can starve an engine with an oil pan not designed with these forces in mind. The baffles in the pan help keep the oil from sloshing around from side to side, and possibly away from the pump pickup point.

If you're just getting started looking for race tires, check with race teams and on race-oriented automotive message boards for a set of used tires with a few days of use left in them. Tires that have hardened by time or heat cycles can be rejuvenated with chemicals available from race shops. Visually inspect the tires before mounting them to ensure that they haven't sustained punctures or flat-spotting.

Dual-purpose tires

DOT-legal race compound tires are dual-purpose street-legal tires that are specially designed for competition. They are the only true race tire in the U.S. that can legally (or reasonably) be driven to and from the track.

Dual-purpose street/track tires embarrass even ultra-high performance street tires at a fraction of the price (especially in smaller sizes).

Race compound tires often carry the *R* designation in the name of the tire (such as A032R, 555R, R3SO3, or RA1) or may simply be so designated by the manufacturer without any *R* used in the name (V700). Unfortunately, there is no clear way of knowing if the *R* on the sidewall refers to the compound or the radial carcass, since almost all radial tires also have an *R* on the sidewall. If in doubt, you just have to do a little extra research on the tire, or consult with your tire retailer.

Dual-purpose tires are available with either

✔ Full tread for street driving and wet racetracks

✔ Shaved tread for dry racetracks

Shaved tires aren't welcome everywhere:

• Shaved tires may be illegal and unsafe for street driving.

• If you have shaved tires for racing, make sure they are legal for your class.

Dual-purpose tires, like the Yokohama A032R (see Figure 5-6), are often designed as wet-weather race tires. Dual-purpose tires use racing tire rubber compounds on a reinforced street-legal carcass. Sturdy, heavy sidewalls can easily offset any weight saved from ultra light alloy wheels, so consider the big picture before settling on a setup.

Figure 5-6:
The
Yokohama
A032R.

I've run Yokohama A032R dual-purpose tires on my MR2 for three years, and they've served me well as a compromise tire for driving to a weekend track day, coping well with the rigors of track use, and still allowing me to drive my car home after the event without changing wheels. A set lasts me about 5,000 miles before they become either too worn and/or heat cycled. Companies like Toyo, Bridgestone, and Kumho offer similar tires. For the drag race fans, Nitto's 555R can be dropped in pressure so it reacts much like a "wrinkle wall" drag tire on launch; at normal inflation, it corners with the best.

Although I personally run my daily driver on dual-purpose street tires, there are a couple of significant considerations to keep in mind before running out and buying a set:

- ✔ These tires usually last less than 7,500 miles on the street before the tread wears below legal and safe depth, or they become hardened from multiple heat cycles.

- ✔ They can be much noisier than normal street tires, much like I imagine monster truck tires would sound at freeway speeds.

Most dual-purpose tires are designed for racing and autocross classes that require street-legal tires. They're also great for track days.

Top competitors in street tire classes treat their tires like racing tires. If they drive the car on the street, they don't use their competition tires. If you have dual-purpose tires for competition or track days, I recommend that you

- ✔ Minimize the street miles on the tires.

- ✔ Complete at least one full heat cycle before driving hard on the track.

- ✔ Use shaved tread if the tires are to be driven only on dry racetracks. (Make sure the shaved tread is legal for your class.)

When There Isn't Any Air There

Modern tires are strong and puncture-resistant. Flats and blowouts are less common than in the bad old days. Still, you're bound to run over a nail (or a hammer) now and then, almost always at an inconvenient time and place. There's never a good time for a flat.

For safe everyday driving, you need either

- ✔ A spare tire and all the equipment to change it

    Pop quiz! Is your spare tire inflated to the recommended pressure? Do you have all the wrenches and jack parts to change it? If you don't know, go out and check right now. I'll wait here until you get back.

- ✔ Run-flat tires with a pressure-monitoring system

    Run-flat tires (see Figure 5-7 for an example) are one of the biggest advances in everyday tire technology since the invention of the steel-belted radial.

Figure 5-7: The Kumho ECSTA MX XRP, a run-flat tire.

The dinky spare tire in most cars lets you drive a few miles to get where you can repair or replace your flat tire. Don't go *anywhere else* on that spare tire! (The speed rating restriction on those space-saving spare tires is designed not so much to prevent a tire blowout as it is designed to minimize wear on your differential from having a tire size that is dramatically different from the one on the other end of the axle.)

Pressure monitoring

Tire pressure monitoring can keep you from driving on under-inflated tires if you have a puncture or neglect your tire pressure.

Tire pressure monitoring systems are available for most cars, either as factory equipment or as an add-on. Most pressure monitoring systems are light and simple, weighing mere ounces, and transmit wirelessly to a monitor mounted in the passenger compartment. You are alerted instantly when a tire loses pressure. Figure 5-8 illustrates a pressure sensor mounted on a rim.

A budget-minded solution that will visually alert a driver to low pressure is a simple mechanical device that screws on to the valve stem of each wheel. This solution has several limitations, however: It can't tell you the exact pressure (the colors change to indicate the approximate tire pressure), and it can't alert you to a drop in pressure from within the passenger compartment.

Figure 5-8:
A tire pressure sensor mounted on a rim.

It is generally a good idea to carry a portable air compressor that can be run off your car's cigarette lighter or similar power source, along with a tire plug kit. While this will not ensure that you will never be stranded on the side of the road, it may be useful for minor punctures or if idiots let the air out of your tires.

A can of *tire repair* (such as Fix-a-Flat) may be substituted for an air compressor, but it has a couple of significant drawbacks:

✔ The stuff is flammable, which makes fixing the tire later a hazard.

Always warn the technician if you've used anything but compressed air in a tire. *Never* just hand the car over and ask for a new tire if you've used a tire-sealing product.

✔ Hardened sealant foam must be removed from the inside of your wheel when the tire is repaired. It's a nasty job.

Removing your spare tire, and carrying a plug kit or can of foam and a roadside service card may be a great way to save unwanted pounds from your car, but being stuck at the side of the road — usually at the worst time possible — is a big trade-off for the added weight of the spare tire and tools.

Run-flat tires

Run-flat tires (also known as *extended mobility tires* or *EMT*) can be driven a short distance at reduced speeds without any air pressure. If you have a puncture, you can drive to a safe place for help. They're standard on street cars when designers eliminate the space and weight of a spare tire and its tools.

A run-flat tire needs air pressure for *normal* driving, like any other tire:

- ✔ You can drive only a few miles for a repair if you don't have full pressure in a run-flat tire. If you continue driving without full air pressure, you will damage or shred the tire (just like a standard tire).

- ✔ Pressure monitoring is essential on a street car with run-flat tires. Otherwise, you might not realize you've sustained a puncture until the tire is completely shredded.

One of the latest industry developments in run-flat technology focuses on new polyurethane tire compounds. Beyond being more environmentally friendly than conventional rubber compounds, and eventually allowing for more consistent manufacturing quality control compared to rubber, the handling and load carrying abilities of future polyurethane tires, when run with low to no pressure, promise to greatly surpass those of rubber compounds when used as a run-flat tire.

Chapter 6

Wheels

*W*heels can dramatically change both the look and performance of a car. The manufacture and sales of aftermarket wheels grows more than any other car industry each year. Cars and SUVs look more alike each year, but changing your vehicle's wheels can give your car or truck an individual character and personality.

Buying Right

Wheels are among the most common, and costly, of modifications. Even the tamest car or truck can benefit from a well-considered set of wheels, but the cost can be considerable — anywhere from a couple of hundred dollars for a used set of factory alloy wheels off eBay to a set of wheels that costs as much as a new car. With this in mind, carefully consider which set of wheels is the best match for your car.

Fit

How the wheels fit is important for both

✓ Performance

Wheels that don't fit may cause erratic and dangerous driving characteristics in your car.

✓ Appearance

Even the best set of wheels looks downright awkward if they don't fit right.

Directly consulting a wheel and tire expert is a good idea. You need the following information.

Basic dimensions

If you're replacing stock wheels with custom wheels of the same size, the first step is to match the basic dimensions of the stock wheels. The custom wheel catalog should list the following dimensions:

- Bolt pattern
- Rim width
- Rim diameter
- Offset
- Backspacing

Bolt pattern

The *bolt pattern* refers to

- The number of lug nuts (or bolts) that hold the wheel on the *hub* (the assembly on the axle that receives the wheel)

  Wheels are made to bolt on using four, five, six, or eight lugs.

- The diameter of the *circle* described by the centers of the wheel's lug holes

The bolt pattern is described by two numbers, like *5x110mm, 5x4.5",* or *5 by 4.5":*

- The first number is the number of *lug holes.*
- The second number indicates the diameter of the circle of holes, in either millimeters or inches.

  If you can't find the diameter of this imaginary circle from your car's manual or another source, you can measure it based on Figure 6-1 and Figure 6-2. (The circle passes through the *center* of the lug holes.)

Make sure the lug hole is machined for the *shape* of your car's lug nuts or bolt heads. Depending on the car, the lug holes usually need to be either

- *Cone* shaped
- *Ball* shaped

Rim width

Rim width describes the width of the rim where the tire sits (the *bead seat*) — *not* the overall width of the rim. This measurement is usually in inches.

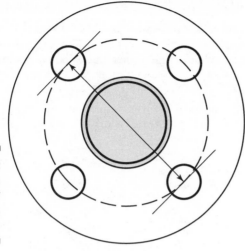

Figure 6-1:
Measuring
the diameter
for four, six,
or eight lugs.

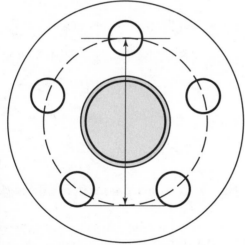

Figure 6-2:
Measuring
the diameter
for five lugs.

Rim diameter

This describes the diameter of the rim where the tire sits (the bead seat) — *not* the overall diameter of the rim. This measurement is usually in inches.

Hub centering

The hole in the center of the wheel should fit snugly around the protruding center of the hub.

A *plastic* wheel center is likely to lose its snug fit under the heat of hard driving.

Position

Aside from the basic dimensions of the wheel, you have to make sure that the wheel is *positioned* (located) correctly on your car. To do this you need to make sure that your wheels have the right offset and backspacing for your car.

Offset

Offset describes the position of the mounting surface based on the physical center of the wheel, as shown in Figure 6-3. The offset can be

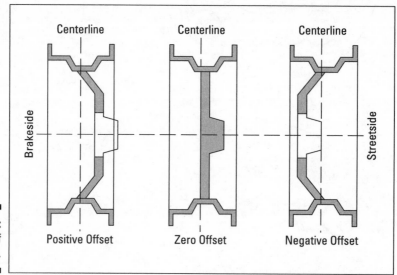

Figure 6-3:
The offset of a wheel.

- ✔ **Positive:** The mounting surface is closer to the front side, or curb side, of the wheel.

    Positive offset (a shallow "dish") is found on almost all front-wheel drive and most modern rear-wheel drive cars.

- ✔ **Negative:** The mounting surface is closer to the back side (brake/drum side) of the wheel.

- ✔ **Zero:** The mounting surface is at the physical center of the wheel.

    Negative and zero offset (deep "dish") can be found on

    - Traditional rear-wheel drive cars and trucks
    - Cars that are going for the Euro deep dish look

Backspacing

The backspacing becomes important if you upgrade your brakes. Larger brakes need more room, so it is important that you make sure your wheels have enough backspacing to fit those larger brakes you're considering purchasing, or else you may have to spend some more money getting another set of wheels as well.

Figure 6-4 shows backspacing among other wheel measurements. Figure 6-5 shows how a big brake can fill even a big wheel.

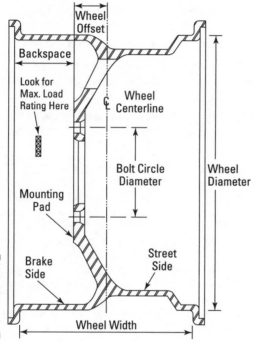

Figure 6-4:
Measuring back-spacing.

Wheel Offset

Backspace

Look for Max. Load Rating Here

Wheel Centerline

Bolt Circle Diameter

Wheel Diameter

Mounting Pad

Brake Side

Street Side

Wheel Width

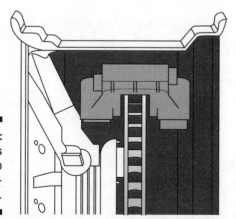

Figure 6-5:
Brakes can fill up the back-spacing.

Appearance

Hundreds of wheel designs are available in every finish and pattern conceivable. If performance isn't essential, you can use any wheel that fits your car and looks good to you.

When you have the right wheels, shop for tires that

✔ **Fit the rims**

✔ **Have the correct width and diameter for your suspension setup**

If you don't actually intend to change your suspension setup, your new tires should have the same *width* and overall *diameter* as the original tires, regardless of your wheel size.

If you change the *wheel* diameter, you can still maintain the stock *tire* diameter and width by selecting the right *aspect ratio.* Chapter 5 explains aspect ratio.

✔ **Have the performance you want**

Consider purchasing tires that are readily available, and preferably in stock at a local store. Getting a flat and then waiting for a four-week backorder is not fun.

Performance

For maximum performance, your first concern should be to choose the best tire based on cost, size, and availability, and then work backward from that to identify an appropriate wheel for that tire. A wheel chosen for a performance car should be

✔ **Correctly sized for the car's appearance and suspension.**

Consider your car's proportions:

• Usually, bigger cars can look right with bigger wheels and still look proportional, but bigger isn't always better.

• Bigger wheels make your *brakes* look smaller, so what you gain in wheel presence you can lose by having dinky-looking brakes.

Some measurements depend on both the wheel and tire.

✔ **Light and strong enough for its intended application.**

Those big, pretty "dubs" look stunning on that parked show car, but can dramatically affect the performance of your car — as in slow it down. If you are building a boulevard cruiser, weight is less of a concern, but consider the condition of your local roads as well.

A well-placed pothole can ruin your whole weekend — and a good part of Monday, too. Big, heavy wheels will also hamper suspension response and will ultimately lead to additional wear and tear on suspension components. Prepare to face big repair bills down the line.

✔ **Big enough for any brakes you are considering for the car.**

Big brakes need big wheels. If some major-league brakes are in your future, make sure they'll fit inside your new wheels *before* you buy the wheels.

Appearance

When appearance is the primary concern, the biggest technical issues generally are how big a wheel-tire combination can be run without rubbing either the fender lining, fender lip, or strut tower at full lock. Many cars can accommodate wheels that are several sizes larger than the original equipment. Usually, you can get the right look without scraping on bumps or in turns by

✔ **Rolling the fender lip.** There are machines that can precisely perform the task.

If you're a do-it-yourselfer and you don't care how good the result *looks,* you can use a baseball bat, as shown in Figure 6-6 — at your own risk of course. Shove the bat between the tire and fender, and literally roll the fender by rolling the bat.

✔ **Modifying the fender liner.**

Thinking about removing or trimming fender liners? Don't. Fix the basic problem instead of hacking fender liners — especially in a modern car. The fender liner

- Protects the suspension and electronic brake/suspension components from water spray, brake heat, and road debris

- Manages airflow under the car for both aerodynamics and engine cooling

If you need to remove or modify fender liners, you've probably made a basic mistake, like these:

- The offset on your wheels isn't right.

- You've lowered your car too much.

- You have an inappropriate wheel and tire combination.

✔ **Installing wheel spacers.**

Wheel spacers fit between your wheels and hubs.

You should use wheel spacers only if you intend to keep your current wheels and increase the *track* of your car for improved handling or looks. If you're buying new wheels

- Don't *plan* on getting wheel spacers.

- Consult with professionals to ensure that you are getting the correct wheel offset for your car so you don't *need* wheel spacers to make the wheels fit.

Wheel spacers are used in a couple of cases:

- When wheels don't have enough *offset*

  A wheel spacer compensates for too little offset by pushing the wheels farther away from the hub.

- To make a lug-centric wheel (one that centers by tightening the wheel lugs rather than a hub-specific mounting surface) hub-centric

Depending on how you car's wheels are bolted on, wheel spacers require either

- Longer wheel studs

  Some wheel studs can be unscrewed for easy removal. Others will require a hydraulic press to remove.

- Longer wheel bolts

  Wheel bolts are an easy swap. Just use the right bolts for the thickness of spacer being installed.

Wheel spacers, as shown in Figure 6-7, have a few drawbacks:

- Wheel spacers add rotating, unsprung weight (absolutely the worst kind for acceleration, cornering, and ride).

- Longer wheel studs or bolts are more prone to shear fatigue (snapping) than standard-length bolts.

  These are weak points for cars that have regular track use.

Figure 6-6:
Rolling a
fender
for more
clearance.

Figure 6-7:
Some wheel
spacers.

In extreme cases, wider fender flares coupled with either air bagged or coilover aftermarket suspensions can produce the look you want.

Performance

If you're mostly interested in performance over appearance, then shopping for wheels is basically a question of how wide a tire you need. Working from that, you can establish the corresponding

- ✔ Wheel diameter
- ✔ Tire aspect ratio (for maintaining gearing and speedometer accuracy)

The wheel should be no bigger than it needs to be to

- ✔ Accommodate a tire of the right width
- ✔ Give the wheel enough extra meat to support the tire's sidewall under extreme cornering loads

If two similar wheels have the correct offset, backspacing, and brake clearance, usually you get better performance with the wheel that has

- Less weight
- Wider rim
- Smaller diameter

The smaller diameter wheel requires a tire with a larger aspect ratio to get the right *tire* diameter and width for your car

Adding a bit more negative offset can widen your car's track while maintaining a correct alignment without spacers and longer wheel studs

When in doubt, contact a tire expert and tap his or her wisdom.

Materials

There are many wheel manufacturing methods. Check each one so you can find the right balance of performance and cost for your car.

Forged wheels

Forged aluminum wheels have a higher strength-to-weight ratio than cast aluminum.

Rays Engineering in Japan has its Volk line of lightweight wheels available in sizes and offsets to fit many popular Asian and some German applications. Rays/Volk made a name for itself in the Japanese Touring Car Series and has brought this race-bred philosophy to consumer-level wheels, starting with the popular TE-37 model and later expanding its offerings of lightweight wheels to include variations on this core design.

Forged wheels are made by compressing a solid billet under extreme pressure. This creates a consistent and strong base from which the rim is spun.

Forged centers were used in two- and three-piece wheels using a cast outer section. However, because the outside of the rim was cast, it remained weaker than a one-piece forged wheel. It wasn't until the one-piece forged wheel became common that the benefits of running a completely forged wheel were fully realized. You can step up in diameter to wheels sized using ultra-low profile sidewall tires without fear of bending your wheels on the first pothole they encounter. Previously, track cars could get away with low-profile tires, but their owners had to switch wheels for the drive home. With forged wheels, you can drive most everywhere on the same wheels and tires.

Forged wheels have a few tradeoffs:

✔ Forged wheels are usually more expensive than their cast and semi-solid forged counterparts.

✔ Though a forged wheel has higher limits than a cast wheel, it may fail more dramatically.

A cast rim *bends* at its limit, a forged rim *shatters*.

In rally racing, many cars use cast wheels that can limp to the next checkpoint when damaged. When forged wheels shatter, they can cause damage to other components of the car, including the brakes, hubs, and axles. It's no fun to be out of a long rally after just a few miles because a broken wheel wrecked the rest of your car beyond repair.

Cast wheels

Cast wheels are generally easier and cheaper to manufacture than forged or semi-forged wheels, so they're often a fraction of the price of a forged wheel. Generally speaking, cast wheels are both heavier and softer (and so more prone to bending) than forged or semi-forged wheels.

The latest cast wheels increase in strength and reduce in weight. For example, a 15-inch Volk TE-37 forged wheel may cost $400 or more; it weighs a bit less than 10 pounds. A comparable Konig Helium cast wheel that costs as little as $92 weighs just over 11 pounds.

Cast wheels are more vulnerable to pothole damage with a low aspect ratio tire. However, the savings from buying a set of cast wheels instead of forged wheels may help offset the cost of a replacement cast wheel if needed.

Semi-solid forged and modular wheels

Modular wheels mate a forged center to a cast outer rim. Many European cars look best on modular style wheels.

Modular wheels reached their heyday in the '70s and '80s with popular applications from BBS for European cars. Sold as a premium wheel, with a premium price to match, modular wheels (which come in both two- and three-piece designs) allow you to

✔ Replace just part of a damaged wheel

✔ Mix and match colors and styles of center sections and outer lips for a unique look

Expect to pay a premium when you have these wheels installed or when tires are mounted. Some shops won't even touch multi-piece wheels because of the special training required and the potential liability.

Multipiece wheels require careful assembly and mounting. A botched job can make the pieces separate at speed with disastrous results.

Speed Star Racing (SSR) responded to the growing popularity of Volk wheels by closing the gap in both price and performance between a true forged wheel and a well-designed, but still softer, cast wheel by offering what it named a semi-solid forged wheel. SSR created its wheels by taking the same type of billet that is used in traditional high-pressure forging, and heating it up to nearly molten state before forcing it into a mold at a much faster rate than traditional gravity or low-pressure casting. The result is a wheel that has a strength-to-weight ratio between a cast and forged wheel, with a price between traditional cast and forged wheels as well.

Want to Super Size That?

If you know hip-hop culture (or if you watched MTV for five minutes last night), then *bling, dubs,* and *spinners* don't need any explanation.

If you bought this book immediately after serving a penance at a remote alpine monastery where television, radio, and contact with the outside world were forbidden, the hot trend in wheels is bigger, flashier, and with separate spinning center sections that continue to rotate when the car has stopped moving, as shown in Figure 6-8.

Figure 6-8:
Spinners. The outer set of spokes spins freely.

Worried about strength, unsprung weight, and contact patch? You can stop reading the chapter right here. Your priorities are all wrong for *stylin' bling-bling rims,* O Corner-Carving One.

The rest of this chapter explains how to select dubs for the right look while keeping the car reasonably practical.

The look

Most often seen on luxury SUVs and big luxury sedans, the hip-hop set has a seemingly relentless appetite for rim diameters that have little practical value other than to make an impression . . . not that there's anything wrong with that.

If the wheel makes the car, then giant chromed wheels make the statement that you are, indeed, living larger. The spinning integrated hub sections are mesmerizing the first few times you see them at a traffic light, and they can make a run-of-the-mill Navigator, Escalade, or Hummer H2 stand out from every other SUV.

To further round out the look, oversized dubs are installed to minimize the wheel gap between the outside edge of the tire and the fender, so the car looks like it's just floating on these huge gleaming discs without any tires.

The look is certainly not for everyone. You need a car with appropriate road presence to not look ridiculous (don't try this with a Yugo). But if you have the SUV or luxury car and the inclination, big wheels can make a big hit.

If you install dubs, don't be surprised when your car is slower to accelerate, harder to stop, and burns more fuel. If these things *helped* performance, Michael Schumacher's grand prix car would be sponsored by Vogue Tyres.

The life

If you've gotta live large, a few guidelines can keep the fun big and the headaches small with dramatically oversized dubs:

✔ Keep the overall *tire diameter* fairly close to stock.

This means that as you *increase* wheel diameter, you must *reduce* the tire's aspect ratio.

• Good news: This is the look you probably want anyway.

• Bad news: You'll feel every pebble in the road, and you're more likely to damage the wheels and tires on bad potholes and railroad crossings.

✔ Make sure your suspension is up to the task of coping with these over-sized, heavy monsters:

- You probably need to compensate for the extra unsprung weight with stiffer spring rates and a heavier duty set of shocks.

- Wheel hubs, steering racks, and bearings will get a workout the factory engineers didn't plan. Keep tabs on these mechanical bits for failure and either upgrade them now or replace them as soon as they show the strain.

- Extra rotating mass reduces the performance of your brakes. Blingin' big brakes are available for popular rides, such as Hummers and Navigators.

✔ Install wheel locks, so you don't have switch back to stock wheels if you don't really want to.

Part IV
Stylin'

In this part . . .

You find everything you wanted to know about body kits, aero components, wings, spoilers, and graphics in this part. You also find detailing tips to keep your car looking and performing its absolute best.

Chapter 7

Fashion Is a Fickle Thing

In This Chapter

▶ Considering mods from mild to wild

▶ Getting graphic

*W*hether the effort you put into enhancing your car consists of years of painstaking preparation, or merely an hour or two of car detailing once every couple of weeks, you want your car to look its very best. For better or worse, your values, self-image, and priorities are reflected to the world in the car that you're modding and (hopefully) improving. Often, this implicit connection between the car and its owner happens in obvious ways — like what car you chose to commit your money, time, and energy into and how you go about doing it — and sometimes it is in more subtle ways — like how your attention to detail, creativity, and ingenuity are reflected in your car.

Mild to Wild

There is a truism in the car scene — cars are modified to be *different*. Yet modified cars begin looking a whole lot alike because many modified cars follow trends within the industry. Some of these trends are global, often originating in Asia for Asian imports and Europe for European models and then finding their way to the United States. Other times, regional trends take off in small pockets at a local level when a particular owner or crew pioneers a look that becomes an instant hit. This look gets adopted elsewhere, on the show circuit and streets all over the U.S., and the rest is automotive history. One thing is certain: Wherever the trends start, by the time they hit Anytown, U.S.A., they're played out, and the scene moves on to the next big thing.

All hope is not lost. Even after the scene has moved on (and this happens on a nearly seasonal basis), originators and innovators are often fondly remembered and respected for their contributions. Cars that are no longer cutting edge eventually either fade from memory and are considered dated, or come back into focus as newly discovered stars when trends come around full circle. The car scene is remarkably cyclical, much like the world of fashion. Give bell-bottoms enough time, and eventually they come back into style. The same is true with old-school trends becoming new again as fresh faces (re)discover innovations from the past.

When you're considering whether to go mild and clean with your car's appearance modifications, or to go wild and really make a statement and show your skills and vision, two guidelines usually ensure that your car and your efforts are respected rather than mocked behind your back: Stay true to yourself and stay true to your car.

To elaborate; if I modify my Honda S2000 to look just like the one from the movie *2 Fast 2 Furious,* and it takes me six or eight months to accomplish my goal, when I am finally ready to unveil my car in all its glory, is it realistic to expect admiration and adoration from my peers? The car says very little about who I am or what my vision of an S2000 is and adds nothing to the scene or community that thrives on a constant supply of new ideas and innovations. Because I put very little of my own creativity into the project, at best the project is ignored by anyone with any sort of informed opinion at all. At worst, I can expect scorn and disdain. This kind of modification path makes me a poseur — whether I have chosen to misappropriate a well-known project like a car from a popular movie, or crib a look from another source that is already established within the import world.

On the other hand, if I had tried something unprecedented with my S2000, even if the finished project was a total flop, I would still get an A for effort in staying true to my unique vision of what an S2000 could be. Most importantly, whether or not others appreciate my creation, the car will far more likely be a lasting success in my own eyes than something that I made to fit the flavor of the month, and then grew bored with along with everyone else.

Ideally, the finished project is unique, tasteful, and admired. The best rule is to *exercise restraint.* Remember quality over quantity. An overly modified car is a caricature of itself. Your car is much more likely to be a hit than the butt of jokes if you

✔ Stay true to the lines and heritage of your car

✔ Understand your car

✔ Modify with an eye toward restraint

I recommend these guidelines:

- **Follow the character of the car.** If you own a mostly stock Honda Accord, adding a huge aluminum wing doesn't make it look like a racecar. It will look like a mostly stock Honda Accord with a huge aluminum wing.

  Rally lights, knobby dirt tires, and big mud flaps don't make a Miata look like a WRC rally car — it will look like a Miata with an identity complex.

- **Follow the lines of your car.** Rough transitions from front to back and styling cues that begin up front and then terminate midway without any apparent rhyme or reason just make your car look busy and cobbled together.

  Don't over-kit the car. If you mix bumpers, skirts, flares, wings, and spoilers from different kits, make sure they actually work together. Many headlights fit certain proportions. Sure, they can be molded to fit most any car, but are they out of proportion in the new application?

- **People respect function.** If a modification increases performance and makes sense for the car, an inelegant or gaudy appearance is more forgivable.

- **Stay within the brand.** If you have a Mazda, look at other Mazdas before considering parts from a Camaro. If you have a Volkswagen, either borrow from another Volkswagen, or look at a Volkswagen-related brand (Audi, SEAT, Porsche) for parts that can successfully carry over. A "Frankencar" made from a dozen different brands looks more jarring than a seamlessly integrated car that is based on parts from the same manufacturer.

- **Sweat the details and keep it clean.** Eliminating such distractions as protective trim pieces, casting marks, and panel seams can help bring out the natural lines of your car. Adorning your car with tacked-on accessory after accessory obscures the natural lines of your car.

  Be very careful about buying replica kits and knock-offs. These rarely fit right and often look off even after spending time and money aligning them.

- **Consider performance and aero components from the car's home market.** A Japanese car generally looks best wearing high-end JDM (Japan Domestic Market) parts that are rarely seen in the United States. Their exclusivity helps create this respect, but Japanese manufacturers just have more experience working with Japanese cars. If you drive a Porsche, look to Stuttgart. This method can cost a small fortune, but the result will please even demanding critics.

- **Keep it balanced.** A $15,000 paint job and $5,000 wheels and tires don't make your $5,000 car look like a $25,000 car. It is better to address all aspects of the car in equal proportion than to go overboard in one or two areas.

✔ **Start with a car that has good lines.** An Acura NSX doesn't need much help looking and performing well. A few pieces from its home market performance parts suppliers or limited release variants make a stock NSX stand out.

✔ **Photoshop is your friend.** Have a friend or someone who is familiar with Adobe Photoshop create an image that simulates your proposed changes. Then print out that image and tape it on your bathroom mirror and near your desk at your office. If, after staring at it for a week or longer, you still think it looks terrific, chances are good that you won't be disappointed with the real thing.

✔ **Maintain.** Cracked, scratched, and sagging fiberglass looks awful. Period. If you won't maintain your car's appearance, don't go for the look.

Go with something that you can realistically maintain. Many drift cars, like the Nissan 240SX (also known as the S13, S14, and Silvia) and Toyota's Corolla GT-S (also known as the AE86, or *Hachi Roku*), look terrific when spray-painted with Krylon flat paint, sporting bumper skins attached by zip ties (so they are easily shed and quickly reattached after contact with barriers and other cars). That's how these cars are raced and kept in Japan, and that's how they look their best here. Utility, oddly enough for this industry, actually wins here. Flat paint and zip ties on a Lincoln Navigator, though, would be far less impressive.

Authentic or not, if your project includes more Bondo, rust, and duct tape than hope or horsepower, the project is probably in violation of some or all of the preceding rules. Review and reconsider.

Graphics

When it's time to go with a new look, you are not limited to wheels, tint, and paint. Visual addendums, in the form of stickers, pinstripes, and full-fledged graphics, are available to those brave souls willing to give it a shot. If you are building a true showstopper, sooner or later you're going to have to accept some risk. While I recommend that risk to be assumed elsewhere, the "different strokes" rule definitely applies in this business. If everyone built cars the same, the industry would be far less colorful. If big and beautiful graphics are indeed in your future, their application and design is best left to a professional. You don't pull your own teeth, nor do you deliver your own newspaper. There are countless shops and individuals who specialize in graphics; as I suggest elsewhere in this book, tap the wisdom of people who have done it before.

Design

There are only a few hard and fast rules for adding graphics to your modified car:

✔ **Keep it classy.**

"Calvin" decals are just plain tacky. You're better than that. Don't do it.

✔ **Keep it logical and truthful.**

- If your Volkswagen's windshield banner reads, "Powered by VTEC," please remove it (unless your VW has a Honda engine with variable cams).

- If your Acura's windshield banner reads, "Powered by Acura," remove that, too. Acuras are powered by *Honda.* (Check under the hood and see which company's name is on the engine.)

✔ ***Kanji* stickers (Japanese characters) don't fool anyone.** For all you know (unless you happen to be able to read and speak Japanese), Kanji stickers say something you really don't want on your car.

The Japanese are guilty of the same *faux pas* as Americans. This English-language gem was a factory sticker on the Toyota MR2 in Japan:

A Man In Dandism. New Rich And Sports. Mature Sporty Personal. More Innovation More Adult. A Man In Dandism. Powered Midship Specialty.

✔ **No parts, no promo.**

Graphics tell the world about the performance parts on the car. For many seasoned show and track cars, this is a necessary evil because sponsors require them in exchange for providing free or deeply discounted parts or services. Some novice enthusiasts believe that graphics featuring performance company logos give their cars added credibility because it looks like the car is so special that it deserves sponsorship.

If your car doesn't have the parts on it, don't use the graphics. A particularly egregious violation of this guideline is a Dodge Neon with "Spoon" as a large vinyl graphic. Spoon is one of Japan's top-tier purveyors of aftermarket performance parts. Most anyone would be happy to have Spoon as a sponsor on a project vehicle — but, last I heard, the company only makes parts for Hondas and Acuras.

Graphics may still be your future, either because you need them for a sponsorship commitment, or because you have found a look that just plain works with the car. If you have Photoshop, make sure that you create a good mock-up of

your car with the graphics you plan to apply *before* their physical application. This is just a high-tech way to sketch out your ideas and make sure that they're what you want before you actually start working on your car.

For great graphics, use either

- ✔ **Contrasting colors:** Graphics in a color that is a sharp contrast with the paint scheme will stand out and be very noticeable.
- ✔ **Subtle shading:** Graphics in colors that are a bit darker or lighter than the color of the finish on your car give a more subtle ghosting effect.

Whether you decide to go for contrasting or subtle graphics, the key is to stay consistent — you can easily do this by cutting all the stickers from the same vinyl.

Custom cutting

To get custom graphics cut, you can provide logos or graphics to a local signage place as a scalable vector graphic file. (Optimally, any scalable high-resolution graphic will do — GIF or TIFF files also work well.)

- ✔ Look for a shop in your area that specializes in vinyl for car applications
- ✔ Ask other modders at the local car shows for recommendations.

Mobile vinyl cutters and installers often show up at import car events the night before the show for last-minute installations.

Installation

Window tint installation shops can be an excellent resource for having graphics applied; they're already good at eliminating little air bubbles that get trapped under stickers. Pricing varies depending on the size of the graphics and where on the car you want them applied.

If you want to apply graphics yourself, you will need the following items:

- ✔ A soft squeegee
- ✔ A spray bottle filled with a soapy water solution
- ✔ A whole lot of patience

If you're applying the graphics yourself, be patient and take your time. The soapy water solution should be applied very liberally so that you can easily position the vinyl.

If you see small air bubbles under the vinyl after positioning and smoothing, either

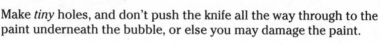

✔ Let the car sit out in the sun to allow the trapped moisture to be released from the vinyl.

✔ Use a blow dryer and X-Acto knife to pop the bubbles.

Heat up the vinyl without burning it, moving the blow dryer as if you were drying your hair, and then pick at the bubble at an angle just enough to pierce the bubble without going all the way through to the paint. It may take several days for the bubbles to completely disappear, and it's a good idea to park the car out in the sun during the first few days after installation. Thereafter, it is a good idea to use a UV blocking polish (I recommend Zaino) not only on the car's paint, but on the vinyl graphics as well, to keep them from fading.

Make *tiny* holes, and don't push the knife all the way through to the paint underneath the bubble, or else you may damage the paint.

Chapter 8

Vanity? Performance? A Little of Both?

In This Chapter

▶ Adding spoilers and other wind diffusers

▶ Utilizing body kits

▶ Lightening your car

*W*hether you believe that form follows function or that function follows form, attaching "racing inspired" add-ons can either enhance or detract from the appearance and even the performance of your car.

Some projects focus on the "show car factor," while others turn their nose up at anything that doesn't make the car faster. Whether you're strictly interested in impressing the driver in the next lane, or you actually intend for aero enhancements to make your car perform better in a racing environment, there are a number of different approaches available for customizing your ride with both simple and not-so-simple body modifications.

Aero Add-ons

Aero add-ons, that is, supplemental pieces attached to existing body work in hopes of improving a car's aesthetics or aerodynamics, come in three areas: front "chin" spoilers, rear spoilers, and side skirts.

Rear-mounted spoilers and wings

Popular jargon uses the terms *spoiler* and *wing* interchangeably, but they have different functions.

Spoilers

The ubiquitous *spoiler* is the little flap or raised protrusion on the rear decklids of coupes and sedans, or on the upper edge of the rear gate on hatchbacks. Although the spoiler is often a cosmetic upgrade designed to tell the world that your car is "sporty," it also has a very specific role in aerodynamics.

Whether a spoiler is needed on your car is matter of

✔ How you use your car

✔ How your car was designed

As the name implies, this device *spoils* the airflow over the top half of the car at the trailing edge of the car's upper surface. The spoiler can keep airflow from *tumbling* and creating a swirling vortex behind the car. This is important for a couple of reasons — without a spoiler, swirling air behind the car can create both

✔ Drag (which can keep the car from moving forward as quickly as possible). Drag is expressed as a numeric coefficient of wind resistance.

✔ Lift (which reduces the car's grip on the road at speed)

Manufacturers have been known to add spoilers to cars that didn't have them in the original design. The Audi TT was released first without any spoiler. It could only be purchased *with* a spoiler after reports began deriding its high-speed stability and inherent rear lift.

Wings

A *wing* on a car is an upside-down version of the wing on an airplane. Instead of lifting, the upside-down wing pushes the car against the ground.

Because the wing must catch an undisturbed flow of air, most wings are mounted on raised pedestals, as shown in Figure 8-1.

Figure 8-1: Airflow and the WRX: Why a tall wing is good.

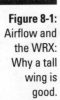

Many wings can be adjusted for rake (vertical angle) so that the amount of downforce (and corresponding drag) can be fine-tuned for a specific application. This is often accomplished with adjustment holes that allow you to alter the angle of the wing's plane for adjustable levels of resistance. Figure 8-2 illustrates an adjustable wing on a Subaru WRX STi, shown in two different positions.

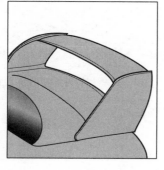

Figure 8-2: Adjustable wing shown in two different positions.

A wing needs to be bolted into the rear trunk of your car. This means drilling holes. This also means that if you get tired of the wing and decide to remove it, you will need to pay a body shop to weld these holes shut and repaint the trunk for you. Choose wisely.

There are several materials from which wings are constructed. In addition to the plastic, fiberglass, and carbon fiber variants available for other body add-ons, wings can also be made from aluminum.

Although these aluminum wings tend to be functional — they are often tall enough to catch reasonable airflow at the back of the car, and many can be adjusted for rake — they also look utterly out of place on a street-driven car. Aluminum wings are fine if you're building a track monster, but putting one on a street-driven car screams *poseur.*

Underbody diffusers

A rear diffuser, otherwise known as a *venturi*, is designed to create a low-pressure or vacuum area under the rear of the car using a physics principle known as the *Venturi effect.* In essence, a diffuser is like an air channel that is designed to accelerate the air out from underneath the back of the car and help to both minimize underbody wind turbulence and to create negative lift at the rear of the car. Figure 8-3 illustrates a sheet metal diffuser as installed on the rear underbody of a Lotus Elise. You can see the twin exhaust tips poking out of the middle of the diffuser.

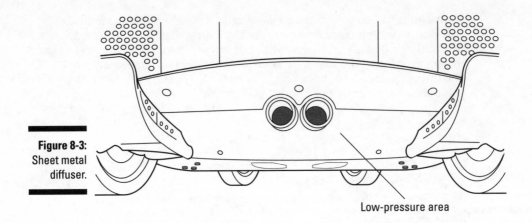

Figure 8-3:
Sheet metal
diffuser.

Low-pressure area

Rear diffusers are available in sheet metal, carbon fiber, and plastic. They are used either with or without a rear wing.

Front add-ons

Although much of the performance aftermarket seems to be visually fixated on the back of the car, with spoilers and wings being the leading indicators of performance (or at least a shallow pretense), managing airflow at the front of the car, either by reducing lift or creating downforce (negative lift), is just as important. As a rule, the more work the wing is doing in the back, the more attention you will want to pay to the front of the car to ensure that the car moves at speed. The front (which is where the steering input is generated), provides as much grip and feedback as the rear.

Air dams

The air dam is the front valence mounted underneath your car's front bumper. If you have no idea what I'm describing, that's okay. Nearly all modern cars have integrated air dams in which the lower-front valence and bumper skin are one seamless piece. Back in the mid-1980s and earlier, in the days of the exposed steel bumper, this was not the case. The air dam's job is to manage airflow at the front of the car, guiding air to the radiator/air-conditioning condenser and/or front mount intercooler and away from the tires, where it would cause lift. Many air dams also provide the mounting location for fog lights or driving lights.

Today, one of the most common ways to give your car a "face lift" is the addition of a new front bumper (with air dam) along with a matching set of side skirts (the plastic extensions that bolt onto your car's side sills under your doors) and rear bumper. These body kits (consisting of the four pieces described and with a front lip sometimes added as a fifth component) can be mixed and matched from a number of different manufacturers for a unique look.

Several tuners have signature designs for front bumpers/air dams that they carry over to a number of different makes and models. For example, the distinctive (in a bad way) Veilside front end looks virtually the same regardless of the car it is found on.

When choosing a front bumper for your car, go with quality/durability (polyurethane excels here; fiberglass will crack, chip, and shatter), aesthetics (flows with the lines of your car), and try to find something that allows you to retain your factory bumper beam and foam support for safety.

Beyond these requirements, keep the air dam's functional purpose in mind. If you are running a front-mounted intercooler or larger radiator, make sure that the bumper skin/air dam that you are buying will provide an oversized opening to give it all the air it needs.

If you live in a state that requires a front license plate, check whether the front bumper allows for a logical mounting location for this.

Splitters

A *splitter* is designed to separate the oncoming air at the lower-leading edge of the car (see Figure 8-4, the splitter is the dark piece jutting straight out from the bottom of the nose of the car).

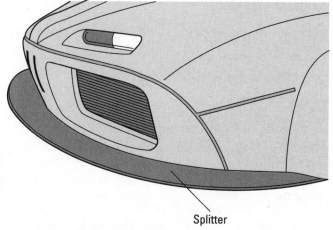

Figure 8-4:
Functional
splitter.

Splitter

By presenting a planed splitting surface, the air doesn't immediately encounter the car's front valance and tumble in front of the car. Instead, the air is channeled

✔ Up above the car's front lip to the radiator

✔ Below the car toward brake ducting or other air channels.

Splitters are available in a number of materials, including

- ✔ Plastic
- ✔ Fiberglass
- ✔ Carbon fiber

Splitters must be mounted securely to the car's bodywork to perform as designed. If they move around at speed, they aren't effective.

For most racers, a splitter is an expendable item that is often broken and replaced. However, weekend enthusiasts need to be careful when negotiating driveways and hills to avoid damaging the splitter.

Canards

Canards (bumper winglets) are designed to provide downforce on the front end of the car. Much like a wing on the rear of the car, canards add drag but help keep the front of the car planted when at speed. Made of plastic, carbon fiber, or fiberglass, canards are relatively inexpensive. However, they flex the paint on the front bumper skin, often resulting in stress cracks in the paint's surface.

Bodyside styling

On the side of your car, wide-body kits and fender flares usually serve the same purposes:

- ✔ Covering bigger and wider wheels than stock
- ✔ Allowing a wider track

Your choice depends on styling, performance, and complexity.

Fender flares

A set of fender flares simply extends the fender lip outwards to avoid rubbing the tire against the fender.

Fender flares are light, simple, and inexpensive, but they usually have a couple of drawbacks. Compared to a full wide-body kit, fender flares usually

- ✔ Don't look as good
- ✔ Don't flow air as well

Wide-body kit

A wide-body kit extends on the idea of fender flares, matching the flared fenders to the rest of the car's body work to allow the car's lines to flow more naturally. Wide-body kits usually

- ✔ Look better than merely adding fender flares
- ✔ Have better airflow around the car

A wide-body conversion can have a few drawbacks:

- ✔ It's costly and labor intensive, because it requires
  - Replacement of many of the factory body panels
  - Extensive paint work
- ✔ A wide-body kit often adds weight to the car.

  Even when the panels themselves are lighter than the factory originals, the extensive molding work needed to make them fit seamlessly with the stock pieces may make the finished body heavier than stock.

- ✔ Damaging a wide-body conversion in an accident is a harrowing prospect because of its relative fragility and high repair cost.

Materials

Not all things are created equal. To meet different pricing, strength, weight, and shape requirements, OEMs (Original Equipment Manufacturers) and aftermarket companies use a variety of materials to create body pieces. The pieces must show some semblance of strength in everyday use, depending on the part, and usually have a paintable surface as well. Polyurethane, fiberglass, and even carbon fiber are used to give a car its form and function.

Fiberglass

Fiberglass has been a staple in the automotive performance aftermarket for many years, and it continues to be used on bodywork despite the gaining popularity of carbon fiber. Fiberglass has a couple of advantages:

- ✔ It's usually the least expensive alternative.
- ✔ Fiberglass has been around for a long time in a variety of automotive and non-automotive uses. Many people can install and repair it.

The negative aspects of fiberglass are

- Fragility in some uses (including its propensity to chip and shatter)
- Weight penalty when compared to carbon fiber

Before manufacturers began to readily experiment with other-than-sheet-metal products, the Chevrolet Corvette was known as a "fiberglass sports car," for the sheer novelty of its pioneering use if nothing else. Lightweight and relatively easy to produce, fiberglass offered some benefits over heavier and more corrosion-prone metals, but had its downside, mainly unpredictable and thorough failure in collisions.

Carbon fiber

Carbon fiber, the material first used by NASA on spacecraft, has become ubiquitous in the tuner scene. Of course, as with most performance add-ons, its popularity has as much to do with its appearance as its performance. From a structural standpoint, carbon fiber has a very high tensile strength to weight ratio, making it an ideal alternative in applications like body panels and aero components where lightweight fiberglass and aluminum might have otherwise been used. Carbon fiber has a naturally shimmering look to its alternating gray and black checkered weave, and many auto enthusiasts prefer to mount it as-is rather than painting over this attractive surface.

However, carbon fiber has its negative aspects:

- Although light and strong, carbon fiber is anything but cheap. The raw material (available in rolls or pre-preg sheets) is expensive.
- For the weave to look cosmetically acceptable, the lay-up process must be flawless and uniform. Because carbon fiber is often kept bare and on display, cosmetic perfection is an important consideration in the manufacturing process.
- Hit at the wrong angle, carbon fiber splinters and shatters where metal would bend and crumple.
- Carbon fiber is both
  - Flammable
  - Electrically conductive
- Carbon fiber's appearance degrades with exposure to ultraviolet rays, becoming brown and hazy.
- When used to make hoods, carbon fiber requires the use of hood pins to prevent it from unlatching and smashing the car's windshield.

There have been numerous instances of ultra-lightweight carbon fiber hoods flying up and smashing the windshield and windshield support pillars (and yet sustaining no damage to the hood itself).

Popular carbon fiber vendors include Fiber Images, Fiber Dynamics, VIS, Madpsi, and Aero Duo. A typical carbon fiber hood sells for $500 to $900 and, depending on model and application, components run between $200 for a budget-level spoiler to well over $1000 for top-shelf limited-run items. When shopping for carbon fiber, keep in mind that not all carbon fiber components are created equal.

Carbon fiber costs vary depending on

✔ Grade of weave

✔ Fitment

✔ Lay-up method

- *Wet lay-up* involves laying up sheets of carbon fiber cloth in resin, much like traditional fiberglass work. The resin is applied with a squeegee in the mold, and gravity sets the carbon fiber in shape as it cures. This is the cheapest and simplest method of making carbon fiber. These products aren't as light and strong as dry lay-up.

- *Dry lay-up* uses pre-impregnated (pre-preg) sheets of carbon fiber that are either set by vacuum bagging or baked in an autoclave to achieve a stronger and lighter finished product.

Dry lay-up carbon fiber can often be distinguished from wet lay-up by the lack of the high sheen from the resin, and the fact that the weave of the fabric can often be felt (in wet-lay up, the additional resin creates a perfectly smooth surface).

✔ Pressure setting

- An *autoclave* is a pressure oven that cures carbon fiber at a specified temperature while using pressure to adhere it to the mold.

- *Vacuum bagging* sets the mold inside a bag in which a pump creates a vacuum, setting the mold under pressure.

A variant on carbon fiber, carbon/Kevlar is the stronger alternative to pure carbon fiber, but is generally heavier as well. Carbon/Kevlar weaves can often be identified by the yellowish weave (the color of the Kevlar strands) against the gray/black of the carbon.

Polyurethane

Long a staple of car manufacturers for its ability to give and to recover from minor impacts, polyurethane is gaining popularity in the tuner world as the material of choice for

- ✔ Bumper covers
- ✔ Side skirts
- ✔ Lower lips

Any part of the car exposed to impact or road debris can be made much more resilient and long lasting with polyurethane than with fiberglass or carbon fiber.

Polyurethane has a few drawbacks:

- ✔ Weight (compared to carbon fiber)
- ✔ Cost
- ✔ Lack of stiffness

  Polyurethane is an inherently flexible/non-rigid material, so it isn't ideal for body components that have large surface areas, such as hoods and trunks.

Chapter 9

Detailing 101

. . . .

In This Chapter

▶ Washing your car

▶ Detailing your car

. . . .

Any true auto enthusiast will tell you that washing your car is a bonding experience.

If your idea of a car wash is having the local dealership hose it down and scrub it with nylon brooms (yes, this really happens), there is really no need to read any further in this chapter.

If you value your car's appearance and don't mind taking the extra time to make sure it looks as good, if not better, than the day you first drove it home, read on.

Car Wash Basics

The best way to wash your car is with a bucket and hose. All the other short-cuts are both a waste of money and a quick way to ruin your car's factory finish:

- ✔ Car washes with brushes can scratch and permanently damage your finish.

- ✔ "Touchless" or "No Touch" carwashes use harsh chemicals to get your car clean.

- ✔ Coin-operated self-serve car washes use reclaimed water that leaves a film all over your car and can leave your finish looking dull and hazy.

If you don't have access to a garden hose, use a coin-op car wash for the initial wash and rinse, but bring a spray bottle filled with filtered or dis-tilled water for the final rinse before applying your polish and/or wax.

You need the right supplies to give your car a good wash:

✔ To keep you car looking its best, use only a liquid car wash solution specifically made for cars.

Dishwashing detergent strips the wax from your paint. It's far too harsh to use regularly. *If* you must remove old wax from your car's surface in preparation for a complete detail, use a degreasing dishwashing detergent like Dawn to strip the wax from the car's paint.

- Don't use dishwashing detergent more than twice a year.
- Only use dishwashing detergent immediately before waxing.
- *Never* use automatic dishwasher soap.

✔ Use lamb's wool mitts that trap dirt within the fibers and keep it away from the paint.

I recommend using two buckets and two mitts:

- One bucket and mitt for the grungiest parts, such as wheels and the lower rocker panels
- One bucket and mitt for the upper part of the car

If you intend to use a single bucket and mitt, make sure you wash from top to bottom — save the wheels and other dirty parts for last.

Don't use an old sponge or rag to wash the car. These are far too likely to drag imbedded particles across the paint and mar the finish.

✔ Don't wash your car in direct sunlight. Water drops that dry on the car's surface etch the paint.

Ideal car washing weather is cool and cloudy, not hot and sunny.

✔ Dry the car with either

- A synthetic chamois product like the Absorber ($9–12 at most auto parts stores)
- A waffle-weave chamois

If you want to impress purists, feel free to use a natural chamois. But a natural chamois requires careful handling and storage, and it doesn't give better results than a synthetic chamois.

Stay clear of silicone *water blades*. They're far too likely to drag leftover dirt and dust across the finish.

Follow these steps to wash your car (don't let the car dry between steps):

1. **Hose the car down with a steady stream of water to remove as much surface dirt as possible.**

2. **Without first drying the car, wash it immediately.**

Use a large bucket (or two) filled with soapy car wash solution and a lamb's wool mitt to wash the car. Start with the roof and work down to the hood and rear deck before moving onto the sides.

If your car has rubber floor mats without any carpet or other fabrics, take them out and wash them *after* you wash the outside of the car. (Never use other detailing products on rubber mats — you don't want to get that stuff on your pedals.)

3. **Rinse the car thoroughly with the hose.**

4. **Dry the entire car with the chamois.**

Don't give the water a chance to dry on its own before you can dry the car. The car should be cool and shaded, and you should wipe away all the water.

Don't forget to dry

- Door jambs

- Wheels

- Seams at the hood, gas door, and trunk openings

A leaf blower works wonders at blowing water out of crevices on your car.

A damp chamois does a great job of removing dust from your dashboard during the drying process, too.

Mr. Clean AutoDry Carwash may be a worthwhile time saver if you have a larger vehicle that is hard to dry with a chamois (some SUVs have very tall roofs), if you are washing multiple cars at the same time, or simply hate drying your car after you wash it. The Mr. Clean system consists of a garden hose attachment with a replaceable water-softening filter and a sheeting agent in the carwash solution (similar to those used in dishwasher detergents). The car dries with a spot-free finish in both shade and sunlight.

The Weekend Detail

Cleaning your car's exterior shouldn't be a chore. Think of it as a time to bond with your car. You'll discover war wounds from normal wear and tear that you will want to address in the process, and perhaps fall in love with those lines on your car that remind you of what inspired you to buy it in the first place. Handing over the "work" of washing your car to an outsider robs you of this opportunity to take inventory of what kind of shape your car is in (such as loose trim, worn tires, and leaking fluids) and could make a big difference in how your car performs later on down the road.

For a complete exterior detail, budget five or six hours to clean paint, trim, glass, and tires.

Paint

Follow four basic steps to thoroughly clean, polish, and protect your car's paint:

1. Washing and drying

2. Clay bar

3. Polishing

4. Protecting with wax or polymer

The following sections guide you through each step to keep your paint great.

Washing and drying

Wash and dry the car thoroughly, as described in the preceding "Car Wash Basics" section.

When you're preparing your car for a full treatment from washing to protection, you can take special steps when you wash:

✔ If your car already has carnauba-based wax on it, you can use a degreasing dishwashing solution instead of car wash solution to help strip the old wax from the paint.

Don't use dishwashing solution more than twice a year, and never use automatic dishwasher soap.

✔ If you're planning to remove a polymer like Zaino or Klasse from your car's finish, follow these three steps to safely wash the car and remove the polymer:

1. Wash the car normally with a mild car wash solution.

2. Wipe off the polymer coating with a mild alcohol solution.

Use common sense when working with alcohol or paint thinners. Experiment with the most dilute solution (about 50/50 diluted with water) before moving up to a stronger dilution, and keep alcohol and other thinning agents away from plastic, vinyl, and fabrics. When using these agents be sure to thoroughly rinse the area immediately following application, and rewax as soon as possible.

Dishwashing detergent doesn't remove polymers and a clay bar needs many passes to remove polymer coating.

3. Rewash the car with a mild car wash solution.

Clay bar

After washing, continue preparing for final protection by removing surface imperfections and contaminants from the paint with a clay bar and lubricating spray.

Clay bars are available for $10–15 from Clay Magic, Zaino, Griot's Garage, and Mothers.

You'll know the clay bar is doing its job by

- ✔ Dirt that shows up on the bar's surface
- ✔ How smooth the paint feels

Follow these rules while you use a clay bar:

- ✔ Fold the bar frequently to expose a fresh surface.
- ✔ Discard the bar if it is ever dropped on the ground.

   Cut your bar into a few pieces so you don't have to throw away a whole bar if you drop it.

- ✔ Use a light touch. If the bar doesn't glide smoothly over the paint, use more lubricating spray and go back over areas that show leftover clay residue to clean up any remaining clay on the surface.

- ✔ Be very selective about products you use to polish your car. The only cloths you should use to polish your car should be either

   - 100-percent USA cotton towels with the tags and ribbing trimmed off.

   - A quality microfiber detailing cloth with any extraneous labels removed.

Polishing

After cleaning the paint by washing and applying a clay bar, polish the paint with a non-wax polish. This step shines the car and prepares it for the final protective coating of wax or polymer.

Use a quality polish and/or glaze, like 3M's clear coat safe polish, 3M Finesse It, or 3M Imperial Hand Glaze. In terms of my personal preferences, there are comparable alternatives, and the Meguiar's brand of polishes comes in a close second (and can more commonly be found in chain auto parts stores), but I generally prefer these 3M products and have used them successfully on many cars.

Follow these rules for polishing:

- ✔ Work in a cool, dry environment away from direct sunlight.
- ✔ Apply the polish with a terry cloth applicator and remove it with either a 100-percent USA cotton Fieldcrest or Cannon brand towel or a quality microfiber towel.
- ✔ Use back and forth motions when polishing, not circular motions.

  Polish with a light touch. It is better to go through multiple passes than to muscle your way through it and mar the finish with too much pressure.

You can polish a car by hand or with a special polisher:

- ✔ *Hand polishing* is what I recommend. It's safer for the paint and more of a bonding experience than going at it with a machine.
- ✔ *Machine polishing* with a random orbit polisher may save some time in preparing your car's finish for the final protective coating. (But why would you want to spend *less* time with your car?)

A random orbit polisher (like those sold by Porter-Cable or through Griot's Garage) is the only kind of power polisher that beginners should try. It's virtually impossible to damage the paint with a random orbit polisher if you follow the instructions with fresh pads and a quality polish.

A *high speed rotary buffer* quickly burns through your paint if you make a mistake. If a high speed rotary buffer is the only tool that has a chance of salvaging badly oxidized or damaged paint, leave it to the pros. Once they've done their best, you can either

  - Maintain the paint with non-destructive hand polishing.
  - Have either the bad areas or the whole car repainted, and *then* maintain the new paint with non-destructive hand polishing.

Protection

After polishing, you can use either a conventional wax or polymer applied with a terry cloth applicator for the final protective coat.

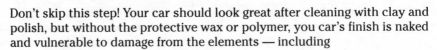

Don't skip this step! Your car should look great after cleaning with clay and polish, but without the protective wax or polymer, you car's finish is naked and vulnerable to damage from the elements — including

- ✔ Oxidation
- ✔ Etching from airborne contaminants

Other than the new breed of polymer protectants, conventional wax technology hasn't changed much over the years. In fact, companies like Zymol often tout that their high-end waxes are derived from formulas dating back to the old coach-building days. Nearly every wax on the market is some form of *carnauba* (a plant-derived wax), blended with combinations of oils and/or silicone, to provide a sealant barrier for your car's finish:

✔ A conventional carnauba-based wax, such as those offered by Meguiar's, P21S, and Griot's Garage, will provide both the final gloss and protective barrier on your car's finish.

Big name waxes aren't always the best, and neither are "As Seen on TV" gimmicks. (Come on, do you really need your car wax to deflect laser beams and shark attacks?) These days, the top surface sealants are names like Zaino, Klasse, and P21S. Klasse and P21S can be ordered online, and are often available through the parts department of new car dealerships. Zaino is available exclusively online by mail order. If you would like the "best of breed" among those paint protectants offered at your local chain automotive store, in my experience, Meguiar's NXT (a polymer blend) works nearly as well as Zaino and Klasse, and is much more widely available.

When you buy wax, don't assume "you get what you pay for." A $1,000 jar of wax probably doesn't deliver results that look 100 times better than its $10 equivalent.

✔ A polymer sealant like Zaino or Klasse allows you to layer the protective coating on your car with multiple applications.

Polymer sealants have a few advantages over conventional carnauba waxes:

- Longer protection

- More UV light protection

- Less dirt trapping on the car's surface

- Less heat degradation

Meguiar's polymer-based protectant NXT (which I have used with good results) is a common and easy-to-use product at a reasonable price.

For these products, it is often a good idea to use

- Back and forth motions when applying the product to *horizontal* (top) surfaces like the hood, roof and trunk

- Up and down motion for the *vertical* (side) surfaces like the quarter panels and doors.

When you use a polymer sealant, make sure that the surface of your car is free from wax and silicone (including residue from the preceding polish). Before applying the polymer sealant, either

- Use a silicone removing spray to prepare the surface.

- Rewash the car with dishwashing detergent.

If you need to remove a polymer like Zaino or Klasse from your car's finish, use a mild alcohol solution.

Detailing sprays

To keep your car looking its best, a quality detailing spray, like those offered by Meguiar's, Mothers, and Zaino, can help make your just-detailed look last longer. Detailing sprays can be used both to remove contaminants like bird droppings and bug splatter in between washings, and to give your car's gloss an extra kick and some additional protection immediately after washing (when you don't have time to do a full wax). Spray on and then wipe off with a quality microfiber towel.

Do not allow bird droppings or bug splatter to remain on your car's surface, especially not in direct sunlight, as these things can etch into the clear coat. Always use water or a detailing spray as a lubricant, rather than attempting to wipe these off your car's surface while dry.

Wheels

Treat your wheels like any other metal part of the car:

- ✔ If your wheels are painted, powder coated, or clear coated, your best bet is to either wax or polymer seal them.

  Dirt and brake dust comes off much more easily after wheels have been waxed or polymer sealed.

- ✔ If your wheels have a polished finish, a quality metal polish like Mothers Mag & Aluminum Polish will do wonders in making them shine and help protect them from the elements.

Stay away from wheel cleaner sprays. The harsh acids can damage your wheels in the long run.

Tires

The most important aspect of detailing tires is inspection. When you're washing the car, inspect the tires for

- ✔ Curb damage on the sidewall, including any nicks or gouges
- ✔ Uneven or excessive tread wear
- ✔ Objects in the tire tread

Getting your tires looking their best just requires spraying a dressing material onto a foam applicator or rag and wiping the sidewall of the tire. (I favor tire dressings that leave a more natural gloss or sheen to the tire, not a greasy look. I like Zaino tire dressing.)

I have a couple of simple rules for tire dressing:

- *Never* allow tire dressing on your tire tread. This makes your tires very slippery and is an accident waiting to happen.

- Stay away from products that are advertised as no-touch sprays and foams. They tend to go on too heavily — when you drive the car, the product gets flung off of the tire surface and onto the paint where you don't want it.

For wheel wells, Griot's Garage offers an excellent dressing that will make your wheel wells sparkle — but don't let it get on your tire tread or driveway.

Windows and lenses

Cleaning windows and lenses is mostly about getting them squeaky clean and avoiding contaminating products.

Glass

Auto glass should be very low maintenance. Wash it with the rest of the car.

Be very picky about what you put on glass windows:

- Don't put any coating containing oils, wax, or silicone on your auto glass. It will distort the optics required for clear vision.

  Zaino claims its Show Car Polish is "99.9 percent optically perfect," so it doesn't distort vision if you use it on glass.

- Don't use traditional household glass cleaners containing ammonia (such as Windex). These tend to leave a residue on the glass and will require significantly more upkeep to keep clean. Additionally, ammonia will destroy aftermarket tint, if you have this on your windows.

- I don't recommend using Rain-X products on the outside of your windshield. These may make your windshield wipers *chatter* (wipe unevenly) when you need to rely on them during a heavy downpour.

Exterior

I use Zaino polish on the outside of auto glass. When fully removed, it gives the glass a bit more sparkle, prevents dirt from accumulating on the glass surface, and helps shed water at speed.

To keep your windshield looking its best, use a razor blade (applied at about a 45 degree angle to the glass) to scrape your windshield down. This minimizes pitting from minor stone chips and impacts. You will be surprised by how much of a difference this can make on an older windshield.

Interior

For the inside of auto glass, use newspaper for an initial cleaning, along with water if needed. A simple pass of a microfiber towel should be all you need for maintenance after that. For more aggressive glass polishing (for example, to remove minor scratches and staining), Zaino Brothers makes an excellent glass polish. Alternately, any non-gel toothpaste works well as a glass polish, and leaves your interior feeling minty fresh.

Plastic

For flexible plastic convertible top windows and lightweight Lexan replacement windows, I recommend

- ✔ Novus or Zaino plastic cleaners for heavy cleaning and small scratches
- ✔ Plexus (available at most motorcycle shops) for regular cleaning

In a pinch, Meguiar's Clear Plastic Cleaner and Clear Plastic Polish are widely available and work okay.

Avoid making sharp creases in plastic windows when you fold a convertible top with plastic windows. Sharp creases damage the UV protectant layer that keeps plastic windows from being sunburned. If your top lets you unzip window panels so you can fold the top without creasing the windows, unzip them every time you fold the top.

Use a penetrating lubricant for sticky zippers (such as bicycle chain wax), but be sure to use the narrow spraying nozzle attachment to avoid getting lubricant on the convertible top. The lubricant will stain your convertible top if it is allowed to remain on the surface. (Canvas tops are by far the most sensitive to staining.) If you must fold the rear window, use a towel between the surfaces so you don't have plastic-on-plastic contact and to decrease the severity of the crease.

Trim

Automotive exterior trim can be divided into basically four categories:

- ✔ **Painted trim:** Treat this like the rest of your car's paint.
- ✔ **Chromed metal trim:** Use a quality metal polish like Mothers Mag & Aluminum Polish or Griot's Garage Chrome Polish.
- ✔ **Chromed plastic trim:** Treat this like the rest of your car's paint.

Never use metal polishes on chromed plastic.

✔ **Unpainted plastic trim:** Give it gloss and protection with either

- 303 Aerospace Protectant
- Autoglym Vinyl & Rubber Care

Avoid getting wax onto unpainted and textured plastic trim — it leads to discoloration.

If you have wax discoloration on your plastic trim, peanut butter does an excellent job of removing wax residue. Smear it on, wipe it off, and wash off the excess.

Convertible and fabric tops

I recommend RaggTopp Cleaner for cleaning canvas or vinyl tops and sunroofs. Follow these steps:

1. To apply the RaggTopp cleaner, wet the top down with a garden hose, spray it with the cleaner, and use a soft nylon brush to work the solution in.

2. Apply the appropriate RaggTopp Protectant for your convertible top (a separate solution is available for both canvas and vinyl). This restores the look of your faded top and makes water bead on it.

   When applying RaggTopp Protectant, wipe away any protectant that gets on other car parts with a microfiber towel and some detailing spray.

3. Park the car in the sun to let the protectant dry.

Interior

The world sees your car's exterior, but your car's interior is how *you* see your car. Some untidiness is okay — particularly when you have kids — but cigarette burns on the seats and fast food stains on carpeting and upholstery damage your driving experience, image, and self esteem.

Cleaning your car's interior can be a rewarding experience. Just think of all the spare change you'll find! Once clean, your car will continue to be a pleasant environment to drive and ride in with just a little maintenance.

Floors

Thoroughly cleaning your carpet and floor mats makes them look and (just as importantly) *smell* much better.

When you clean your floors, move the seats all the way up, all the way forward, and all the way back so that you can clean every bit possible. You may find a buck in change, too.

Carpet

To clean carpets and carpeted floor mats, I recommend these steps

1. **A good vacuuming to remove loose dirt first. Gently loosen anything that may be stuck, if you can.**

   You should only use shampoo to remove stuff that you can't simply lift off with your fingers or vacuum out.

2. **An application of a mild carpet shampoo, such as**

   - Autoglym Interior Shampoo
   - 303 Carpet and Upholstery Cleaner

   Before you use any carpet cleaner on your whole carpet, try it in a hidden area first so you can be confident it won't damage the carpet.

   A good quality nylon upholstery scrub brush can be a big help in removing tricky stains.

3. **If you have a wet/dry vac, vacuum the shampoo out of the carpet before it dries.**

4. **Vacuum the carpet again after it has dried.**

Cleaners and conditioners can get all over the soles of your shoes and cause your feet to slide off the pedals:

- Never use a rubber protectant on rubber mats or pedals.
- Never attempt to detail your pedals.

Fabric

For cloth and velour upholstery on seats, side panels, and roof linings, I recommend

- A thorough cleaning with the easy-to-use interior cleaner solution from Griot's Garage. (It also protects against future stains.)

  You may need to work carefully with a good nylon upholstery scrub brush to loosen stubborn stains.

- Regular maintenance with Griot's Garage Interior Wipes.

Clear plastic

For clear plastic (such as most gauge lenses), I recommend the same steps inside as outside:

- ✔ Novus or Zaino plastic cleaners for heavy cleaning and small scratches
- ✔ Plexus for regular cleaning

Plastic and vinyl

For vinyl upholstery and harder plastic surfaces (such as dashboards), I recommend one of these products to both clean and protect:

TIP

- ✔ Zaino leather polish

    Zaino leather polish has a couple of advantages:

    - It has a UV barrier to help prevent cracking and fading.
    - It doesn't leave a greasy appearance.

- ✔ 303 Aerospace Protectant
- ✔ Autoglym Vinyl & Rubber Care

Generally, a quick wipe down with a wet chamois or microfiber is all the maintenance needed to keep vinyl surfaces looking their best between applications of protectant.

Leather

For leather seats, Lexol or Zaino leather cleaners and conditioners are excellent for

- ✔ Gently cleaning your leather
- ✔ Keeping leather soft and pliant

Weather seals

For interior rubber seals and weather stripping, I recommend either

- ✔ Zymol soft seal conditioner
- ✔ BMW Gummi-Pflege (available at your local BMW dealer's parts department)

Under the Hood

When you're cleaning around your engine, it's best to use a wet rag and a lot of elbow grease.

Don't use *steam cleaning* or a *pressure washer* under the hood of your car. They'll saturate critical engine components with moisture and may strip away protective coatings.

If you absolutely must use a hose under the hood to get the engine compartment clean, take precautions against soaking sensitive parts:

✔ Use the *least water* and the *lowest pressure* possible.

✔ Avoid accidentally soaking the electrical parts:

- Seal all electrical and ignition-related parts and intakes in plastic bags.

- Always aim the water flow *away* from the parts, never at or over the parts.

If you flood an electrical part with water, it may not work even after it dries out. Even clear water carries or loosens crud that can permanently damage electrical components.

Part V
Slowing Down

The 5th Wave   By Rich Tennant

"Did you have an appointment?"

In this part . . .

1 guide you through the mods you need to help slow your car down just as well as it speeds up.

Chapter 10

Slowing Down

• •

In This Chapter

▶ Maintaining your brakes

▶ Deciding to upgrade your brakes

• •

There's an old racing adage, "slow in, fast out," that directly applies to the importance of brakes in winning races. Your car's stopping power is vitally important and shouldn't be left as an afterthought, to be dealt with only after everything else from neon underbody lighting to huge wings have been added. If you haven't thought much about your car's brakes, visit your local racetrack sometime and take a look at the brakes of the cars turning the fastest laps. Odds are that the stopping power on those cars has received as much of the tuner's attention as the car's handling and power delivery.

Of course, the importance of braking transcends the drive to turn ever-faster lap times on a race circuit. If the difference between losing a car (and possibly life and limb) to a catastrophic accident depends on the ability to slow down a car from speed, then you shouldn't be surprised that brakes must be upgraded to match your car's increasing performance envelope.

If there's one area in particular where performance enthusiasts scoff at the show crowd, it's at the number of cars with enormous turbos, lowered suspensions, gigantic wheels, and tiny factory brakes with stock calipers.

Bonus points for cluelessness are awarded to people who paint stock calipers and cross-drill rotors for that "race ready" look.

Not every street performance car is woefully under endowed in the braking department. Street drivers who are in the know pay attention to the importance of braking.

Deciding Whether to Upgrade Your Car's Brakes

When you're deciding whether you need to upgrade brakes, or what to upgrade to, it helps to approach the issue with two viewpoints in mind:

- How do you use your car?

    You need to know whether your car primarily is a

    - Daily driver
    - Weekend plaything
    - Dedicated track car

- How much power have you added?

    Your car needs the ability to scrub off speed to complement its ability to pile speed on.

Most street driven cars can benefit from upgraded

- Brake pads
- Brake lines
- Brake fluid

Cars that are mostly driven on weekends, and that see some form of high performance driving, may add

- More aggressive upgraded pads and rotors
- Caliper upgrades

Dedicated track cars need all the previously listed upgrades. In addition, you may also add

- Ducting
- Master cylinder brace
- Proportioning valves (for controlling brake bias)

Bigger brakes don't automatically provide *shorter* stopping distances. Your one-time minimum stopping distance is determined mostly by your car's *grip*. If your car can lock its wheels or activate ABS, it probably has enough braking power for the car to stop *once* as hard as your wheel/tire combination allows. If you repeat this process several times, or ride the brakes down a long hill, the stopping distances increase as the brakes absorb more heat than they can shed (the sign of *brake fade*). During hard driving, the concern isn't whether you can pull off just one braking event, but whether you can slow the car down again and again consistently and controllably.

Chapter 11 covers upgrades other than brake fluid.

Brake Fluid

Brake fluid is one of the easiest and most important brake upgrades, yet it is also among the most overlooked items.

Brake fluid needs to be *fresh* to do its job. Water content in brake fluid increases by one or two percent per year of use. Water decreases the *boiling point* and the effectiveness of your brake fluid. Your car is past due for a fluid flush if the brake fluid in the reservoir looks either

- ✔ Brown
- ✔ Tinged with black

If you can't remember the last time you had the brake fluid changed, your car probably is due for a change.

Even if you don't think your car will experience the rigors of heavy repeated braking at the track, driving down a long hill that requires you to constantly apply the brakes can show the limitations of water-saturated brake fluid.

Fresh, quality brake fluids, like those offered by Motul, ATE, or Brembo (even Ford has a highly regarded high temperature brake fluid), make a world of difference in your brake system's performance.

Specifications

Brake fluid is graded by the Department of Transportation (DOT) with a DOT number rating. DOT numbers are based on both *chemistry* and *performance*.

A brake fluid may *exceed* the minimum performance that its DOT number promises, so it pays to compare the actual specifications of DOT-graded brake fluids, even if they have the same DOT number.

Brake fluids fit into two basic families of chemistry:

- ✔ DOT 3, 4, and 5.1 are *glycol-based* fluids.

  The heat resistance of glycol-based brake fluid drops drastically as it absorbs a tiny percentage of water, even from air. Some fluids lose almost 200 degrees of boiling resistance when they're saturated with invisible water.

Glycol-based brake fluid is *hygroscopic,* which means it attracts and absorbs water, even from the least obvious sources:

- Through tightly closed bottlecaps

  As soon as you break the seal on a fresh can of brake fluid, the clock is ticking. If you don't know how long ago the can was first opened, it probably shouldn't be used in a high-performance car.

- Through brake-system seals

  Water *condenses* on hot brake seals when they cool down. Even if you haven't driven your car in the rain, water from the air collects on your brake seals after a little hard work (or hard fun).

  - Just from the air

✔ DOT 5 is *silicone-based.*

Silicone-based brake fluid doesn't absorb water from the air, but water can still get into the system and

- Significantly lower the boiling point of the brake system

- Cause internal corrosion

Glycol- and silicone-based fluids must *not* be mixed. Never, ever use DOT 5 silicone-based fluid in a brake system that isn't designed for it.

Brake fluid performance is classified by three properties:

✔ **Wet boiling point** is the temperature at which the brake fluid boils (changes from liquid to gas) when it is fully saturated with all the water it can absorb *(wet).*

Wet boiling point is probably the most important property of brake fluid for everyday driving. In the real world, your brake fluid will never be perfectly "dry."

Glycol-based brake fluid can invisibly absorb up to about three percent of its weight and volume of water.

✔ **Dry boiling point** is the temperature at which perfectly fresh new brake fluid (without any water) boils.

✔ **Viscosity** determines how easily a brake fluid flows within the system.

Glycol-based brake fluid (DOT 3, 4, and 5.1)

Glycol-based fluids are the traditional liquids in hydraulic brakes. Glycol-based fluid decreases in boiling temperature as it takes on water (for example, during everyday driving).

Fresh, DOT-approved, glycol-based fluid is either clear or light amber.

Check your car's owner's manual to find out what kind of brake fluid is specified for your car. Depending on your car's age and design, it probably recommends one of these glycol-based fluids:

🖊 DOT 3

There's no harm in using a high-temperature DOT 4 fluid instead of DOT 3. But DOT 4 fluid generally absorbs moisture more readily than DOT 3, so the boiling point of a DOT 4 fluid can drop quickly to a DOT 3 fluid's boiling point.

🖊 DOT 4

🖊 DOT 5.1

This glycol-based fluid is specifically designed for ABS brake systems, which have *modulators* (control valves) that aren't happy with standard DOT 3 and DOT 4 fluids.

If your owner's manual doesn't specify DOT 5.1 fluid, don't assume that any DOT 5.1 fluid is better than every DOT 4 fluid.

Never use silicone-based DOT 5 brake fluid instead of DOT 5.1 (or instead of DOT 3 or 4).

Table 10-1 lists some popular glycol-based brake fluids by *dry* boiling point. Table 10-2 lists the same fluids by *wet* boiling point.

Table 10-1	Dry Boiling Point of Brake Fluids
Brake Fluid	*Dry Boiling Point*
DOT 3 Minimum	401F
DOT 4 Minimum	446F
Castrol LMA DOT 3/4	446F
DOT 5.1 Minimum	500F
Valvoline SynPower	502F
Motul 5.1	509F
AP Racing 551	527F
ATE TYP200	536F
Ford Heavy Duty DOT 3	550F
Castrol SRF	590F
Motul RBF600	593F

(continued)

Table 10-1 *(continued)*

Brake Fluid	Dry Boiling Point
Brembo Racing LCF 600	601F
NEO Synthetic Super DOT 610	610F
Cobalt Super XRF	620F

Table 10-2   Wet Boiling Point of Brake Fluids

Brake Fluid	Wet Boiling Point
DOT 3 Minimum	284F
Ford Heavy Duty DOT 3	290F
AP Racing 551	302F
DOT 4 Minimum	311F
Castrol LMA DOT 3/4	311F
Valvoline SynPower	343F
DOT 5.1 Minimum	365F
Motul 5.1	365F
ATE TYP200	392F
Brembo Racing LCF 600	399F
Motul RBF600	420F
NEO Synthetic Super DOT 610	421F
Castrol SRF	518F

Silicone-based brake fluids (DOT 5 only)

Silicone-based DOT 5 fluid doesn't easily absorb water, so it may maintain its maximum boiling point longer than glycol-based fluids.

JDM and European specifications, and enthusiasts, sometimes call for "DOT 5" brake fluid when they mean glycol-based US-spec DOT 5.1. If a specification calls for "DOT 5," make sure you know whether it means

✔ Silicone-based DOT 5

✔ Glycol-based DOT 5.1

DOT 5 fluid doesn't eliminate the need for regular brake fluid changes:

- Silicone-based fluid doesn't attract water, but water still sneaks into the brake system and lowers its boiling point.

- Because silicone-based fluid doesn't absorb water, water in the brake system tends to form drops or bubbles and corrode the brake system.

The common uses for DOT 5 silicone brake fluid are

- Show cars (because it won't damage paint)
- Karts
- Motorcycles
- U.S. military vehicles
- Bicycle brakes

Maintenance

Like motor oil, brake fluid needs to be

- Checked regularly
- Replaced occasionally, according to how you use your car

Checking fluid

Every time you take your track car out, or according to the schedule set out in your street car's owner's manual, you should take a couple of steps to make sure your brake fluid is ready for action:

- Check your brake fluid level

  If you need to top off your brake fluid regularly, something is definitely wrong and you have a leak in the system. Get this fixed right now. A leaking brake system is a recipe for disaster.

- Visually inspect your brake fluid.

  Good brake fluid is clear or light amber, not dark and opaque.

Most brake fluid ruins almost anything it touches, including paint. Take all necessary precautions when checking and filling your brake fluid to prevent dripping it onto your car's paint.

Replacing fluid

Follow these guidelines for changing your brake fluid:

- ✔ If your car sees track use, flush and refill your brake fluid both before and after every track event.

- ✔ For normal street use, follow your manufacturer's recommendations. Many car manufacturers specify changing (completely replacing) the brake fluid every one or two years.

Follow your car manufacturer's instructions to fully bleed air out of your brakes when flushing and filling the brake fluid. Brake systems don't work well with air pockets trapped in the system. Trapped air bubbles can lead to soggy pedal feel and erratic brake performance.

Chapter 11

Basic Braking Bolt-Ons

*Y*ou've got to be able to go slow to go fast. This captures the importance of brakes, from both a safety and a performance standpoint. If two cars have the same power, the car with stronger brakes will turn faster lap times because it can brake later and deeper into corners.

If you've got more "go!" than "whoa!" your car simply isn't as fast as it could be.

Wheel Components

The brake parts that connect to the wheels do the hard work of changing speed to heat.

Pads

Brake pads are the easiest component to upgrade in the brake system.

Brake pad compounds are formulated with a number of compromises:

✔ Pad wear

✔ Rotor wear

An abrasive brake pad compound may wear down the brake rotors faster than a stock brake pad, so rotors may require replacement instead of simply *turning* (smoothing) the rotor surfaces.

✔ Effective heat range

For street driving, you must check more than a pad's maximum heat tolerance and fade characteristics. Street brake pads must be effective at *low* temperatures so that you can stop quickly in an emergency during normal driving.

✔ Noise

Some high-performance and racing brake pads squeal loudly when you use the brakes. It doesn't hurt their performance, but the racket may be embarrassing. Squealing brake pads aren't automatically better performers. For racing, brake pad makers often just don't bother either

- Fine-tuning brake pads and materials to minimize noise

- Designing pads to work with anti-squeal shims

✔ Dust

Brake dust can be messy and corrosive, and it can resist your best efforts to keep your wheels clean.

- Some brake pads produce more dust than others.

- Some brake dust can be more stubborn and harder to clean off your car's wheels than others.

✔ Price

Many brake pads on the market outperform stock pads without the day-to-day problems of driving a pure racing brake pad on the street. If you're a weekend warrior, these pads improve maximum braking performance with a livable compound that still performs well on the street. Companies like Porterfield, Pagid, Hawk, Carbotech, Endless, and Project Mu produce a wide range of pads for popular cars, trucks, and SUVs.

Rotors

Rotors need not be a daunting item to buy, provided that you follow a few simple guidelines, as I discuss in the following subsections.

Cross-drilling

Unless you're using period-correct brake pads that release gasses when hot, cross-drilled rotors don't improve performance.

Cross-drilled rotors were invented when brake pad compounds released gases when they were hot (a phenomenon called *outgassing*). The gas pressure actually pushed the pad away from the rotor surface. Cross-drilling allowed a passage for these gasses to escape. Modern brake pad compounds usually don't release gas under load, so you usually don't need cross-drilled brake rotors. Some high-end car manufacturers have cast cross-drilled rotors along with painted red calipers, but this is done more for marketing than because it improves performance.

If rotor holes actually are drilled instead of cast (this includes most cross-drilled aftermarket rotors), the rotors are prone to cracks, and ultimately failure around the drilled holes.

Figure 11-1 illustrates a cross-drilled brake rotor. The holes are cross-drilled radially on the rotor surface (not on the mounting hub).

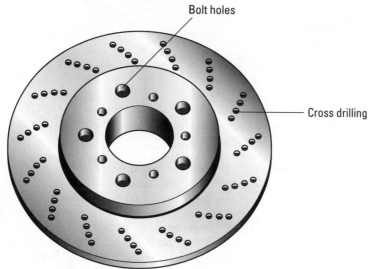

Bolt holes

Cross drilling

Figure 11-1:
Cross-drilled
rotor —
avoid this!

Slotted rotors

A *grooved* or *dimpled* rotor surface may make brake pads less likely to *glaze* (crust over with burned material) under high heat. But these features are more of a marketing gimmick than a benefit to the performance-minded enthusiast. They look cool, but grooves and dimples work like a cheese grater on the brake pads, wearing them more quickly than a smooth surface rotor.

If your rotors are glazing over, the culprit probably is your brake pad compound. You will be better served changing to a more aggressive pad compound rated for a higher heat range.

Figure 11-2 illustrates a slotted brake rotor. The slots are the straight grooves on the rotor surface.

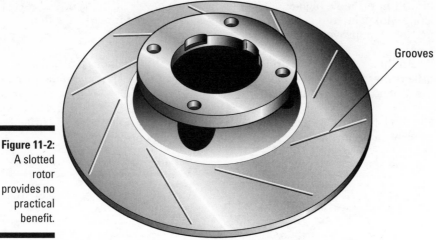

Grooves

Figure 11-2:
A slotted
rotor
provides no
practical
benefit.

Floating rotors

A two-piece floating rotor has an aluminum *hat* (center section) to reduce unsprung weight and rotational mass.

These rotors generally cost more than traditional one-piece cast rotors. The benefits that you can expect to see with a two-piece floating rotor include quicker suspension response from the reduction in *unsprung mass* (weight that isn't carried by the suspension), less *gyroscopic effect* under turning (which feels like a tug on the steering wheel during cornering), and possibly even quicker acceleration from a reduction in *rotating mass* (the mass that turns as the car moves). It's up to you to determine whether these benefits justify the expense of upgrading to two-piece floating rotors.

Endless, Project Mu, AP/Lockheed, and Alcon all make excellent quality two-piece rotors to suit most budgets, for a wide variety of applications. These kits are available either as rotors designed to be used with factory calipers, or as a complete caliper and rotor package.

Internal cooling vanes

Generally, a rotor with internal cooling vanes (usually called *vented* rotors) between the inner and outer rotor surface does a better job of

✔ Drawing heat away from the rotor's face

✔ Preventing the brakes from overheating and fading

Figure 11-3 illustrates a cutaway view of a vented brake rotor. The channels provide more surface area by which the rotors can shed heat. Solid rotors have no such channels because they're solid all the way through.

Cooling vanes

Figure 11-3:
A vented
rotor.

Oversize rotors

All things being equal, a larger rotor has more surface area than a smaller one and can better dissipate heat than a smaller rotor. Of course, all things being equal, a larger rotor has a weight penalty that works against both unsprung and rotating mass to harm both handling and acceleration.

The front rotating assembly of a car (wheels, tires, rotors, and hubs) works like a gyroscope. Adding mass here can add gyroscopic forces that reduce your car's steering and handling response.

Cryogenic treatment

Cryogenic treatments freeze the rotor with liquid nitrogen to better align the internal molecules and resist wear.

Cryo treating often extends the life of brake rotors, but it may not be justified by the price of replacement rotors.

Calipers

Calipers are upgraded, generally at the same time as rotors, to

- Fit bigger rotors
- Provide more clamping force

A caliper's job is to squeeze the brake pads against the rotor surface (thereby slowing the car), so the caliper must be able to exert a strong and steady pressure on the rotor even under extreme loads and high temperatures. As with most braking system components, the caliper's number one enemy is heat.

Generally speaking, calipers are affected by heat a couple of ways:

✔ The number of pistons and the caliper's design dictates how much clamping force the caliper can exert on the rotor. Larger and more numerous pistons mean

- Greater and more even clamping power
- More resistance against being pushed apart by heat accumulation

✔ The size/mass of the caliper, relative to the brake rotor, plays a part in its clamping ability. The greater the caliper mass, all things being equal, the better the caliper resists either

- Coming apart under greater heat loads
- Failing to hold pressure as the brake pad is pushed away from the rotor surface

Figure 11-4 illustrates a popular model of Brembo brake calipers. They feature exceptional clamping power, while still maintaining a reasonably low profile.

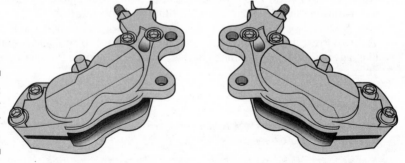

Figure 11-4:
A popular caliper upgrade.

Calipers are manufactured in these different ways:

✔ **Billet calipers:** This type of calipers is considered the strongest because the solid billet material from which they're made is the most dense and uniform in its strength. These calipers have an excellent strength to weight/size ratio. Not surprisingly, these often are the most expensive calipers.

✔ **Forged calipers:** This type of calipers is shaped under high pressure using solid or nearly solid material.

✔ **Cast calipers:** This type of calipers is made from a mold. Cast calipers are the weakest.

Although many factory calipers are a cast design, they usually have substantial mass. Stock calipers may be bulky and heavy, but generally they usually

- ✔ Cope fairly well with heat
- ✔ Are well constructed

Larger calipers and rotors often require either

- ✔ A larger capacity master cylinder
- ✔ A brace that minimizes flex in the standard master cylinder

Race-spec calipers aren't automatically good for street driving. They're designed to hold brake fluid in under extreme pressure. A dynamic seal that can hold pressure on one end as well as it does on the other is a true engineering marvel, and it's usually a compromise is achieved by favoring pressure retention on one end. A race caliper is more likely than its factory stock counterpart to allow moisture migration in through the seal, so the brake fluid must be flushed each time the car is driven in the rain. Not a big deal for the race guys, but awfully inconvenient if you have to drive to work in the rain three days in a row.

You can't see water that has been absorbed into your brake fluid. So make sure to stay on top of regular brake fluid changes, especially if you've been driving in a lot of rain or snow.

Cooling

Your brake system depends on dissipating heat to the air. Good airflow to your brakes can reduce _fade_ (loss of braking power) in heavy use. Some cars are designed with excellent brake ventilation.

Ducts

Tubing or molded plastic ducting underneath the car can channel cool outside air to the brake rotors. Delivering more cool air to the brakes helps the brakes shed heat, so that they're less likely to fade under heavy use. Proper ducting can be one of the least expensive and easiest brake upgrades to carry out on your car. You can install tubing anywhere that you can fit it that will receive cool outside air and not interfere with the wheel, brakes, or suspension components.

Figure 11-5 illustrates a home-made brake venting system — inexpensive brake-duct tubing directing air from the front of the car to a rear brake rotor.

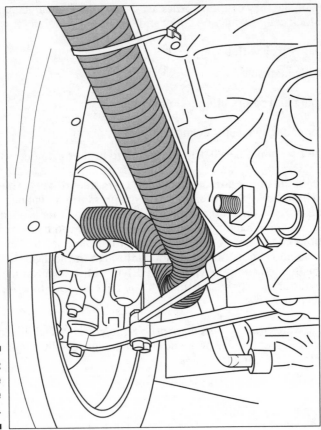

Figure 11-5:
An example
of brake
ducting.

Follow these guidelines to install duct intakes:

- Like a cold air intake, place the duct near one of the car's surfaces that sees constant air flow at speed. (On my Toyota MR2, I used the factory fog light holes in the front valance.)

- Look for a short, straight path for the tubing.

- Deliver the cold air to the inside facing edge of the brake rotor.

- Try to cool both the caliper and rotor by aiming the air delivery towards the back of the brake assembly.

Figure 11-6 illustrates the materials needed to create brake ducts:

- Tubing

- NACA ducts to cosmetically blend in with the car's exterior and channel air into the hosing

- Metal funnel-shaped nozzles to direct the air at the brake assembly

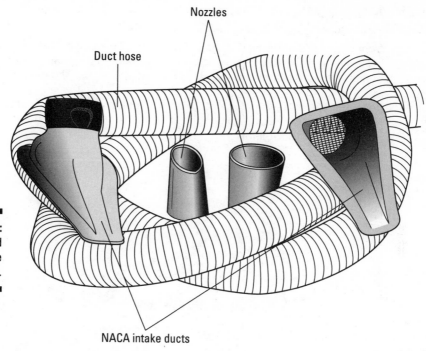

Nozzles

Duct hose

Figure 11-6:
All you need
for brake
ducting.

NACA intake ducts

If there's no place to squeeze in ducts at the front, you can install them on the side of the car.

Ducting can have an undesired side effect: Brakes may take longer to reach their minimum effective operating temperature, especially on a cold day.

An effective brake duct should

✔ Draw air from an area that can provide sufficient volume at speed to completely wash these parts in a steady stream of cool air

✔ Tolerate the tremendous heat generated by your car's brakes while staying flexible

✔ Resist punctures and leaks if it

• Contacts the suspension components underneath the car

• Is hit by rocks and road junk

Don't use a *dryer vent hose* for brake ducts. A dryer vent hose simply isn't tough enough for brake ducts. Brake-ducting hose sells for around $5 per foot from your local race supply shop.

Dust shields

To help rotors shed heat, you can trim or remove the factory dust shields from your car's hubs, as shown in Figure 11-7. This will better allow your brakes to shed heat under repeated hard braking. Trimming, removing, or bending the dust shields is necessary if you plan to install larger rotors.

If you have upgraded to a remote reservoir coilover (the shock absorber reservoir is mounted away from the strut body) you can safely remove these dust shields without shortening the life of your gas-filled shocks.

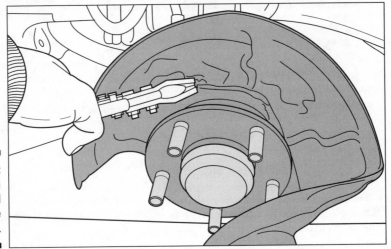

Figure 11-7:
Removing a dust shield from a brake assembly.

Factory dust shields often are also *heat shields* that protect other suspension parts, such as ABS sensors and shock absorbers. Removing dust shields may send more heat to other suspension components, which may reduce their performance or shorten their lives.

Brake drums

Many trucks, SUVs, and inexpensive cars have *drum* brakes on the rear wheels. These are okay for driving to the store, or an occasional hard emergency stop on the street, but they aren't the best setup for hard, fast track driving.

If your car has rear drum brakes (new cars have not come with front drum brakes in many years) you can improve their performance by either

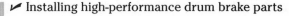

✔ Installing high-performance drum brake parts

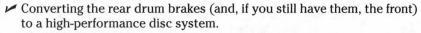

Many front wheel drive cars can be competitive with front discs and drums in the rear, because over 70 percent of a car's braking is done with the front brakes. Lightweight cars like older Civics and Integras are examples of this. So if you are on a tight budget when modifying your front wheel drive car, upgrading the front disc brakes is very often adequate.

✔ Converting the rear drum brakes (and, if you still have them, the front) to a high-performance disc system.

Because it's much more difficult to modulate drum brakes, it is much preferable to upgrade to discs, if they are offered for your model.

High-performance drums and shoes

When was the last time you heard a performance enthusiast telling his buddy about the new titanium Alcon brake drum upgrade he just installed on his ride? Never. While a drum brake from a respected manufacturer may stand up to rigorous racing conditions, the ability to modulate drums is next to non-existent. If your budget allows, and you have anything but an ultra-light front wheel drive car, consider swapping to discs where feasible.

Bigger brake drums usually

✔ Offer little or no modulation

✔ Increase your car's unsprung weight

Finned aluminum brake drum upgrades may be available if there isn't a practical way to switch to disc brakes. You may also find an upgraded brake shoe for more performance.

Disc conversions

Unless you're the first person who has ever tried to make your kind of car go faster, there's probably already a proven method to change your car's drum brakes to discs.

Disc brake pads are easier to change than drum brake shoes.

Depending on your car, you usually can convert to disc brakes with either

✔ An off-the-shelf aftermarket disc brake package

✔ Factory-stock disc brake parts

Factory brake disc conversion parts for your car may come from

• Faster models

• Newer models

• Options that weren't originally installed on your car

Check a few key items when you consider any disc-brake conversion:

✔ A conversion changes the performance and capacity of the rear brakes and their wheel cylinders, so it probably needs an appropriate

- Master cylinder

- Proportioning valve

If the proportioning valve isn't exactly right for your car, a disc-brake conversion may not stop as well as standard drum brakes.

✔ Some disc-brake conversions don't have a parking brake.

Driving on the street without a parking brake may be illegal, unsafe, and really, really inconvenient.

✔ Like any brake hardware upgrade around the wheels, the disc-brake conversion must be correct for your car's wheels and suspension:

- The bolt pattern must match your car's wheels.

- The brake system must fit inside your wheels.

- The brake conversion shouldn't change your car's *track* (distance between wheels at the same end of the car) unless you actually intend to change your suspension's geometry.

Control Components

Your brake pedal is connected to hydraulic devices that regulate the force applied to your brakes.

Master cylinder

The brake master cylinder itself plays a part in overall braking performance.

Replacement master cylinder

An older or undersized master cylinder doesn't enable the highest-spec calipers and pads to work to their potential. If your car is older, consider installing one of the following:

✔ **A standard replacement brake master cylinder and booster**

✔ **A master cylinder from a higher-spec version of your car (if available)**

If a turbocharged or supercharged stock version of your car exists, chances are high that the factory includes a beefier brake system on the faster model. If your car is the standard model, your larger brake master cylinder and booster are only a phone call away at your local dealer's parts counter.

✔ **An aftermarket master cylinder designed specifically for your after-market caliper and rotor upgrades**

If you need an aftermarket master cylinder, leave the sizing and specific application to the professionals that design brake systems. Choosing the wrong master cylinder can

- Reduce brake capacity and cut the stopping power of your new calipers.

- Reduce your ability to *modulate* brakes (detect by feel where they begin to grab and lock the wheel)

Even if your brakes are super powerful and perfectly proportioned front to rear, you can't get the most stopping power from your brakes if they work like an on/off switch.

Master cylinder brace

A simple brace can prevent movement of the brake master cylinder when you stomp the pedal hard. This may provide a more firm and direct pedal feel and aid in your ability to modulate your brakes. Although a finely tuned brake pedal does not itself reduce stopping distances, the information that it conveys to the driver aids in stopping shorter. These braces usually are available for under $100.

Figure 11-8 illustrates a master cylinder brace, as installed on a car. The brace in this illustration, mounted to the factory strut tower, prevents flex at the master cylinder by using the set screw at center to provide constant support to the master cylinder, restricting fore and aft movement under hard braking.

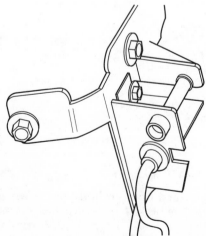

Figure 11-8:
Brake
master
cylinder
brace.

Proportioning valves

Proportioning valves are used to adjust *brake balance* so that one end of the car doesn't lock up much before the other. Mounted as a dial in the cabin, the proportioning valve allows the driver to balance the amount of braking force from front to back.

Not all cars need a proportioning valve. To decide whether your car is a good candidate for a proportioning valve, look at your tire temperatures by using a pyrometer. Your brake balance may need adjustment if

- Your tire temperatures are even side to side, but vary significantly from front to back
- The front end tends to skid under hard braking when turning
- The rear end feels very loose under braking
- Tires are getting flat spots on only one end of the car

When a proportioning valve is used, the brakes at the end of the car that is being worked harder are more likely to fade with repeated hard stopping.

Figure 11-9 illustrates a simple screw-type proportioning valve that adjusts brake bias using the red adjustment dial to feed more brake pressure from one end of the car to the other. The amount of absolute pressure remains constant, but the ratio front to back can be adjusted.

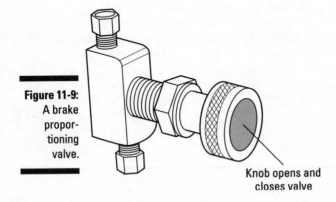

Figure 11-9:
A brake propor-tioning valve.

Knob opens and
closes valve

Brake booster

A *brake booster* assists you when you press your brake pedal. When you push a little, the booster pushes more. The brake booster usually gets its power by saving a vacuum in a canister.

If you hang around with people who enjoy appearing European, you may hear a brake booster called a *servo*.

Brake boosters aren't often upgraded. In some cases, they can be downgraded or completely removed to provide better brake feel by allowing you to modulate the brakes at the verge of lock up without having to factor in this extra assist.

If you intend to use your car on the street, stick with your factory brake booster and use different *pad compounds* that provide more feedback under braking.

ABS

ABS, or Antilock Brake System, is essentially an electro-mechanical method of brake modulation. Nothing more, nothing less. When it detects a locked wheel, it *pulses* the brakes on and off at the verge of locking the brakes to prevent a skid — and it does this much faster than you could ever pump the brake pedal manually.

ABS doesn't improve your car's best stopping distance, and it doesn't improve brake feel.

The benefit of ABS is that when the car is controllable under heavy braking; brakes aren't locked, so the car can be steered even under heavy braking. When the brakes are locked and the car is skidding, the steering input spins (*rotates*) the car without actually changing direction.

Like any evolutionary appendage on cars, ABS started off in a rather crude fashion with some simple two-channel sensor systems that were more of a hindrance than an aid to spirited driving. ABS has became more sophisticated over the years, expanding to four channel, and eventually, tying in with ASR (Anti-Slip Regulation) and TRC (Traction Control) systems, the ABS sensors at each individual corner of the car provide feedback to prevent a skid or spin by applying braking force to one or more wheels while simultaneously applying throttle to other wheels.

In a two channel ABS system, sensors are mounted at the front wheels only, and the computer assumes that if the front brakes need to be pulsed, then the rear wheels do as well (there are no sensors at the rear). With three channels, the front wheels each get a sensor, and the rear brakes are treated as a single unit, receiving only a single channel for both of the rear wheels. Four channel ABS provides a separate sensor for each wheel.

If your car doesn't have ABS, master the skill of *threshold braking.* This involves bringing the brake pressure to the verge of lock-up, and then backing off and squeezing the brakes on again to maintain control of the car while using the brakes to their full potential. From both a safety and performance standpoint, time spent mastering this technique will serve you well.

If your car has ABS, try to get comfortable with the brake pedal pulsing (sometimes accompanied by a light on your dash) indicating that the ABS is doing its job. If you're tempted to lift off the pedal when you feel this pulsing, don't. Instead, train yourself to keep your foot on the pedal and focus on your steering.

On the street, ABS is intended to keep your car controllable in an *emergency,* such as a panic stop or an unexpectedly slick road. If you're frequently activating the ABS system in normal driving, you're driving far too aggressively. In everyday driving, you should allow enough margin for

- ✔ Yourself
- ✔ Other drivers
- ✔ Slick roads

When changing or upgrading brake components — whether pads, rotors, calipers, or full kits — know in advance how they will affect your ABS system. In particular, familiarize yourself with your car anytime you make a change to your brake system.

Lines

Brake lines are hydraulic pipes that connect the master cylinder to the wheel cylinders in the calipers.

The function of a brake line is to contain the brake fluid so the fluid can push against the wheel cylinders when you push the brake pedal.

Some brake lines (particularly older rubber lines) *swell* under pressure — instead of the brake fluid pushing the caliper, the fluid stretches the brake lines like a balloon. That doesn't much reduce the maximum performance of the brakes, but it degrades the brake pedal's feel — when you press the brake pedal, it's hard to tell whether you're pushing the wheel cylinders or just bulging the brake lines. Unless the lines are so deteriorated or damaged that they're at risk of bursting under pressure, this isn't a big problem if you're just cruising to the store. However, in a high-performance car, it means the brakes will be hard to modulate for maximum performance.

Rubber

Rubber brake lines are a simple, efficient option for everyday driving. For hard driving, they may not be the best choice.

Stock rubber brake lines are very likely to swell when you use the brakes hard, because rubber lines aren't very rigid when they're new, and they tend to get less rigid as they get older. They may also swell *inside* (where you can't see it) and reduce responsiveness. This deterioration is visible in these ways:

- ✔ Cracking
- ✔ Ballooning

Stainless steel

Stainless steel brake lines resist ballooning under pressure. Some models have a Teflon or Kevlar outer sleeve to prevent punctures and abrasions to the steel inner liner.

Stainless lines give you the most from your braking system — whether your brakes otherwise are bone stock or modified. There's no downside to upgrading to a quality set of DOT-approved stainless steel brake lines, whether you're

- ✔ Looking for better pedal feel
- ✔ Simply replacing brake lines have been on the car for a few years

When shopping for stainless lines, look for lines that

- ✔ Mount firmly and securely to the factory locations
- ✔ Use secure, quality fittings
- ✔ Include a Teflon or Kevlar outer sleeve to help prevent abrasion

Part VI
Corner Carver

The 5th Wave   By Rich Tennant

©RICHTENNANT

"First thing I'd do is scale back on the carbon fiber and switch from helium to nitrous oxide."

In this part . . .

I guide you through creating a mean handling machine that can chew up and spit back out any set of corners that you can throw at it.

Chapter 12

I Just Want to Hang (Onto the Road)

The best way to get to know the handling dynamics of your car is by experience behind the wheel. Period. With that said, an understanding of the physics involved in getting a car to do what you want it to do, and an understanding of how to react when your car catches you off guard, can make the learning process a whole lot faster and more enjoyable. If feeling like your car is out of control makes you feel squeamish, or if your responses to a spin or slide are anything but smooth and calculated, have no fear; a little knowledge goes a long way.

Understeer

You are driving your car and approaching a turn at high speed. There isn't nearly enough time to slow down. You turn the wheel, and the car continues to run wide. Before you know it, you have crossed over the double yellow line and into oncoming traffic. Just as car is about to plow through the guardrail on the other side of the road, as you brake and it scrubs off speed, it begins to respond to your steering inputs and gradually arcs back over into the correct lane and continues on.

You have just experienced understeer, as illustrated in Figure 12-1. This is how most, if not all, cars are set up from the factory. They run wide when pushed too hard. Back off a bit, and the car steps back into line.

Racers may say that an understeering car is *pushing* or *tight*.

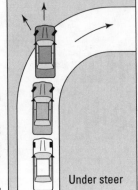

Figure 12-1:
What
happens
when a car
understeers.

Under steer

Oversteer

You are approaching a high-speed turn, again going far too fast. You enter the turn and begin to feed in the steering inputs, perhaps even lifting off the throttle a bit in an attempt to slow down. Like a pendulum, the rear end of the car begins to step out of line and swing wide. As it does so, the front takes a tighter arc. You are now pointed directly at the inside of the corner, with the tail of your car hanging well into the oncoming lane. Brake or lift off the throttle, and the tail comes completely around, spinning the car 180 or even 360 degrees. Feed it a bit more throttle and the tail end of the car regains grip and the car steps back into line.

This is oversteer, as illustrated in Figure 12-2.

Racers may say that an oversteering car is *loose.*

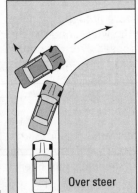

Figure 12-2:
How your
car reacts
during
oversteer.

Over steer

Controllability

It makes sense that auto manufacturers usually design cars to understeer. After all, natural human instinct tells everyone to *slow down* when a car won't go around a curve. This is appropriate for a car that understeers; but in a car that is inclined to oversteer, the driver must do the exact opposite. That is, if I have entered a corner far too fast, perhaps because the corner appeared to be more gradual upon entering and then become a much tighter bend than I had anticipated (this is known as a *decreasing radius turn*), then as the back end of the car swings out on me, I will lightly press the accelerator to transfer weight back onto the rear wheels of my rear-wheel drive car in order to regain traction and try to save the situation. For most people, pushing down the gas pedal when they have found themselves going too fast is counter-intuitive — yet it just might save the day in an oversteer situation.

So understeer is better, then? Not quite. It is nearly impossible to modulate the brakes of a car to effectively steer by braking. However, a skilled driver can change the car's trajectory by easing on and off the throttle, allowing an oversteering car to receive inputs from two sources — the steering wheel and the gas pedal.

A car that lets go at all four corners simultaneously (one that is "neutral" in handling character) is considered perfect. That said, a car that is decidedly neutral under one set of road and weather conditions might veer off into understeer or oversteer as conditions change. The perfect solution would be to have the perfect driver — one that could recognize and cope with whatever handling attitude his or her car takes. However, most drivers turn into Elmer Fudd in an emergency, not James Bond, so understeer is the rule of the day for auto manufacturers, insurance companies, and product liability lawyers.

Both understeer and oversteer are related to the issue of *absolute grip* (how much grip is available to any tire at any time). To appreciate how grip comes into play, consider the job of the tires to steer, brake, and accelerate:

✔ **On a front-wheel drive car:** The majority of the car's weight, namely, its engine, sits over the front wheels — the same wheels used to drive the car. This gives the front wheels great grip in accelerating under slippery conditions, up to a point:

- As the car accelerates, the weight shifts off of the front wheels as inertia makes the car squat back on its rear wheels, unloading the front end.

- The wheels that accelerate the car are also the same ones that provide *steering input*.

Under braking, the front-wheel drive car can regain more steering control and grip.

✔ **On a rear-wheel drive car:** The weight of the car slides backwards on acceleration, like on a front-wheel drive car. This means that if the rear end swings wide (oversteer), the only way to transfer weight back to the rear, and thereby reestablish grip at the rear, is by feeding in more throttle.

In a racing environment, you can often save an oversteering situation in a couple of different ways. You can track off in a straight line (off course) and slow the car under braking, or you can increase the radius of the corner by drifting wide and then tracking off, without using the brakes, in order to slow the car. However, on a public road, tracking off may not be an option if it means allowing the car to drift into oncoming traffic, off a cliff, or into a tree. For this reason, the safest course is going to be to keep the car in its lane of travel and reestablish grip at the rear with appropriate throttle inputs.

Chapter 13

Basic Handling Bolt-Ons

• •

In This Chapter

▶ Adjusting your car's handling

▶ Reducing body roll

▶ Upgrading cornering response

▶ Stiffening your car's chassis

▶ Improving suspension feel and feedback

▶ Delivering power to the pavement

• •

*W*hether your car makes 100 horsepower or 1,000, the feeling of being connected to the road and being able to push your car deep into corners as the lateral G-forces pile on is largely a function of suspension response. Whether or not you agree with BMW's claim of building the "Ultimate Driving Machine," this boast is aimed not at making more power than its competitors, but in the feel of the car and the ability of the motor, brakes, and suspension to work in unison to improve the driving experience. If you want your car to be your version of the ultimate driving machine, you will be wise to look carefully at how your car's suspension is working for you, or in some cases against you, in your quest for unparalleled driving enjoyment.

Wheel Control

Your car's suspension is not designed simply to provide cushioning to the passengers riding in the cabin. You car's suspension is also designed to maintain correct wheel and tire geometry and contact in response to changes in road surface and weight transfer.

Although a go-kart with no suspension would corner terrifically on a perfectly smooth surface, throw in a dip, bump, or pothole, and it would be skipping sideways mid-corner. For this reason, don't wait until your suspension is thoroughly soggy and completely shot before upgrading. Long before your stomach gets tired of the undulations, your car's handling performance will already have suffered.

A *strut* is just a combination of a shock absorber and a spring. You can get high-performance struts with the spring and shock absorber features you want — just remember that you're replacing *both* the spring and the shocks.

Shocks

Shocks are an ideal initial suspension upgrade because upgrading shock absorbers or inserts is

- ✔ Cost effective
- ✔ A quick way to dramatically improve your car's handling characteristics when the stock shocks are worn
- ✔ Useful to fine-tune your car's cornering attitude

Popular shock replacements are available from such makers as Koni, Bilstein, KYB, and Tokico.

Adjustable shock absorbers have an adjustment knob on each shock absorber that allows you to change stiffness for

- ✔ **Compression:** The amount of effort it takes for the shock to be compressed as the suspension moves up.

  Increasing compression resistance usually increases grip and makes the ride less comfortable.

- ✔ **Rebound:** The amount of effort it takes for the shock to release as the suspension moves back down.

  Reducing rebound resistance usually increases grip and makes the ride less comfortable.

This allows you to fine tune your suspension for more or less understeer by changing the *damping* (compression and rebound) settings front to rear — for example, running a softer suspension in front and more firm in back, or vice versa, to change the cornering attitude of the car.

Most factory struts and shock absorbers are hydraulic, meaning that they convert kinetic energy (movement) into thermal energy (heat) by forcing fluid to flow through restricted outlets and valve systems, thus generating hydraulic resistance. Inside the case is either twin-tube (one tube inside the other) or single-tube (*monotube*) construction that houses the valving.

From a performance standpoint, monotube shocks generally have high-pressure gas chargers and beefier valving than their twin-tube counterparts. However, unlike a twin tube-shock, if the outer casing of a monotube is dented, it will cause the shock to fail. The twin-tube design is generally unaffected by small dents to the outer case.

You can set up the car for greater comfort while driving around town, and then crank up the stiffness for higher performance driving at the track. This is done by turning an adjustment knob found on the shock body for each of the four individual corners of the car.

Expect to pay between $400 and $600 (U.S. dollars) for a set of quality adjustable shocks.

Shocks are fairly easy to replace on most cars, but you need a spring compressor to replace the factory springs. For this reason, it's a good idea to go ahead and upgrade both springs and shocks at the same time, as well as replacing the brake lines. In some cases, the brackets for the stock brake lines must be bent or cut to remove the strut assembly that houses the shock absorber. (This is a common problem with Toyotas.) This is a good opportunity to inspect the condition of your brake lines and install braided stainless steel lines if you want them. See Chapter 11 for more about upgrading brakes.

Springs

Springs are used to lower the ride height (for instance, when you're upgrading to a larger wheel and tire package) and are also useful in helping to reduce body roll by stiffening the spring rates. Generally speaking, the stiffer the spring rates (the amount of resistance a spring is set for against compression), the softer the sway bar settings can be to achieve similarly flat cornering response.

Towing zone

Nearly all tow service clubs like AAA have strict rules for refusing tow services on even mildly lowered cars. If your car is lowered, you should plan on either

↳ Carrying a few sections of 2x4 wood blocks (to drive up on) in your trunk should you need a tow (and sweet talking the driver)

↳ Using a lowering system that allows you to raise the car (for example, coilovers with adjustable perches)

If you have any say in the matter, and have time to wait for the right truck, it is generally easiest to tow a lowered car on a flat bed truck (not the kind of tow truck that uses a *hoist*).

To minimize the risk of damage, opt for the flatbed and/or tip the tow truck driver well.

Eibach, H&R, Suspension Techniques, Intrax, GAB, and others offer lowering springs for a variety of applications for between $200 and $400. A good shock and spring package can make a world of difference in how your car performs. While it can often be daunting to pick out the right spring and shock combination for your car, to make your life easier, consider the following: Your goal with lowering your car is not to drop it as far down as possible. Generally, your range of adjustment will be 0.5 to 2 inches using traditional lowering springs. Any lower, and you will need to adjust the height of the perch itself by using a ride-height adjustable coilover suspension.

Failing to heed this warning will result in a number of negative consequences:

- ✔ If you drop your car too low, there will not be enough adjustment for the alignment to be set back to where it needs to be.

- ✔ Shock absorbers will fail quickly because they won't be able to cope with such a narrow and harsh range of compression and rebound stroke.

- ✔ Your car will suffer from ferocious *bump steer* (when the car jumps sideways mid-corner as it encounters a bump or dip in the road) as your suspension bottoms out (literally runs out of available travel) and contacts the bump stops with every road imperfection and undulation.

If the lower control arms have dropped past the horizontal, you have lowered your car too far. Raise it back up to restore the handling.

If you have lowered your car too far, where the control arms are now past the horizontal, a set of roll center adjusters (aluminum spacers that mount at the bottom of the strut tube) help correct the suspension geometry and ward off bump steer.

If your car uses leaf springs (few modern cars do — mostly trucks rely on these), you need a leaf spring upgrade, not a traditional wound coil spring. Many aftermarket shops geared toward off-roading will be able to provide customized leaf spring arrangements depending on your needs.

If you lower your car, stick to two guidelines:

- ✔ Don't drop more than an inch.

- ✔ Get shocks that are valved to match stiffer springs.

Although a "slammed" car with the tops of the tires tucked underneath the fender lips may look cool, odds are that it is both illegal for road use and a terrible performer, because the suspension alignment settings are way off and the amount of available travel needed for the shock to work properly is next to none. This causes excessive tire wear, poor handling, traffic citations, and prematurely worn shocks.

When shopping for springs, you have two types to consider:

✔ **A progressive rate spring:** The coils aren't evenly spaced on this type of spring. A progressive rate spring is softer on initial compression, but tightens up under load. This allows the car's suspension to soak up small road surface imperfections and irregularities, but still hold a steady line under hard cornering. These are ideal if your car exclusively or primarily sees street use.

✔ **A linear rate spring:** This type has a constant spring rate. The benefit of running a linear rate spring is that because the compression rate is fixed, you may find them to be more predictable on initial turn-in. Linear rate is for smooth roads and track/autocross junkies who want to eliminate the first bit of squish that is associated with progressive rate springs.

Don't cut the factory springs and assume that the end result is just as good as a well-engineered lowering spring. A cut spring often has two big problems:

✔ An inappropriate spring rate

✔ Frequent bottoming out onto the bump stops, making for vicious bump steer and erratic handling

You must get your car's suspension aligned after installing lowering springs.

Coilovers

A *coilover suspension* basically gives you a matched lowering spring and shock absorber combination with the added benefit of adjustable ride height and spring rates through a moveable spring perch or perches.

Coilovers can improve your car's suspension in several ways:

✔ Unsprung mass often is reduced.

✔ Suspension travel often is increased.

✔ The car can be *corner balanced.*

To corner balance a car, it is set on four scales (one under each tire). Weight is moved around on the car and heights adjusted until the car's *cross weights* are even (which is a big aid for handling at the limit). If you car is used to turn primarily in one direction (for example, oval track racing) then the corner balancing may be adjusted accordingly. It is relatively pointless attempting to corner balance a car without the ability to offset weight with ride height. Unless your car is in a competitive class in which a weight must be carried to meet class minimums or competition requirements (in which case, chances are, you are racing on coilovers anyway), and that weight can be moved around, corner balancing a car without coilovers is an exercise in futility because you won't have enough moveable weight to work with.

Many coilovers feature the following additional upgrades over stock:

- ✔ **Pillowball spherical bearings:** These bearings in upper mounts give a more communicative and direct handling response.

  The pillowball mounts replace the spherical bearing rubber-encapsulated mounts found on most stock cars (in which the rubber acts as an extra isolating cushion to aid in reducing vibration to the chassis).

- ✔ **Camber adjustment plates:** These provide higher degrees of negative camber than would be available when aligning the stock suspension.

Within the upper echelon of coilovers, you'll find models that include

- ✔ Remotely mounted shock reservoirs
- ✔ Electronic adjustment modules for setting the damping rate from within the car's cockpit
- ✔ Dual perch adjustments for altering the ride height without compromising overall suspension travel

You must get your car aligned after installing or changing the height on coilovers.

You should have your coilovers installed professionally by a shop that also offers alignment and corner balancing services. A coilover is only as effective as the shop that installs and adjusts it. While a properly installed and adjusted coilover can greatly enhance your car's handling dynamics, an improperly installed or aligned coilover under-performs even a stock suspension.

Sleeve coilovers

The sleeve coilovers use the factory strut perch and incorporate a threaded aluminum sleeve with a coil spring and moveable locking perch that can be adjusted up and down by moving a collar on the threaded strut casing. They sell for around $350 to $450. They provide the ability to height adjust each of the four corners of the car and, when coupled with adjustable shocks, match the damping rate accordingly.

If your budget allows you to choose between a lowering spring and shock upgrade or a threaded coilover and shocks, but you cannot justify the jump up in price to a full coilover, go with a threaded sleeve type coilover. The threaded sleeve type coilovers are preferable to a simple lowering spring in that they allow ride height adjustment and corner balancing while a lowering spring does not.

Full coilover

A full coilover actually replaces the entire factory strut assembly with a light-weight steel or aluminum body. These full strut replacement coilovers also feature a matched spring and shock combination.

A number of companies offer full coilover suspensions, including TEIN, Zeal, Penske, Ohlins, JIC Magic, and others. Expect to pay from $1,200 to more than $5,000 for a quality coilover suspension.

Suspension Components

Suspension tuning doesn't stop with the springs and shocks. To really get your car dialed in, you'll want to look at a wide range of other components in your arsenal, including sway bars and end links.

Sway bars

Most modern performance-oriented cars come equipped with factory sway bars. The sway bar makes the *outside* spring seem stiffer in a corner, which is what you usually want.

Sway bars make up for the amount of lean and roll you would otherwise experience with relatively soft street springs.

If you're seeking flatter cornering with less wallowing in the turns, then you should consider upgrading your car's factory sway bars.

Many sway bars are available with adjustment holes in the end link mounting tabs. These are tremendously useful tools for dialing in the handling attitude of the car, from understeer to oversteer.

Sway bars are available for a number of popular cars by companies like Suspension Techniques and sell for $300 to $600 a pair. Sway bars nearly always come with upgraded polyurethane bushings for even crisper handling response.

If your car was not equipped with a factory sway bar, or if the bar to which you are upgrading is considerably stiffer than stock (some aftermarket applications can be up to 200 percent stiffer than stock), be sure to have the mounting tab reinforced before installing the new bars.

The beauty of upgrading to stiffer sway bars is that they not only have a minimal impact on ride quality, but also they allow the use of softer springs so that a car can be set up for a cushier around-town ride and a flatter cornering attitude.

Stiff springs and a very stiff sway bar can reduce *body roll* so much that the car's breakaway is hard to predict. Roll gives you some warning before you run out of grip.

Most sway bars can be installed with basic hand tools.

End links

End links connect the sway bar to the strut body. Most factory end links contain a rubber bushing to help reduce sway bar twisting and flexing.

Upgraded end links, especially when preloaded during suspension setup, can help you get the most from the sway bar's performance.

Aftermarket end links are often manufactured with two critical improvements:

- ✔ A sturdier build with a threaded shaft that allows you to set the amount of preload on the sway bar.
- ✔ The squishy rubber bushing is replaced with a pillowball bearing for more responsive sway bar performance.

Chassis Reinforcement

A stiffer chassis is a more responsive chassis. It really is as simple as that. You can dial compliance back into your suspension to compensate for added chassis rigidity, but from a driver's standpoint, there is no such thing as a chassis with too much rigidity.

Of course, from a builder's standpoint, you can overdo it. Stiffening a chassis to the point of metal fatigue, building it so stiff that it won't allow for minor suspension variances, or compromising crashworthiness are all serious concerns. However, because the average enthusiast is more interested in fortifying an existing chassis rather than designing and building from the ground up, the relatively mild tweaks described in this chapter are safe and effective.

Strut braces

Strut braces are used to reduce the amount of flex in the factory strut towers (the part of the chassis housing the factory strut assembly). Under hard cornering loads, especially with ultra-sticky race tires, the strut assembly is pulled laterally at the strut top. Over time, the chassis fatigues and allows the strut tower itself to flex, resulting in deflection in the suspension.

A strut brace, as the name implies, ties together the strut towers and, in some cases, braces them against the firewall or another part of the car's chassis (this third point is called a *triangulated brace*), to reduce flex and movement at the strut towers. Made of aluminum, carbon fiber, or steel, strut tower braces are available for most popular cars and trucks for between $50 and $350, depending on application and construction method. These braces take mere minutes to install with basic hand tools.

The seat-of-the-pants benefit to the driver is a firmer and less flexible-feeling chassis with better turn-in response.

Tower braces

Strut tower braces are typically used to connect the upper two front strut mounts together at the top. Some manufacturers also make an upper strut brace for the rear strut tops. The front bar is by far the more important of the two because the car receives its steering response from the front suspension, so this is where the flex can most noticeably deteriorate a car's handling response.

Lower arm brace

The *lower arm brace* is a bar that ties the front and rear lower control arms to the chassis to prevent flex at the lower arms. Think of the lower arm brace as a complementary piece to the upper strut bars. A lower arm brace costs around $100 to $150, and it can, like the strut bar, be installed in minutes with basic hand tools.

Foam

Chassis-strengthening foams, such as FoamSeal and Bellco, are made for filling the side sills and/or transmission tunnels on cars with a stiffening structural polyurethane foam. This two-part foam, after it's cured, has the consistency of very dense plastic and can help reduce torsional movement in the chassis.

Foam reinforcement has several practical drawbacks:

- ✔ Installation is a one-shot deal — if installation is botched for whatever reason, it cannot be reversed.

- ✔ Foam must be installed at the ideal room temperature in a very narrow window of time and is extremely messy to work with.

- ✔ The side sills or other cavities that have been filled with foam can no longer be repaired with welders because the foam is flammable.

- ✔ Long-term corrosion impact is a concern. Many of these foams block the factory drain holes unless care is taken to ensure that these are not blocked during the foaming process.

Expect to pay $150 to $400 to have your car foamed. Installation centers are few and far between in the U.S. (Japan still leads the way here), and foaming should not be attempted on your own.

Seam welding

Modern mass-production cars are put together on assembly lines by robots. Spot welds join the various bulkheads making up the car's chassis (the component sections of the body). These welds are in spaced intervals along the car's structural seams and are fired off by robotic welders in rapid succession as the car moves down the assembly line. The net result is a reasonably strong structure that can be produced quickly, and if needed for repair purposes, can have the tack welds broken apart (for example, to replace a damaged rear trunk or quarter panel).

One way to fortify your stock body car, short of converting to a tube chassis, is to reduce the gaps in the welds — a process known as *seam welding*. Welding the seams on your car's chassis increases its stiffness, responsiveness, and safety. However, seam welding may make repairs impractical or impossible if the seams ever need to be taken apart to straighten the car after a collision.

Seam welding a chassis is no small endeavor:

- ✔ You must strip the car down to the bare shell, although this can be done in sections.

- ✔ You must remove all sound-deadening materials that might be in the way — including the stubborn tar strips covering much of the inside of your car.

- ✔ When you're finished, you must prime and paint the weld before reinstalling everything you want.

Suspension links

The moving parts of your suspension usually have special end links that allow them to move smoothly. You can customize these links for a combination of control and comfort.

Bushings

Bushings perform the same function for your car as the cartilage between the joints in your body. Some bushings providing cushioning, like the discs in a spine, while other bushings provide a pivot point for rotation, like a knee or elbow joint. Your street car has rubber bushings and mounts throughout the suspension system to provide vibration damping and movement to the metal suspension components, such as the struts, control arms, sway bars, and even engine and transmission mounts. Over time, factory rubber suspension and engine mount bushings can dry, crack, and rot away. Fortunately, stiffer, longer-wearing and more responsive suspension bushings are available to help make your car's suspension perform its best. One of the popular upgrades is a set of polyurethane bushings from Energy Suspension or Prothane, which cost between $20 and $100.

These bushing kits are available for upper and lower control arms, sway bars, steering racks, and engine mounts. They come in car- and truck-specific applications and are both stiffer and more resilient than the factory bushings, offering a tighter-feeling suspension with less wheel hop and sharper steering response. For serious racers, Delrin and aluminum bushings take the same concept a step further and eliminate any bushing compliance or bind that might otherwise exist in the factory suspension.

You can fortify your own engine mounts by reinforcing the factory rubber bushings with liquid polyurethane. I suggest liquids that are durometer rated at shore 60 or 80.

Although inexpensive to purchase, bushings can be a huge pain to install, and they need to be pressed out with a hydraulic press, burned out with a blowtorch, or cut and chiseled away with a lot of colorful language. If possible, leave this job to the pros or give yourself a weekend to change the bushings out — and make sure you have access to a press.

Spherical rod ends

Precision-formed spherical rod ends (also known as *Heim* joints in the U.S. and *Rose* joints in the U.K.) eliminate the slack and softness of bushings in joints for the most precise adjustability and feedback from your suspension.

This is an unpleasant modification in a street car. Spherical rod ends transfer noise, vibration, and the tiniest of bumps from your tires directly through the suspension to the body shell.

Performance Differentials

Some cars come equipped with a factory limited slip differential (LSD), while others make do with an open differential. Regardless of which one is in your car at the moment, either can benefit from upgrading.

An aftermarket LSD is still one of most dramatic handling improvements you can make to your car.

An open differential always applies the same amount of torque to both drive wheels. So, when under hard cornering, if one of the wheels breaks traction, the open differential actually continues to feed power to the wheel that has no grip.

A limited slip differential sends more torque to the non-slipping wheels, allowing those wheels to make the maximum use of available power in negotiating the corner.

Whatever path you take, installing an LSD can be a big project. It requires opening the transmission or rear axle. Expect to pay at least the price of the LSD to cover the cost of labor for the installation. Then add the cost of special gear oil and maintenance.

Limited slip differentials come in three flavors:

- Viscous fluid
- Clutch
- Gear

The right differential for your car depends on your car's design and how you use it.

Viscous (fluid type)

Most factory limited slip differentials (LSD) use a viscous elastomer fluid to control the amount of power being fed to the drive wheels. When one wheel starts to slip, the fluid thickens and slows the spinning of the disc for the slipping wheel and matches it to the speed of the wheels with grip.

Viscous fluid takes a while to react. Under hard cornering, keeping the throttle buried while the LSD catches up can be a nerve-wracking experience.

The benefits of a viscous type setup include its

- Mechanical simplicity
- Long service life (provided that the fluid is changed regularly).

The negatives are

- Slow reaction speed
- Lack of user adjustability

Most serious performance enthusiasts bypass the viscous type LSDs in favor of gear or clutch type units.

Clutch type

The clutch type LSD uses a series of stacked internal clutch plates to provide varying degrees of slip before locking up, and it can be tuned by the end user during installation by changing the orientation of the clutch discs.

If you're looking for all-out performance, the clutch type LSD is the way to go. It provides the most predictable control, which is why nearly every *drift car* (the ones that spend more time going sideways than going straight) relies on clutch type LSDs.

Kaaz and ATS offer fast acting clutch type differentials that bring the car back in line with a mere feathering of the throttle — blip the accelerator and the LSD locks up and sends you on your way with no delay. These LSDs are available for around $799 to $1,000 and come in three configurations:

- ✔ 1-way works only under acceleration.

- ✔ 1.5-way works under acceleration and gives up to half lock on deceleration.

- ✔ 2-way fully locks under both acceleration and deceleration.

The benefits of a clutch type LSD are that it

- ✔ Reacts fastest

- ✔ Allows full lock when active

- ✔ Can be user-tuned to change the aggressiveness of its response

The negatives include

- ✔ A relatively short service life on the clutch packs (these should be serviced every six months to a year and require opening up the transmission to do so)

- ✔ The need for frequent fluid changes with expensive fluids to keep the clutch packs in good working order

- ✔ Noisy clutch chatter on engagement

- ✔ A very specific break-in procedure involving driving the car in figure 8s for a long period of time

  Even drivers with iron stomachs need an airsickness bag for this.

Failure to properly break in a clutch type LSD will shorten its life and increase the amount of chatter you feel and hear because the clutch pack mating surfaces will not mate properly.

Gear type

The gear type LSD, including those made by both Torsen and Quaife America, is also known as a *torque-sensing differential*. It works off of a planetary gear to bind the differential according to a built-in gear bias

If you want a worthwhile performance improvement with a long service life and minimal hassle, a gear type LSD can be a great alternative to either an open differential or a factory viscous limited slip:

- ✔ It reacts faster than a viscous limited slip.
- ✔ It doesn't need the routine maintenance and adjustment of the clutch type limited slip.

The gear type LSD has one major shortcoming: When one wheel has lost all traction — for example, when a wheel has lifted off the ground or in snowy/icy conditions — it reverts back to functioning as an open differential because it lacks any torque on the side of the free-spinning wheel to achieve its locking effect. For this reason, many cars that come with factory option Torsen LSDs also come with available electronic traction control to help supplement the LSD in slippery conditions.

Traction Control

If you are not using a standalone ECU and would like to add traction control to your car, and in particular if you are interested in traction control as a performance enhancement, Racelogic is the system to get. Although many late model cars come factory equipped with traction control, enthusiasts often find that these systems act more as a "big brother" to curtail spirited driving rather than adding to the driving experience. Racelogic offers a user tunable system that can be adjusted on the fly for variable assist, and also comes with a plug-in module for launch control to help minimize wheel spin under hard launching. Full throttle "no lift" shift control is also an available option.

In essence, the Racelogic system works with ABS sensors to detect slip, and then reduces engine power for a fraction of a second until control is regained. For cars without factory ABS, the necessary sensors can be retrofitted to allow for installation.

On high-horsepower cars, like the MKIV Toyota Supra, the factory traction control from the mid to late 1990s was sorely lacking. With the Racelogic system, users can pull the fuse for the factory traction control, and get state of the art performance for their high horsepower cars on the street, strip, or track.

Chapter 14

Get on the Diet!

In This Chapter

▶ Utilizing weight distribution to maximize performance

▶ Removing excess weight from your car

*T*he most effective and dramatic performance increase you can make to any car, truck, or SUV is absolutely free. Whether you drive a Jeep Cherokee or a Lamborghini Diablo, a Honda Civic or a Chevy Camaro, one modification can improve all aspects of vehicle performance, including acceleration, braking, and cornering ability, costs you nothing, doesn't generally void your warranty, is street legal in nearly every jurisdiction, and in most cases is 100-percent reversible. It even improves your gas mileage and reduces wear on your engine, brakes, and suspension components. Sound too good to be true?

Reducing the amount of weight in your car makes a big impact on its performance (see the sidebar, "Less is more," for an example). You've felt the difference in how a car performs, for example, on the way to the airport with the whole family and a ton of luggage crammed inside, compared to driving when you're alone in the car. The difference is night and day.

Usually, it's impossible for most car modders to achieve a magnitude of difference, but even small weight savings add up to a surprising improvement.

As a rule, the best money ever spent on making your car go faster is, and will always remain, the money that you spend on improving your abilities as a driver. Many times I have seen examples of this, like the talented instructor in a rented Dodge Neon (the one with the automatic transmission and all season tires — not the ST-4) who passed a Porsche 911 on a tight road course. That being said, dollar for dollar, as far as modifications to the car go (as opposed to modifying the driver's ability), weight loss tends to yield the greatest overall returns in all aspects of performance.

Less is more

The 1995 Mitsubishi 3000GT VR-4 was, in its day, and remains today, a technological *tour de force.* Equipped with a 3.0-liter V6 twin turbocharged engine pushing out 320 hp and 315 ft-lbs. of torque through an all-wheel-drive drive train featuring all-wheel steering, adjustable suspension, adjustable exhaust, and active aerodynamics, the VR-4 was Mitsubishi's ultimate sports car.

Yet a British sports car called the Lotus Elise absolutely demolishes the Mitsubishi in every aspect of performance with a paltry 1.8-liter naturally aspirated four-cylinder engine, putting out a comparatively meager 190 hp and 138 ft-lbs. of torque.

How does the Lotus do it? Weight — or the lack thereof. Whereas the Mitsubishi tips the scales at nearly 3,800 pounds, the Lotus weighs in at a featherweight 1,975 pounds.

Mass is the critical variable that allows a sub-200 hp car to perform as though it is packing over 400 hp under the hood. The physics are straightforward: The lower the mass, the less force it takes to move the car forward or to slow down when the car is in motion. Lower mass also exerts lower lateral forces under cornering, allowing the car to carry more speed through corners.

Dr. David's Four-Step Diet

While you may be miserable driving a car everyday without at least the basic creature comforts (including a fully functional dashboard, factory carpeting, a stereo, as well as power windows, door locks, and accessories), you can save a worthwhile amount of weight without going to extremes.

I recommend reducing weight in stages:

1. **Remove the items that can easily be put back in if you want them.**

    I can easily reinstall my spare tire, tools, and jack if I want them. I have an auto-club card, a cell phone, and a tire repair kit with a small portable compressor, so I'm comfortable with leaving the spare tire and jack out of the car. Other options include

    - Removing unused factory seats when not in use
    - Removing heavy audio equipment that can be quickly taken out and reinstalled, such as subwoofers and amplifiers
    - Draining your windshield washer reservoir at a sunny track day, then refilling on the way home

2. **Remove anything that's broken and that you'll never repair.**

    For example, if you have a broken power window motor on a rear door, and you don't plan to fix it, you can remove the window motor.

Skimming the fat

On my 1993 Toyota MR2 Turbo, which weighs 2,882 pounds stock with full engine fluids but no driver and an empty gas tank (this is how cars' weights are usually listed), I've dropped more than 300 pounds while keeping a full interior with all of the stock power-assisted features, stereo, carpeting, and sound deadening. I replaced heavy factory parts with lighter-weight performance parts, such as

✔ Lightweight wheels

✔ Carbon fiber body panels

✔ A smaller battery

✔ Carbon/Kevlar racing seats.

My aftermarket goodies cost money, but these parts were taken out for free:

✔ Air conditioning (50 to 75 pounds)

✔ Cruise control (5 to 10 pounds)

✔ Spare tire, jack, and tools (20 to 40 pounds)

✔ Power antenna (2 to 5 pounds)

✔ Rear spoiler (5 to 15 pounds)

3. **Remove factory options that you didn't want or don't need.**

4. **Depending on your budget and performance goals, you can continue reducing weight by**

   • Buying lightweight replacement components, such as forged aluminum wheels, carbon fiber body panels, a lighter battery, and racing seats

   • Removing comfort items that you want but can live without, such as air conditioning and stereo systems

Balancing the Scale

Not all weight loss is equal, so look for targeted changes for the most performance improvement for your money. When reducing weight on your car, pay careful attention to your car's overall weight distribution. Try to achieve as close a balance as possible, both front-to-back and side-to-side. When you have finished your weight-loss regimen, if your car is equipped with a height adjustable coilover suspension, it can often be beneficial to have your car corner-balanced (height adjusted per corner) at a racing alignment shop with you in the driver's seat. This can often make the difference between a light car, and a light car that handles well with you driving it.

Rotating weight

Pound for pound, the most noticeable weight loss is in the reduction of *rotating mass* — any component that must go around and around for the car to move forward.

The amount of power that your car actually produces at the wheel (*whp*, or wheel horsepower) will be 15 to 30 percent less than what the manufacturers list as your car's advertised bhp. The 15- to 30-percent loss can be accounted for in the power it takes to rotate the moving parts of the driveline assembly and the frictional losses associated with this movement.

When car manufacturers list horsepower ratings for cars, they nearly always list them as *bhp* (brake horsepower). bhp is measured by placing the engine on an *engine brake* that measures the engine power with none of the driveline components attached. To gain back some of this lost power, reduce the mass that your engine needs to turn.

Total weight

You can save power and improve the car's responsiveness by installing light-weight versions of these rotating parts:

✔ **Forged wheels**

Big *bling-bling rims* usually add a lot of rotating weight to your car. They're for style, not for speed.

✔ **Driveshaft for front engine, rear-wheel drive configured cars**

The driveshaft carries the power from the front of the car to the rear drive wheels, if applicable. Driveshafts are generally made out of a metal alloy, but some new cars, such as the new Nissan 350Z, now have carbon fiber driveshafts. There are a couple of advantages to carbon fiber:

- Reduction in rotating mass (carbon fiber is lighter than metal).

- Safety — the carbon fiber driveshaft is designed to break apart on impact rather than penetrate the passenger compartment.

✔ **Flywheel**

Chromoly flywheels are lighter than stock and often can weigh as little as half as much as the stock unit.

✔ **Brake rotors**

For your brakes to do their job, they need mass to absorb and dissipate the heat generated by the friction between pad and rotor in slowing down a car. The less mass there is at the rotor, the more this heat will get channeled elsewhere — like into the caliper, raising the temperature of the brake fluid and causing potential failure at the piston seals.

With today's technology and prices, your best bet is to upgrade to a two-piece rotor:

- The rotor surface (swept area that touches the brake pad) is a longwearing, heavy iron surface.

- The inner *hat* (the part of the brake rotor that mounts to the wheel hub) is made of aluminum.

Two-piece rotors from vendors like Endless and Project Mu for popular Japanese cars can

- Shave critical pounds off your car's brake system without unduly compromising braking performance

- Work with your factory calipers

Steer clear of blinging titanium rotors and ultra lightweight waved and contoured rotors. This technology remains unproven and expensive.

✔ **Tires**

Some tires are much lighter than others. Because tires are the farthest out on the wheel/hub assembly, their weight can have a bigger impact on rotational mass than components located closer to the center (such as lightweight lug nuts).

✔ **Lug nuts**

Never use an impact wrench on lightweight aluminum mounting hardware. These must be hand *torqued* (tightened) to the specified torque. They're far too fragile for the rigors of the impact wrench.

Braking the bank

If you have a Porsche and deep pockets, you can reduce braking mass without compromising braking performance by installing Porsche's very own carbon ceramic brake system (PCCB). Weighing in at half the weight of their cast-iron counterparts, the Porsche carbon ceramic brakes utilize a cross-drilled, carbon fiber reinforced ceramic rotor with special composite pads.

This six-piston (two in front, four in the rear) brake upgrade is one of the few performance upgrades that really doesn't have any drawbacks when you install it:

✔ It lasts the life of your car (Porsche estimates 160,000 miles of normal use).

✔ It improves suspension feel and acceleration.

✔ It even reduces fuel consumption.

How much fuel will you need to save for these brakes to pay for themselves? A paltry $17,000 to $23,000 for the parts. Of course, as this technology becomes more common, you can expect to see these prices decline rapidly.

Centering weight

The most important place to remove rotating weight is farther from the center. Concentrating rotating weight closer to the *center* lets it spin faster.

All things being equal, a smaller diameter wheel spins more quickly than a wheel with a larger diameter. A larger diameter wheel hurts rotating weight because it moves the weight of the rim and tire farther from the center.

If you've seen a figure skater spinning fast, you've seen what happens when the rotating weight moves closer to the center:

✔ When the skater folds her arms in, she spins faster.

✔ When the skater's arms are stretched out, she slows down.

Unsprung weight

Reducing the mass that moves up and down in the suspension increases the suspension's ability to respond to variations in the road surface. (It's called *unsprung weight* because it doesn't ride on the car's springs.) Reducing unsprung weight reduces the suspension's *inertia* (resistance to movement) so that it can move up and down faster, which allows the car to maintain its composure over uneven road surfaces.

Every part of the brake assembly on the wheel hub is unsprung.

With independent suspension, some heavy parts (such as differentials) are supported by the body instead of the suspension. Body-mounted parts don't count as unsprung weight. This is one of the advantages of *independent suspension,* found on nearly all passenger cars. The exceptions usually are the rear axles of

✔ Trucks and SUVs

✔ Traditional American rear-wheel drive cars, such as Mustangs and Camaros

✔ Some older front-wheel drive cars

A non-independent rear suspension on a front-wheel drive car usually is called a *beam suspension.*

You can reduce unsprung mass by installing lightweight replacements for

✔ **Wheels**

✔ **Brake calipers**

✔ **Brake rotors**

Huge brake rotors look great behind spoked wheels, but an oversized rotor increases both unsprung and rotating mass.

✔ **Suspension assembly**

On an independent suspension, an aftermarket *coilover* (height adjustable strut and spring assembly) is often lighter than the factory strut assembly that it replaces. Many coilover suspensions are smaller and use aluminum bodies to reduce weight.

✔ **Control arms**

✔ **Sway bars**

A hollow aftermarket bar of a larger diameter performs at least as well as a heavy solid core factory sway bar.

Static weight

Static weight is the mass that sits on the car's springs. You can improve your car's performance by

✔ Reducing static weight

✔ Relocating static weight

Reducing weight

For better acceleration, cornering, and braking, reducing weight anywhere on your car is a good thing. But some areas have more impact on your car's performance.

Weight that's high

Reducing the highest weight above the ground makes the most improvement in the car's *center of gravity,* which makes the most improvement in its handling. The lower the center of gravity, the better. You can lower the center of gravity by reducing weight high in the car as follows:

✔ **Replace a heavy glass sunroof or T-top with carbon fiber replacements.**

✔ **Replace heavy side- and rear-window glass with Lexan.**

Don't use a Lexan windshield. It scratches easily.

Make sure that your local vehicle laws allow plastic replacement windows.

✔ **Roll down all windows during a competition.**

This lowers the weight of the window glass without having to remove the windows.

Usually windows *must* be rolled down in competition for safety.

✔ Remove the sunroof or T-top panel for motor sports events.

✔ Replace steel hood and trunk lid with carbon fiber.

For legality and safety, always

- Check your local vehicle codes
- Use hood pins.

✔ If you drive a convertible, consider removing the heavy convertible top mechanism and using a removable fiberglass hardtop only when you need it in bad weather.

✔ If your battery is mounted up high, consider switching to smaller, lighter, dry-cell type battery, or relocating your battery further down in the car.

✔ Lower the whole car by either

- Installing shorter springs
- Adjusting coilover suspension to a lower ride height

When lowering your car's suspension, be sure to have your car realigned because the alignment will have changed.

Weight at the ends

Reduce weight at the *ends* of the car. Pound for pound, weight that is farther from the car's center of gravity makes the car more resistant to changing direction. Usually, you can reduce weight of parts like exhausts and batteries.

Pay special attention to weight that's located either

✔ Behind the rear axle

✔ In front of the front axle

If you have pop-up headlights, consider eliminating the extra weight of the motors that operate the headlights by either

- Replacing them with *fixed* (non-moving) headlights
- Removing the motors and leaving your headlights up all the time

Check for DOT-approved replacement headlights. Many fixed headlight replacement kits for pop-ups aren't DOT approved and don't work as well as stock lights.

For a track-only car, consider removing your headlight motors and manually cranking the lights up and down when needed.

On my own car, along with the weight loss that you can't see (carbon-Kevlar shell type racing seats, lightweight sway bars, coilover suspension, and stripped-out air conditioning to name a few), you can see the carbon fiber hood, engine cover, trunk lid, wing, headlight covers, and rear view mirrors. Additionally, the windshield wipers were removed, and the pop-up headlights have been modified to stationary, eliminating the need for the motors that drive them. The Volk forged rims are approximately nine pounds each. I take the T-top off at the track.

Never remove or modify the bumper beams in your car if it's street driven. They're required for channeling impact forces into the crumple zones of your car's body in an accident.

Reducing mass from the ends of the car improves the car's *polar moment of inertia.* That means the car can change direction faster (for example, slicing left and right through a tight slalom). This is why mid-engined cars have historically been praised for their transitional handling responsiveness. With the big mass of the engine located in the center of the car, a mid-engined car can make quick movements from one direction to the other faster than a conventionally configured car. Although both a conventionally configured front engined, rear-wheel drive car and a mid-engined car can have 50/50 weight distribution, the mid-engined car carries its weight at its center while the front-engined car off-sets the weight of its engine up front by placing the weight of its other driveline components at the rear.

Other weight

Reduce weight in and around the center of the car (including the cabin). This is the least important location for dropping weight, but it still improves your performance.

✔ If you are running a full roll cage in your car with adequate side protection, and your car is never to be used on the street, gut your door beams and use shell-style doors.

✔ Remove your spare tire, jack, and tools for motor sports events.

✔ Remove any other unneeded items from your car. You'd be surprised how much useless stuff you're carrying.

Most comfort and convenience items are located in the cabin. Often substantial weight savings can be found in the following areas:

✔ A standard power seat can weigh more than 75 pounds. You may be able to drop 150 pounds or more by replacing heavy power seats with fixed-back shell-style racing buckets that weigh less than ten pounds each.

Look for racing seats with TUV or FIA certification.

✔ Bumpin' stereo systems with big subwoofers can easily add over 200 pounds to your car. Either leave them out or make them easily removable if you care about performance.

Relocating weight

You can lower your car's center of gravity and reduce its polar moment of inertia by moving components *lower* and *closer to the center* of your car.

Many stock batteries are in the worst possible location for weight distribution: High in a front corner of the car. You have a couple of options:

✔ Use a *battery relocation kit* to place this heavy item in a better position for handling (for example, moving the battery to the rear trunk to aid with fore/aft weight distribution).

✔ Invest in a lighter dry-cell battery from a company like Hawker or Odyssey. These batteries have the same cranking power as stock batteries, but weigh considerably less.

Dry-cell batteries have a couple of limitations:

• They aren't suitable if you either live in a colder climate or allow your car to sit for long periods with the battery connected.

• They may not be an exact fit for your car without some modifications. You must ensure that the smaller battery is securely mounted and that the car's battery connectors match the battery's own terminals.

Part VII
Let's Go!

The 5th Wave — By Rich Tennant

©RICHTENNANT

"I swapped out gauges from my treadmill. Want to know how many calories we just burned in the last quarter mile?"

In this part . . .

For those of you who skipped straight to this part, power is what you are after, and tips for making power are what you shall receive. From basic bolt-on modifications to more involved and expensive power adders, including forced induction, I take you through the recipe for adding power to your car.

Chapter 15

Basic Power Bolt-Ons

. . . .

In This Chapter

▶ Modifying the elements of combustion to get more power

▶ Opening up your car's air intake

▶ Improving your car's exhaust efficiency

▶ Strengthening the spark that sets it all off

. . . .

*W*ho says that power upgrades must be expensive, involved, illegal, and fragile? There's an old saying in the go-fast world: "Cheap, fast, and reliable . . . pick any two." Inexpensive, reliable monster power upgrades are few and far between, but many simple modifications yield some extra power without either compromising reliability or forcing you to take a second mortgage on the house.

Combustion Theory

Three critical elements limit your engine's maximum power output:

⮑ Fuel

⮑ Spark

⮑ Air

The power derived from all three items can be improved with simple bolt-ons.

Increasing airflow (improving the engine's ability to move air before and after combustion) usually pays the biggest dividends. The internal combustion engine is a giant air pump. The more air the engine takes in on the intake side and pushes out on the exhaust side, the more power it can produce.

What's going on inside your engine is a series of small, carefully timed explosions. Each explosion requires

⮑ The proper proportion of oxygen and fuel

⮑ A spark at just the right time

The combustion cycle consists of four distinct actions that happen sequentially inside each cylinder, as illustrated in Figure 15-1:

- **Intake:** When air and fuel are introduced into the combustion chamber through the intake valve.

- **Compression:** When the air-fuel mixture is compressed (for a more powerful explosion) prior to combustion.

- **Ignition:** When the spark plug fires a spark to ignite the compressed air-fuel mixture.

- **Exhaust:** When the combustion chamber is emptied of exhaust gases through the exhaust valve.

The Four Stroke Cycle

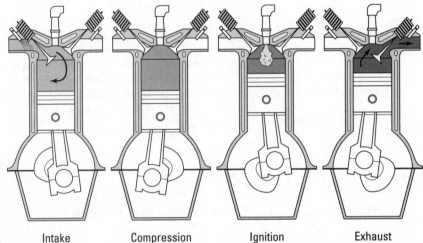

Intake	Compression	Ignition	Exhaust

Figure 15-1:
The combustion cycle.

When tuning your car, it's best to have control over all three combustion elements (air, fuel, and spark). A change in one element almost always requires a corresponding set of changes in the others for an increase in consistent and reliable power:

- As you add air, you should be able to add fuel to keep the ratio consistent.

- With more air and fuel in the mix, you should be able to control the *light-off point*, or ignition point, of the mixture.

Modern cars are adaptive and flexible — within their limits:

- When you add a little air to your late model engine, the engine management system changes the fuel delivery and ignition to account for the change. That is, your car "learns" that something's different and accounts for the altered operating parameters. When this adjustment occurs, a wonderful thing happens — extra power is made!

✔ The engine management system's learning ability is limited to a range that's close to the factory parameters. Most modern cars can account for changes of 5 to 15 percent in operating parameters. This range is fine for relatively minor modifications such as bolt-on air intakes, exhaust components, and upgraded ignitions. But it doesn't allow your engine to compensate for 200 percent more air from the turbocharger that magically appeared under the hood one sunny afternoon.

If you (and local law enforcement) don't mind extra noise, you can easily produce more power by increasing airflow. Most modern cars deliver enough fuel and spark to use more air. To minimize noise (both inside the cabin and outside the car), engineers typically reduce the engine's ability to quickly bring air in and expel it.

Air Intake

The designs for performance intake and exhaust follow many of the same principles. The idea is to keep the gases moving quickly and efficiently before and after combustion. The more air you bring in and the faster your engine ingests it, the higher the volume of air it needs to quickly push out again. Typically, your factory air intake is designed to be quiet and filter extremely well — meaning that it is very restrictive and impedes an open airflow.

Figure 15-2 illustrates a typical factory air intake. In this image, you can see the intake box, the replaceable paper air filter, and the restrictive maze of black plastic tubing that quiets the sound by impeding airflow.

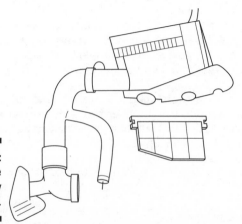

Figure 15-2:
Restrictive
factory
intake.

An air intake is a relatively inexpensive and widely available modification for most cars. An open-element air intake upgrade is usually the first performance modification that most enthusiasts add to their cars — for good reasons:

- Installation is easy.

- An open-element performance air filter creates a pleasing sporty induction sound.

- Open-element performance air filters reduce the maze of plastic tubing and boxes in the factory intake plumbing, giving a cleaner appearance under the hood.

- The mod is easily reversible.

- It eliminates the need for replacement paper filters.

- The engine gains additional power:

    - A normally aspirated car gains up to eight horsepower over a particularly restrictive factory intake.

    - Turbocharged and supercharged cars may add up to 15 horsepower from an intake alone.

- The car gets better gas mileage. Normally aspirated, turbocharged, and supercharged cars can expect a noticeable improvement — usually a couple miles per gallon — which often covers the cost of the intake over time.

- You get a more exciting performance from the car. Even cars that gain only a couple horsepower feel like they gained more with the improvement in throttle response and sound.

Check the CFMs (*cubic feet per minute,* a measure of flow capacity) dictated by the size of your turbo, intercooler, air-metering device, and/or throttle body. Many manufacturers keep these specs on file after testing their filter elements on a flow bench. By verifying that your filter flows the appropriate number of CFMs for your turbo's or engine's breathing requirements, you can avoid starving your engine of the air that it needs. If your turbo flows 600 CFM and your intercooler can support as much as 800 CFM, it does you no good to have a filter element that limits you to 300 CFM.

If you're running a turbo, check with the manufacturer of your turbo kit to ensure that the intake you intend to use provides the necessary air mass for your turbocharger. Failing to feed your turbocharger with as much air as it needs is likely to greatly shorten its life span.

There are several ways to upgrade your car's ability to breathe and make more power:

- Drop in a performance air filter.

- Add an open-element air intake.

 ✔ Add a freer-flowing intake manifold and/or throttle body.

 ✔ Put in more aggressive intake and exhaust camshafts.

The following subsections take a closer look at each of these upgrades.

Drop-in performance air filters

Drop-in performance filters are made of either foam or cotton/gauze elements and fit in the factory air box.

These filters flow only slightly better than a traditional paper filter because they keep the restrictive factory plumbing in place. But they have a few advantages:

 ✔ Longer service life than a standard paper filter

 ✔ Slightly better flow characteristics than a standard paper filter

 ✔ Legal almost everywhere

Figure 15-3 illustrates a popular K&N filter that's designed to fit in the factory air box.

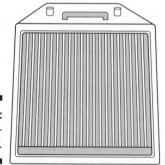

Figure 15-3:
K&N drop-
in filter.

Open-element air intake

An open-element air intake takes up where the drop-in air filter element leaves off: It essentially goes straight to the root of the problem — the convoluted maze of factory intake piping and resonators — and eliminates it entirely in favor of a shorter and more direct means of feeding air into the turbo or throttle body/intake manifold. By using either a cotton/gauze cone filter, a mushroom-style foam filter, or a hybrid filter element attached to a large diameter pipe aimed at a location in the engine bay that sees significant volumes of fresh air movement, the open-element air intake helps your engine breathe more easily.

The factory air intake plumbing restricts the engine's ability to breathe freely — a common analogy for the situation is that it's like trying to run a marathon while breathing through a straw. Eliminate the restrictive factory air intake plumbing by adding an open-element air intake, and imagine how much better your engine can pull in air and make power.

An open-element air intake will generally help with throttle response and, perhaps more so than outright power gains, add a pleasing (to most enthusiasts' ears) induction sound to the engine under acceleration. An air intake can also significantly clean up the under-hood appearance of your car and make it easier to see and access components of your engine bay.

However, as with any performance modification, there are risks and trade-offs involved. Some trade-offs include the fact that many open-element intakes will draw in air that is not properly shielded from under-hood heat, thus reducing overall power instead of adding to it — you need cold air to see power gains. Nearly all of these intakes also do a worse job of filtering out dirt than do the factory units. It may not be a catastrophic difference, and in the long run, the extra dirt may or may not be significant.

Some intakes also let in rain if they're positioned low in the engine bay where they may be subject to splashback (or even submersion) during a heavy downpour, virtually guaranteeing engine damage. Lastly, these open-element filters are highly visible and may or may not subject you to scrutiny from local emissions authorities or your local dealership service center.

Three major design constraints in an open-element air intake need to be accounted for in order to make power:

✔ Filter material

✔ Location

✔ Piping

Filter materials

You find three basic groupings of air filtration elements in open-air intakes:

✔ Cotton/gauze filters

✔ Foam filters

✔ Hybrid filters

Cotton/gauze filters

Pleated cotton/gauze filters, as pioneered and popularized by K&N, are the most common open-element air intakes on the market. They're also known as *cone filters* because of a common shape, but they're just as often available in barrel or cylinder shapes. Figure 15-4 illustrates a typical cone filter installed. Note that the piping leading to the throttle body is much shorter than the factory piping was.

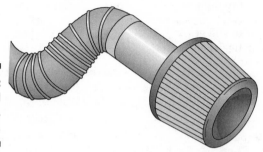

Figure 15-4:
A typical cone intake, as installed.

Cotton/gauze filters stop a comparable amount of contaminants compared to disposable a paper element filter while flowing much more air than a disposable paper filter. Some cotton/gauze filters require periodic cleaning and oiling with a special tacky oil that holds dirt and dust at the filter's surface.

When using a cotton/gauze filter element that requires oiling, a dirty filter actually stops more particles than one that's brand new. The particulate matter builds up on its surface and keeps the finer particles from being pulled through the pleats. However, a dirty filter flows less air than a new or freshly cleaned filter element.

Foam filters

Mushroom-style foam filters, as shown in Figure 15-5 (note the mushroom-like shape), have been popularized by the HKS green filters. Foam filters often flow more air than most cotton/gauze filters, but they also allow more contaminants into the engine than do cotton/gauze filters of similar size and orientation.

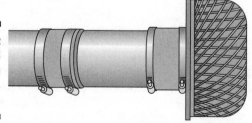

Figure 15-5:
HKS mushroom style intake, as installed.

Hybrid filters

Hybrid filters combine two filtering mediums. There are a couple of combinations on the market:

- ✔ ITG uses a dual-density foam element. A loose density (more free-flowing) outer layer of foam covers a denser inner foam element; it looks like a foam version of the traditional cotton/gauze cone filter. You can see the two different densities of foam in Figure 15-6.

  The dual-density elements provide the best of both worlds by combining the superior flow of a mushroom-style foam filter (as compared to a traditional cotton/gauze filter) with filtration similar to that of a cotton/gauze filter.

- ✔ Other companies place a foam slipcover over traditional cotton/gauze filters. This is a highly ineffective method of trying to create a hybrid filter element because the resulting filter is even more restrictive than a traditional cotton/gauze filter. The use of these slipcovers is best left to the serious off road crowd.

Hybrid filters are more restrictive than either a mushroom or traditional cone filter because air must pass through both layers before it enters the intake pipe.

Figure 15-6:
ITG hybrid
intake.

Location

An open-element air intake needs to be located where it can get plenty of cold air and also stay relatively dry and clean to protect your engine from dirt and water. For this reason, many performance open-element air intake kits position the filter element near forward-facing openings in the car's grill or bodywork so that they are exposed to a steady supply of cool air when the car is moving.

If any part of the intake system (especially the filter) is located near the hot side of a turbo, or immediately adjacent to the exhaust manifold or down pipe, it should come with some kind of shielding or shroud to prevent radiant heat from raising the temperature of the air entering the intake. Unfortunately, many air intakes use metal pipes (which absorb and retain heat) and unshielded filter elements. The cooler the air is, the denser it is. Keeping the air cool allows for more oxygen to be drawn into the engine, so cooler air ultimately means more power. Plan on making the appropriate modifications to keep the intake charge cool if you're considering an intake that doesn't

- ✔ Use a silicone or rubber pipe (instead of a metal one)
- ✔ Provide heat shielding

When shopping for an open-element filter to replace your factory intake plumbing, be wary of any intake that places the filter at a low or otherwise exposed point in the engine bay. For example, many performance enthusiasts will eliminate the factory fog light and use the hole left in the front valence as a spot for drawing in fresh air. While this forward-facing location is optimal from an airflow perspective, it also all but ensures that water will be sucked into the engine when you're driving in inclement conditions. Your open-element filter shouldn't be located where it's likely to pull in water if you get caught in a heavy downpour or drive through a small snowdrift. Water doesn't compress like air, so engine parts may bend or break when trying to compress the water (a phenomenon called *hydrolock*). Although air bypass kits are offered by companies like AEM to prevent hydrolocking your engine, it's a much better idea to simply place the filter in a location that avoids the risk entirely. Look for a source of fresh and constantly circulating air, but don't go overboard. If your filter element is jammed into the car's bodywork just inches from the ground, odds are you'll be in trouble if the car is ever driven in heavy rain.

Piping

Air likes to move in a straight line. Air slows down as it is forced to take turns (particularly tight ones). For this reason, pipes that route air should

- ✔ Be as straight as possible, with smooth, gradual bends
- ✔ Avoid excessive length or tapering before reaching the throttle body or air metering device.

Some intake pipes feature a chamber to store air just before the throttle body. Factory air intake tracts often feature such chambered air pockets, so there's reason to believe that they can be functional, if only to reduce intake noise. The jury is out on whether stored air can also increase airflow for performance.

Avoid sharp transitions anywhere in the pipe. Ideally, the path of the air stream should transition smoothly as it proceeds from the intake into the engine. If the size of the intake changes, the change should be gradual instead of sharp. Sharp lips in the pipe cause turbulence in the airstream. Watch out for these problem areas:

 ✔ A lip where the aftermarket (not from the car's original manufacturer) intake pipe meets the stock throttle body or air metering device

 ✔ A sudden step down from an excessively large pipe into a narrower factory inlet

Figure 15-7 illustrates an excessively sharp transition in sizing coupled with a bend in the pipe — this combination would create turbulence in the airflow, slowing the velocity of the intake charge.

Figure 15-8 illustrates a much smoother transition.

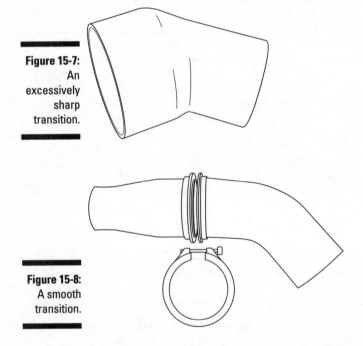

Figure 15-7:
An excessively sharp transition.

Figure 15-8:
A smooth transition.

Intake manifolds and throttle bodies

As the air mass moves further towards the engine itself and eventually into the combustion chamber, it must pass through the throttle body and into the intake manifold. The throttle body, which includes a throttle plate that opens and closes as you press and release the throttle (see Figure 15-9), can be a major bottleneck to air flow on some cars. If the intake piping must step down significantly when it reaches the throttle body, chances are that the engine can benefit both in terms of power and throttle response by upgrading to a larger throttle body.

As with most of the air intake modifications discussed in this chapter, you are trying to eliminate the weak link, or most restrictive element, in the air path. You can often source throttle bodies from other vehicles by the same manufacturer and adapt them to your car for increased airflow capacity. A common upgrade is to source a throttle body from a larger displacement motor to replace the factory unit. In Japan, many tuners rely on the throttle body of the Infiniti Q45 (Nissan Cima), one of the largest mass-market eight-cylinder motors sold domestically in their market. They adapt these throttle bodies not only for use in other Nissan/Infinity applications, but also for various other Japanese car makes and models. In the U.S., the prevalence of large displacement Mustangs and Camaros ensures a steady supply of big bore throttle bodies to U.S. tuners for this purpose.

Throttle plate

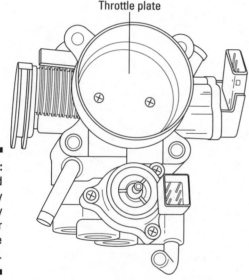

Figure 15-9:
Upgraded
factory
throttle body
with larger
throttle
plate.

From the throttle body, the air moves on to the intake manifold (see Figure 15-10 for a stock intake manifold) where it is distributed to each of the cylinders in (hopefully) equal parts. In order to increase the capacity of the intake manifold to carry more air into the motor for combustion, many tuners incorporate a larger *plenum* (a chamber where the air collects) in the manifold. A barrel or surge tank shape is often used to help more effectively feed the air in equal proportions to the intake runners for each of the cylinders. (See Figure 15-11 for a JUN surge tank style intake manifold.) By varying the length and size of the runners (and all of this is an exacting science), tuners can not only deliver more air to the engine and make more power, but also improve throttle response and gain power in the important useable areas of the power curve. The JUN surge tank and Phoenix's Power surge tanks are both excellent examples of modified intake manifolds that have proven effective for Japanese vehicles — in particular, those using forced induction.

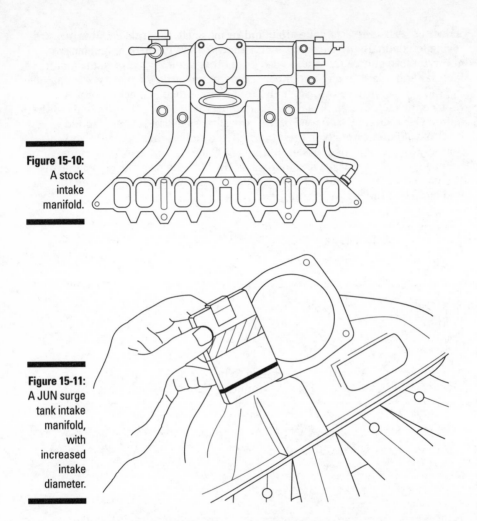

Figure 15-10:
A stock
intake
manifold.

Figure 15-11:
A JUN surge
tank intake
manifold,
with
increased
intake
diameter.

A cheaper approach, which also maintains the factory units, involves boring out the factory throttle body, inserting a larger throttle plate into the increased bore, and then extrude-honing the factory intake manifold. The extrude-hone process, which widens the air path by forcing an abrasive media through the intake manifold, will allow your engine to move higher air mass.

Camshafts

From the intake manifold, the air travels to the intake valve (precombustion) and the exhaust valve (post-combustion). By utilizing a more aggressive camshaft (cam for short — see Figure 15-12) on both the intake and exhaust side that features greater duration and/or more lift, the intake and exhaust valves can remain open longer, which allows for more air to move through the cylinder head efficiently.

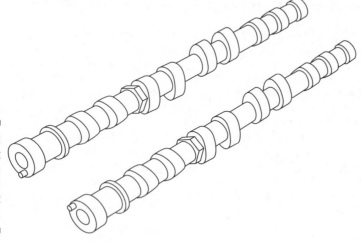

Figure 15-12: Aftermarket performance intake and exhaust cams.

Generally, the cam gears will also need to be upgraded in order to properly degree the new camshafts for your application. Because selecting and installing camshafts, as well as tuning for them, is best left to professionals, it is a good idea to get help in selecting the right components to match your turbo/engine and drivability needs. An improperly matched camshaft can not only ruin your car's idle characteristics, making it a chore to keep a steady idle, but it can also move your power band well outside of the useable range for your turbo and/or driving style. When in doubt, consult with those that have been down this path before.

Some engines are *interference engines* when they leave the factory (like most Hondas). What this means is if the timing belt were to break, the valves will collide, causing engine damage. Other engines are designed to be non-interference. If you have a non-interference engine and elect to install more aggressive camshafts, chances are you will be changing to an interference design by so doing and will need to stay on top of regular timing belt changes.

If you plan on keeping your car normally aspirated in your quest for power (no superchargers, turbochargers, or nitrous), a camshaft upgrade, usually coupled with an increase in your engine's compression ratio, is the single most effective way to meaningfully raise your horsepower. The gains you get from a well-matched set of camshafts will generally dwarf those of the other bolt-on modifications. Generally, an added advantage of upgrading to more aggressive camshafts is that your engine breathes more freely at high revs.

Given the choice, it's often a good idea to stay away from reground cams that rely on a stock camshaft that was upgraded by having material welded on to the cam lobe and then ground down to the new specification. These cams tend to wear much faster than cams that start from fresh billet blanks. If the new set of cams you are thinking of buying for your car involves a core exchange or deposit, chances are good you're being sold a reground cam.

Because most cams allow you to raise the factory rev limit, it is often a good idea to invest in a set of upgraded *valve springs* (the spring that pushes the valve) and *retainers* (holds the spring in place) as well as *head studs* (the bolts that hold the head on the block) to cope with the added cylinder pressure and minimize the risk of floating a valve (contact between the valve and the piston — a very bad thing). Another upgrade includes switching from *shim over-bucket* valve shims to either a *shim under-bucket* design or a *shimless* design. Basically, the shim allows for valve adjustment (that is, increasing the lift) and there are different methods by which this is achieved. For high rev applications, shimless is the safest (in terms of engine longevity) followed by shim under-bucket and then shim over-bucket. If you're interested in pursuing a conversion of one to the other, consult with your local engine builder.

Exhausts

The exhaust path on your car begins as the hot exhaust gases leave the cylinder head through the exhaust manifold. From there, the gases are directed downwards under the car, are cleaned and quieted, and eventually emerge out of the tailpipe. The complete exhaust system basically consists of

- **Exhaust manifold,** which consists of *runners* that channel the exhaust away from each cylinder and into a *collector*.

- **Down-pipe** (for turbocharged cars; normally aspirated cars have longer runners and don't require a down-pipe), which carries the gases down under the car to the rest of the exhaust system.

- **Catalytic converter** (commonly called a *cat*), which cleans the exhaust gases before allowing them into the atmosphere.

- **Muffler section,** which helps to quiet the harmonic frequencies that otherwise contribute to exhaust noise by deflecting the gases through a series of chambers. A performance muffler, by contrast, eliminates or reduces the number of these chambers in favor of a free-flowing design that works primarily off the absorption principle, like a resonator.

The exhaust noise is reduced by routing the gases through

- A muffler

- One or more in-line *resonators* (think of these as mini-mufflers; the old timers called them *glass packs*) A resonator, as the name implies, reduces the resonant harmonic frequencies in the exhaust stream using the principle of absorption by fiberglass packing around a perforated metal core.

✓ **Tailpipe** (or exhaust tip), which is the final exit point after the exhaust gases have left the muffler. The tip itself is primarily cosmetic and can be changed either to make your otherwise stock exhaust system look more sporty than it really is, or to put a humble façade on an otherwise free flowing exhaust in order to maintain a car's *sleeper appearance* (stock appearance, with plenty of performance hidden inside).

Figure 15-13 illustrates a complete exhaust system for a front-engine car, minus the exhaust manifold. You can see how the exhaust gases pass through a catalytic converter to remove harmful pollutants (carbon monoxide, nitrogen oxides, and hydrocarbons) and then move on to a muffler that acts to reduce noise. The resonator also acts to reduce noise. Not all cars have resonators, but nearly all cars have mufflers — with at least one exception, the Dodge Neon SRT-4, a turbocharged four cylinder powered car that manages to attain legal decibel levels with just a resonator.

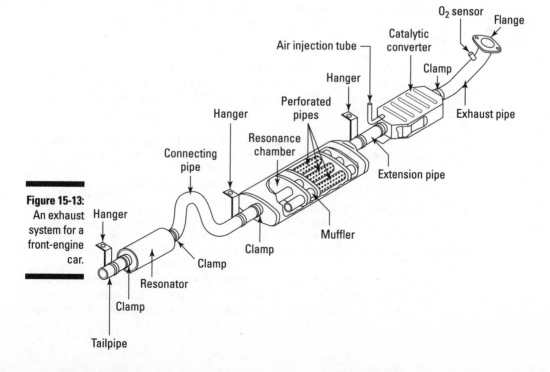

Figure 15-13: An exhaust system for a front-engine car.

Figure 15-14 illustrates a complete exhaust system for a mid-engine turbocharged car, including the exhaust manifold, the turbo, and the wastegate, but no catalytic converter.

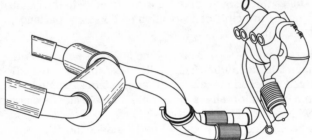

Figure 15-14:
A complete exhaust system for a turbo mid-engine car.

Generally, turbo cars use less restrictive mufflers than their normally aspirated counterparts because

- A freer breathing exhaust path helps spool the turbo and reduces turbo lag.
- The turbocharger itself quiets the exhaust gases.

While in the 70s and 80s, tremendous power gains could be seen from removing catalytic converters; those days are long behind us. As technology marched forward in the design of emissions equipment, catalytic converters became increasingly efficient. In fact, catalytic converters have become so efficient that removing them in favor of a test pipe yields relatively minimal gains in all but the most extreme applications. As such, you would be well advised to look elsewhere for power gains, rather than trying to hunt down a couple of horsepower by removing equipment that serves a very important purpose: keeping our environment clean.

Along the exhaust path, you may also find sensors to monitor the exhaust gas mixture as it leaves the engine. These sensors may check for

- Oxygen (usually identified by the chemical symbol for free oxygen, O_2)
- Exhaust gas temperature

There are minimal differences between the exhaust path of a turbocharged and a non-turbocharged car. The differences occur at the exhaust manifold:

- In a normally aspirated car or a supercharged car, when the combustion process has been completed and the gases have left the cylinder head, everything from that point on is simply a method of clearing the exhaust fumes from the car. Figure 15-15 shows an exhaust manifold for a four-cylinder non-turbo mid-engine car. This device is for the normally aspirated version of the same kind of car whose complete exhaust system (set up for a turbo) is shown in Figure 15-14.

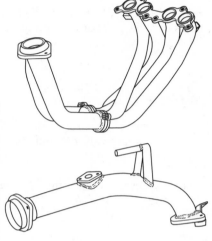

Figure 15-15:
Exhaust
manifold for
a non-turbo
four-cylinder
mid-engine
car.

✔ In a turbocharged car, exhaust gases are reused after combustion. These gases are piped to spin the exhaust side of the turbocharger. The more pressure these exhaust gases apply, the faster the pinwheel turns.

Proper routing of exhaust gases on a turbocharged car has a major impact on both

- Maximum power
- Turbo lag (the delay between pressing the throttle and getting extra power)

There is nothing wrong with making your own exhaust system at a local muffler shop — provided you do it right. Building your own can be an excellent way to save money if you already have the right resources, but mandrel-bent tubing, quality mufflers, and a skilled welder don't often come cheap. Don't be surprised if a good custom system, if built to the same standards as a top-shelf aftermarket equivalent, costs more than an off-the-shelf product that is made for your car. Off-the-shelf systems are made with specific *jigs* and *patterns* for your car. With jigs and patterns, a fabricator can cut, bend, and weld an exhaust system with just a few quick steps. If your buddy tells you that he made a quality exhaust at the local muffler shop for $100 and a six-pack of beer, be very skeptical. Sometimes, you really do get what you pay for.

Some advertisements state that exhaust systems and parts are "50 state legal." This refers strictly to state *emissions* requirements as dictated by the air resources board:

✔ The exhaust system may run afoul of local vehicle code ordinances about exhaust sound levels.

✔ There's no easy way to prevent a misguided law enforcement official from harassing you if neighbors complain about your performance exhaust system, whether or not your system is technically legal.

Header/exhaust manifold

The exhaust manifold (also known as an *exhaust header*) is the first in a series of pipes encountered by the exhaust gases after combustion. The two distinct sections in a manifold are the runners and the collector:

✔ Each cylinder usually pushes its own exhaust gases into a *runner* (a separate segment of pipe). A four-cylinder car has four runners, a six-cylinder car has six runners, and so on.

✔ Gases from separate runners come together in the *collector*.

Designs

Common upgrades for normally aspirated, turbocharged, and supercharged engines include

✔ Increasing the diameter of the exhaust manifold pipes for better flow with less restriction.

✔ Engineering equal-distance runners so that the exhaust gases travel the same distance from each cylinder. (These are called *equal-length manifolds*.) These runners operate under the premise that exhaust gas pulses leave the cylinder head at the same time and travel at the same velocity, and should therefore travel the same distance as they exit the motor. This reduces or eliminates back pressure, so that all the cylinders can evacuate their exhaust charges as efficiently as possible, without one cylinder interfering with others.

Aftermarket tubular manifolds should be carefully evaluated for durability. A durable manifold has

✔ Thick flanges to resist warping and leaks.

✔ Sufficient bracing to prevent cracking (especially if the manifold supports the weight of a turbocharger). Bracing should be used at common stress points on the manifold and down-pipe. These include the areas used to support the weight of the turbo and external wastegate. The heavier the turbo and larger the wastegate, the more bracing the manifold will need. Bracing should be fabricated in such a way as to allow a bit of expansion, but not allow so much movement as to cause the pipes to crack under stress. Common brace points include bracing to the cylinder head at the valve cover and bracing to the engine block.

Figure 15-16 shows a brace that uses the engine block to support the weight of the turbo — it's the triangular piece that's supporting the piping in front of the snail-shaped turbo (on the right) by connecting it firmly to the engine block (on the left).

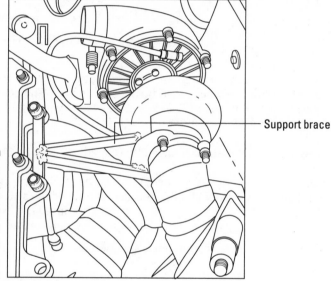

— Support brace

Figure 15-16:
The weight of the turbo is supported by this triangular brace.

Most upgraded exhaust manifolds are made of tubular steel with individual pipes (runners) for each cylinder. Pipes can be shaped by either mandrel bending or crush bending the steel tubing:

✔ Mandrel bending doesn't narrow the tubes internally while bending to shape.

Mandrel-bent pipes are more expensive than crush-bent pipes, but their superior flow increases exhaust efficiency.

✔ Crush bending creates a narrow section inside the pipe where it is crushed into shape. The narrow section reduces exhaust flow and can contribute to back pressure.

Materials

The usual standard cast manifold is less expensive to manufacture than individually welded tubular manifolds featuring mandrel bends. However, cast manifolds usually

- ✔ Have unequal-length pipes and sharp bends that reduce exhaust flow
- ✔ Weigh more than tubular replacement manifolds

The standard cast exhaust manifold has a couple of advantages over tubular replacement manifolds:

- ✔ Cast manifolds are quieter and less likely to crack or corrode.
- ✔ Cast manifolds generally do an excellent job of keeping the exhaust hot.

    Tubular manifolds can retain heat with the liberal use of either thermal wrap or ceramic coating.

    Usually, you shouldn't use thermal ceramic coatings on the inside of exhaust manifolds — especially on turbocharged cars. The coatings have been known to flake off. The debris may harm your engine if it finds its way into the turbo or cylinder head.

Tubular exhaust manifold materials have different advantages and trade-offs:

- ✔ Stainless steel has excellent corrosion resistance; it's less likely to rust through than is conventional mild steel. However, stainless steel is more likely to crack at stress points (such as welds) because stainless steel expands and contracts more dramatically with heating and cooling.
- ✔ Mild steel is less likely to crack, but it's vulnerable to corrosion when left untreated.

    You must take care to prevent corrosion from prematurely killing a mild steel manifold. Several different coatings can be used to both prevent corrosion and maintain exhaust heat inside the manifold:

    - Ceramic coating is used both as a corrosion barrier and to prevent heat from radiating out of the manifold, thereby keeping the exhaust gases hot and moving rapidly. Exhaust gases slow as they cool, and then begin to tumble, creating unwanted turbulence in the exhaust stream.

    - Thermal wrap (see Figure 15-17) is a heat barrier that is wrapped around the outside of the manifold and held in place by metal clips. A thermal wrap can take the shape of a tape form, a reflective heat blanket, or even an expensive and custom-formed Inconel barrier. Note that tape wrap has a tendency to absorb and trap moisture against the manifold's surface and should be treated with a special solution provided by the wrap manufacturer to avoid retaining water.

• High temperature exhaust paint is used as a corrosion barrier and for cosmetic purposes, but should not be relied on for heat management benefits. Paint is the least expensive solution, but it is susceptible to scratches and should be inspected periodically because scratches in the paint will quickly lead to the onset of corrosion.

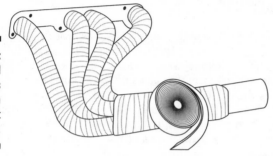

Figure 15-17: Thermal wrap retains heat in exhaust manifolds.

Regular spray paint should not be used on exhaust manifolds or other exhaust system components, as it is not designed to cope with the extreme temperatures in your engine bay.

Not sure which kind of steel was used in the construction of your manifold? Try the magnet test!

✔ If a magnet sticks, the exhaust manifold is mild steel.

✔ If a magnet doesn't stick, the exhaust manifold is stainless steel.

If your car is primarily a show car and you want your stainless manifold uncoated, use some rubbing alcohol to remove all fingerprints, oil, and dirt from its surface before you get it hot. When the manifold goes through its first heat cycle, it has that nice tint to it like the pipes on custom motorcycles. Without the alcohol rub, the oil from fingerprints and such burns into the metal surface and detracts from its appearance. Clean the manifold with rubbing alcohol at least twice:

✔ Once before you begin installing the manifold

✔ Once immediately before you start the engine for the first time after the installation

Exhaust mounting hardware gets *hot!* Take steps to avoid power-robbing (and potentially dangerous) exhaust leaks:

✔ Always use locking fasteners when mounting your manifold — these should come with your kit.

✔ Double-check and retorque (tighten to correct torque) all of your mounting hardware after the manifold has been through a few heat cycles. Even properly torqued hardware can come loose when the metal expands and contracts with heat and cool down.

Exhaust systems

The beauty of exhaust system modifications is that they rarely have to be a one-shot deal. Because most exhaust systems are themselves modular, your upgrade strategy can be modular as well. Because horsepower is addictive, often the best move is to start from the back end of the car and work your way closer to the engine as the power craving sets in and the siren song of car modding becomes irresistible. With this in mind, a simple axle-back system will start you down the road to the look, sound, and performance of a modified exhaust, while leaving room to grow. You can then consider a cat-back exhaust system, or even a header-back system, if your application demands it.

If you want to improve your car's performance, look for a lighter exhaust system that flows better (a straighter, wider path) than your standard exhaust. A high-polished great looking exhaust system that weighs more than stock and doesn't improve flow is never going to provide the performance results that a much lighter and higher-flowing system can give you.

When shopping for an exhaust system, make a point of looking for a system that uses

✔ Mandrel bent tubing

✔ High-grade tubing made with either

- Stainless steel
- Titanium

✔ Joints made with either

- **Quality TIG (tungsten inert gas) or machine (fully automated) welds.** These provide cleaner, more consistent welds than can be achieved using a MIG (metal inert gas) welder. Opt for TIG welds when the welds will be visible and will not be ground down and chrome plated or ceramic coated.

- **V-band couplers.** These couplers take the place of flanges, gaskets, and bolts in exhaust assembly. They allow for the quick and easy removal and reinstallation of exhaust components. Figure 15-18 illustrates a few V-bands.

✔ Features to prevent cracking in the manifold or pipes, such as

- **A flex pipe.** This is a braided steel section of exhaust piping designed, as the name implies, to allow the exhaust piping to flex in order to prevent vibration and movement from cracking the piping itself, or spreading up to the manifold and cracking that. Figure 15-19 illustrates a flex pipe.

- **Rubber vibration isolation mounts.** These mounts are used to provide dampening from road vibrations — to prevent the vibrations from cracking the exhaust system components. They are most commonly used at the *exhaust hangers,* the metal rods used to support the weight of the exhaust where the exhaust mounts to the chassis. Figure 15-20 illustrates a couple of rubber vibration isolation mounts supporting a section of exhaust piping. The rubber mounts are situated on either side of the pipe, hanging the pipe from the bottom of the car by thick hangers welded directly onto the pipes.

✔ A straight-through muffler for maximum flow

Figure 15-18:
V-band
couplers.

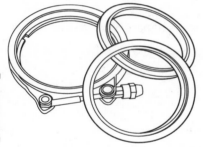

Figure 15-19:
Flex pipe —
the braided
section in
the middle
can flex.

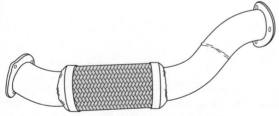

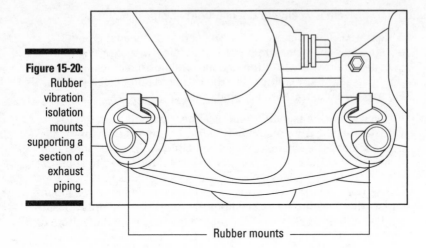

Figure 15-20:
Rubber
vibration
isolation
mounts
supporting a
section of
exhaust
piping.

———— Rubber mounts ————

For easy installation and legal compliance, check whether the aftermarket exhaust system

✔ Uses the same mounting points and hardware as your standard exhaust

✔ Conforms to state emission regulations by either

• Using factory emissions equipment

• Carrying an Air Resources Board exemption number for your state

Axle-back exhausts / rear-sections

As the name implies, the *axle-back exhaust* replaces only the portion of the exhaust system behind the rear axle. Usually, these systems include

✔ Muffler

✔ Tip

✔ A bit of pipe

Figure 15-21 illustrates a typical axle-back exhaust, with a flange at the back for connecting to the catalytic converter (or the intermediate pipe before the cat), a couple of hangers, a straight-through muffler, and a big, shiny tip.

These systems provide the lowest performance gains of the possible exhaust modifications, but are generally the least expensive and most road-friendly of the bunch.

If you want a modified look without the noise, legality issues, and cost of a full exhaust, an axle-back system may be the right solution.

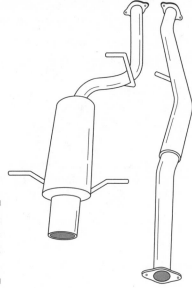

Figure 15-21:
WRX axle-
back
exhaust.

Cat-back exhausts

A *cat-back exhaust* replaces the exhaust system behind the primary catalytic converter.

In many states, it is legal to modify only the exhaust system behind the catalytic converter. If you plan to run your car on the streets, odds are you'll be shopping for a cat-back exhaust instead of the turbo/header-back exhaust systems.

Figure 15-22 illustrates a cat-back exhaust consisting of two segments: The axle-back segment on the left (notice it is almost identical to the axle-back exhaust shown in Figure 15-21), and another segment of pipe on the right (with an in-line resonator) that connects the muffler section to the catalytic converter.

Figure 15-22:
WRX cat-
back
exhaust.

A cat-back exhaust usually offers a little less performance improvement than does a more comprehensive exhaust upgrade, but eliminating the pipes behind the cat still pays large dividends by

- Replacing the restrictive factory muffler with a more free-flowing variety
- Enlarging the rear-most pipes
- Reducing the number and severity of bends in the system behind the catalytic converter

From the outside, a cat-back exhaust is every bit as impressive as a turbo-back or header-back system (except for the street-legal noise level). In most cases, a cat-back system tells the crowd you mean business with

- A better looking exhaust tip
- Polished muffler
- Beefy pipes
- Throatier sound

Turbo back/header back

A turbo-back or header-back exhaust system optimizes exhaust flow without regard for the emissions devices (including catalytic converters) that usually are found in a street exhaust system. The turbo-back or header-back exhaust includes (as the name implies) all of the exhaust pipes from the turbo and header to the exhaust tip.

When installed as a complete package, many turbo-back and header-back exhaust system aren't street legal.

Figure 15-23 illustrates a turbo-back exhaust system. The axle-back segment (with straight-through muffler) is in the middle. The cat-back segment (with in-line resonator) is on the left. The down-pipe (with a large flange that connects it to the header) is on the right. The small piece at the front is the up-pipe, which in this application (the Subaru WRX), replaces a catalytic converter that Subaru has placed before the turbo. Most turbos do not have a cat before them. The ports in the up-pipe are made to house sensors, such as an oxygen sensor and an exhaust gas temperature (EGT) sensor.

Exhaust system modifications are tricky from a legal standpoint. First, they are one of the modifications that are most likely to get you in trouble for violating vehicle code noise ordinances. Second, because your exhaust consists of several critical emissions components, tampering with or removing these components can net you big fines and "fix it" or moving violations tickets:

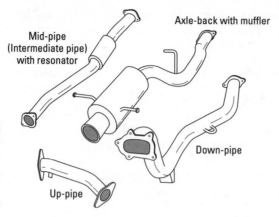

Figure 15-23: WRX turbo-back exhaust.

Mid-pipe (Intermediate pipe) with resonator

Axle-back with muffler

Down-pipe

Up-pipe

✔ For street driving, it is usually illegal to replace your catalytic converter with a less restrictive high-flow catalytic converter unless your factory catalytic converter is clogged or damaged and needs replacement.

Many automotive shops won't remove a functioning catalytic converter.

✔ If you live in an area that tests individual cars for emissions compliance, it is never legal to replace your factory catalytic converter with either

- A *test pipe* (straight through piece of tubing)

- A *hollowed-out catalytic converter* (stock catalytic converter in which the ceramic honeycomb material has been punched out)

Many turbo/header-back exhausts are designed for "off road use only" — they're too loud for street driving under most laws. Systems without catalytic converters often exceed local street noise laws; the cat normally does an excellent job of absorbing exhaust noise in addition to cleaning the exhaust gases.

A shiny exhaust tells the world that you are all about performance to the extreme. It also advertises to law enforcement that you might be packing illegal mods under the hood.

Ignitions

Common ignition upgrades are based on the idea that your car's stock ignition system isn't fully lighting the air/fuel mixture.

If your car isn't suffering an ignition misfire, the old adage "if it ain't broke, don't fix it" applies here. Most modern cars neither need nor benefit from common ignition upgrades. A standard ignition system in perfect working order usually can keep up with power modifications.

For most folks, these ignition upgrades are the equivalent of filling Mom's minivan with 100-octane unleaded race gas: It probably doesn't hurt anything, but there are better ways to spend the cash.

Grounding kit

Grounding kits (or *ground wire kits*) are basically designed to improve the factory electrical grounds by using some combination of

- ✔ Heavier gauge wire
- ✔ More grounding points
- ✔ A junction ring or box

Figure 15-24 illustrates an upgraded grounding kit, consisting of beefy ground wires that are well insulated and ground off the major engine accessories, including the starter, alternator, engine block, and so on. The circular metal ring mounts to the batteries ground, and from there, the other wires extend out to the engine accessories, supplementing the factory grounds.

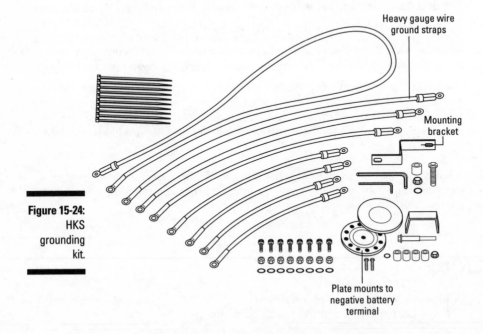

Heavy gauge wire ground straps

Mounting bracket

Plate mounts to negative battery terminal

Figure 15-24: HKS grounding kit.

Ground wire kits are advertised as adding horsepower and smoothing out throttle response, but they're just recovering power that has been lost from corroded or loose factory grounds. Grounding kits may be worth a shot if you have money to burn and have run out of ways to try to improve your car's performance, if the car has a persistent ignition misfire (as diagnosed on a Dyno), or if a visual inspection reveals that the wires are heavily corroded. Otherwise, consider grounding kits a cosmetic engine-bay enhancing mod, not a performance mod.

You can make your own grounding kit with stereo wires and high-end terminal connectors. However, avoid placing wires where they might melt or become worn through. The potential of grounding out an engine's electrical system and starting an engine fire or frying the ECU is an ominous one, and an automobile's electrical system deserves the appropriate amount of care when making modifications.

Amplifier

Ignition amplifiers are designed to work either with a factory setup or upgraded grounding kit to provide a stronger spark for lighting off the combustion mixture. Think of an ignition amplifier as a supplementary amplifier for your ignition — just like having a supplementary amplifier for your car stereo — and you have the basic concept.

Ignition amplifiers usually do their intended job very well and provide a measurable increase in spark. Figure 15-25 illustrates an ignition amplifier. It connects to the factory ignition coil, or it may be sold with an aftermarket high voltage coil.

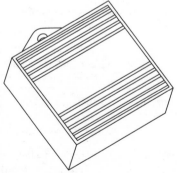

Figure 15-25: An HKS ignition amplifier. This one works with the stock ignition coil.

Spark plugs

Simply installing an ignition amplifier usually doesn't increase power, but an engine with an ignition amplifier can be tuned to take advantage of the stronger spark. An engine with an ignition amplifier can run spark plugs at a colder heat range and with a wider gap than would otherwise be possible.

Running colder plugs allows the engine to better resist detonation when tuned to the ragged edge. Running plugs with a wider gap allows more of the air/fuel mixture to be exposed to the spark, allowing for a more even combustion.

The temperature rating of a spark plug describes how well insulated it is. Because a colder heat range plug has less insulation, it cools off faster between firing and the introduction of a fresh charge of the air/fuel mixture. A hot plug can ignite the air/fuel mixture before the plug actually fires. This is called *pre-ignition*, a form of detonation. Detonation is what destroys motors. So, you want to run as cold a plug as you can in order to ensure that the plug cools down as quickly as possible after it has fired. But if your ignition is not capable of providing enough spark energy to fire your plugs consistently, for example if the gap is too wide or the plugs are too cold, your plugs will foul and become useless.

An ignition amplifier can help remedy the problem. If your car has worn ignition components (this includes the cap, the rotor, the spark plugs, and the spark plug wires) that are overdue for replacement (check the owner's manual) and/or has corroded factory grounds, then your best bet is to address these first. If your factory ignition components are new but you're still seeing evidence of pre-ignition or erratic ignition performance on the Dyno (as evidenced by excessive jaggedness at the top of the power graph), then an ignition amplifier might be well suited to your application.

See Table 15-1 for the relative merits of the many different materials used in spark plugs.

Table 15-1	Spark Plugs	
Material	*Pros*	*Cons*
Copper	Best performance, very cheap	Need to be changed very frequently (every time you change your oil)
Iridium	Copper-like performance with longer life	Expensive and can come apart (electrode separates) if not manufactured correctly
Platinum	Long life with less cost than iridium	Still expensive (but less so than iridium) and not appropriate for turbocharged cars running a lot of boost
Everything else	None	Gimmicky multi-electrode or conventional plugs — avoid at all costs

Chapter 16

Building a Strong Foundation

In This Chapter

▶ Strengthening the driveline

▶ Starting with a healthy engine

A street car may go 100,000 miles or more without big mechanical problems. This often is because the car is designed to be *understressed* — the parts are tougher than they absolutely have to be, and the average driver doesn't often use them as hard as possible. If there's a part that has a little flaw, or is badly worn, the problem may not be noticeable while just driving to the store.

Any weak points hidden under the surface will make themselves known in short order when you add power. A clutch that was perfectly happy with half the power quickly throws in the towel when the power is doubled. A car that never lacked for traction suddenly does the peg-leg burnout, spinning a single wheel, if you don't upgrade to a limited-slip differential. Engine mounts that seemed perfectly fine now strain and break from the engine torquing under load. Even the suspension begins doing funny things as you begin experiencing wheel-hop from the tires clawing for traction with insufficiently resilient bushings.

A performance car usually puts its parts under heavy loads that may break stock or worn parts. You may need to revise and revamp nearly every aspect of your car's driveline to make it drive and feel like it should — a smooth, powerful, predictable, and reliable performer.

For safety and reliability, make sure that your car's parts are up to the extra power you plan to install.

Engine Essentials

The following items can help make extra power possible and reliable.

Basic maintenance

Before you install a performance enhancer, get your engine in tip-top condition:

- ✔ If you have put off changing spark plugs, installing an ignition cap and rotor, or making a valve adjustment, this is the time to act.

- ✔ Change the fluids to make sure that you are running in peak condition.

  - • Use synthetic motor oil of the correct grade for your engine.

    Synthetic motor oil better resists thermal breakdown and *coking* (breaking down and caking of motor oil at high temperatures) inside a turbo.

  - • Use fresh, correct coolant.

Testing

Don't bother upgrading an engine that is anything less than 100 percent healthy. If there is any doubt about the general health of your engine, perform the following tests.

If test results show your engine isn't in tip-top condition, don't try increasing power before you have it fixed. Adding performance on a shaky foundation is a recipe for certain disappointment.

Compression

A *compression test* involves looking for *variances* among the cylinders. You attach a pressure gauge to each cylinder's spark plug hole and check the pressure readings they produce:

- ✔ Compression that's too low indicates that the piston is not sealing correctly.

- ✔ Compression that's too high might indicate carbon build-up on top of the piston.

A technical manual for your make and model can provide the specific variance range (factory tolerances) for your car's engine.

Leak down

A *leak down test* checks for pressure by removing the spark plugs and then feeding pressurized air into the cylinders with the piston at top dead center. By listening for and noting leaks, you can check to see where pressure is escaping.

If your engine has air leaks when you test it, trace down the cause of the leaks:

✔ Leaks between *adjacent cylinders* may indicate either

- A blown head gasket between cylinders

- A valve stuck open

✔ Leaks at the *exhaust pipe* may indicate a burnt or stuck exhaust valve.

✔ Leaks at the *throttle body* may indicate a bent or stuck intake valve.

✔ Leaks at the *oil filler* or *dipstick* may indicate either

- Broken piston rings

- A damaged piston

✔ Leaks at the radiator filler cap (look for bubbles) will indicate either

- A leaking head gasket

- A cracked head

Dyno evaluation

To verify that everything is running smoothly and that the engine is in tip-top shape, many enthusiasts also make an appointment at a local Dyno facility to do a baseline Dyno run. This test has two uses:

✔ It uncovers problems in the car's basic state of tune.

✔ It provides a baseline for measuring increases as you modify your car.

It is important to confirm the static timing (with a timing gun — see your mechanic for this) on your car before attempting to modify for more power. Any changes made in the ignition tables will be premised on the static timing being accurate.

Idle should be within factory specs when cold and when warmed up. If not, look for leaks and perform the necessary troubleshooting before adding boost. Few things are more frustrating than troubleshooting an install only to realize that the problem had been there all along and is unrelated to the installation of the new components.

Before running your car on the Dyno, it is a good idea to spray down any engine component that holds pressure (such as vacuum lines, intercooler pipes and connectors, and connections at the throttle body) with a mixture of soap and water in a spray bottle. If the soap bubbles up anywhere, this will help you identify leaks at common problem areas, including cracks in hoses or connectors that may not be otherwise visible. Be careful not to spray near electronic components.

Fuel

There may be enough headroom in the factory fuel system to work with a modest power increase. Remapping or adjusting the factory fuel map keeps the mixture at a safe ratio for proper combustion. Even this usually requires (at least) retuning of the factory ECU with one of the following:

- Piggyback fuel controller
- ECU reflash/chip upgrade
- Standalone ECU replacement

Chapter 20 is an introduction to the world of ECU upgrades.

Gauges

Gauges can give you the warm feeling of knowing that your engine is healthy and warn you when it isn't. These gauges that help you monitor the health of any high-performance engine:

- Oil pressure

  Some cars, such as some Mazda Miatas, come from the factory with *binary* oil-pressure gauges. It looks like a gauge, but it only works like the usual warning light. The "gauge" just shows "normal" oil pressure unless there's almost *no* oil pressure.

- Oil temperature
- Coolant temperature

Driveline Upgrades

Driveline upgrades are a necessary evil to cope with the extra power. In short, the power you add under the hood needs to find its way to the pavement for it to do you any good. For that to happen, everything from the clutch to the transmission, axles, and driveshaft have to be capable of coping with what your engine is churning out. Basically, driveline mods are approached either through the experience of others, or through a series of educated guesses, to eliminate weak points in your car's driveline.

You're rarely the first person ever who has thought of making your car cope with tremendous amounts of power. There are even guys who have managed to make incredibly quick cars out of Yugos — and somehow the cars hold together (at least, for a while).

Clutches

With big power comes a surprising new addition to your car . . . a new aroma wafting through the cabin. The intoxicating perfume known as *eau de Clutch* is the result of too little clutch for too much power.

A clutch consists of the clutch disc and the clutch cover, between which, you find the pressure plate and diaphragm spring. Figure 16-1 illustrates the various parts of the clutch and their placement relative to the engine and the (manual) transmission on a *front-engine* car. (This placement is reversed on a rear-engine car.)

Keep the following points in mind when you're considering a clutch upgrade:

✔ A clutch is a wear-and-tear item. For this reason, all things being equal, buy local. Your ultra JDM ride is no less authentic if the clutch was made in the United States.

When a clutch wears out, the convenience of receiving a new friction disc, fly wheel, or hub pressure plate within days — rather than waiting months and being forced to buy a complete new clutch kit — more than makes up for using a non-JDM part on your JDM ride.

The United States is a leader in high-performance clutches. Many Japanese-branded clutches are either made by U.S. manufacturers or based on their designs.

✔ Buy the highest quality clutch you can afford. This is particularly true if you must drop the transaxle on your car to replace your clutch. Price doesn't always dictate quality, but skimping on a clutch makes little sense when the labor bill is likely to be at least as much as the cost of the parts.

Clutch upgrades usually have a few problems:

✔ You may break *other* driveline parts that are protected by a gentle stock clutch.

✔ The clutch pedal requires more effort than a stock clutch.

✔ High-performance clutches usually are more difficult to use *smoothly* in everyday driving. You may find that

• Passengers don't think you're a good driver.

• The car's speed is hard to control in start-and-stop traffic without frequent stalling.

Friction material

The clutch disc on most stock cars is made from an organic friction material that allows smooth engagement, a long life, and inexpensive replacement. When shopping for an upgraded clutch, I recommend looking for a friction material that better resists heat than the stock organic variety. Several companies, including ACT, Clutchmasters, and Centerforce, offer clutches with modified friction surfaces incorporating more heat-resistant Kevlar, carbon, or some combination thereof that will allow the clutch disc to be *slipped* (partially engaged) without immediately disintegrating.

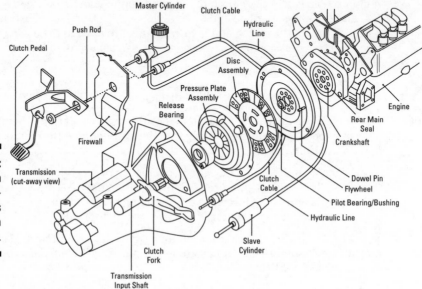

Figure 16-1: Diagram of a front-engine car's clutch system.

Pressure plate

The pressure plate on most stock clutches is designed to handle the torque loads of a stock car when an average consumer drives it.

To increase clamping power and cope with increased torque load, it is often a good idea to switch to

- ✔ Stiffer diaphragm spring
- ✔ Sturdier pressure plate

Hubs

Most stock and many milder performance clutches feature a sprung hub. Springs are placed at the center of the clutch disc to

- ✔ Reduce transmission noise caused by vibration
- ✔ Reduce wear on the clutch splines
- ✔ Smooth out the clutch engagement

Many performance-minded enthusiasts forgo sprung hubs to reduce the weight of the clutch disc (eliminating the springs makes for a lighter rotating mass) and the corresponding payoffs are

✔ Faster gear changes

✔ Quicker engagement

✔ Elimination of spring failures

If you aren't a hardcore racer, don't consider a *four-puck* unsprung clutch. These make your left leg develop muscles that dwarf your right leg, and your drivetrain won't appreciate the extra wear and tear from such an aggressive configuration. Even if you are a hardcore racer, you should probably consider stepping up to a nice twin or multi-disc clutch.

Multiple discs

At the top of the clutch food chain, the twin and multi-disc clutches can be easier to use than other high-performance clutches because they distribute mass of the clutch disc over more than one disc, rather than simply relying on a single beefy disc.

Multiple clutch discs usually have several benefits:

✔ Lighter clutch pedal effort (closer to stock)

✔ Less driveline shock

✔ An integrated lightweight flywheel, which

  • Minimizes rotating mass

  • Improves throttle response

These make rev matching on downshifts a dream.

A lightweight flywheel usually adds at least $400 to the cost of a high-performance single-disc clutch.

There are a few reasons you may decide against a multi-disc clutch:

✔ They're usually far more expensive than single-disc clutches (expect to spend from $1,000 to $4,000 on one), though they usually have an integrated *lightweight flywheel,* which is at least a $400 item if you buy it separately. (Flywheels are covered elsewhere in this chapter.)

✔ They tend to be noisy when the discs chatter against each other.

✔ They operate very much like an *on/off switch* when they engage.

Figure 16-2 illustrates an unsprung twin disc clutch assembly.

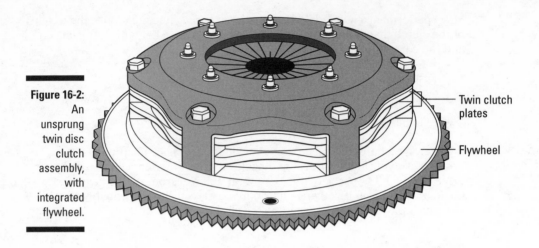

Figure 16-2:
An unsprung twin disc clutch assembly, with integrated flywheel.

Twin clutch plates

Flywheel

The twin or multi-disc clutch has much more surface area than that of a stock clutch, but both pedal effort and strain on the driveline is kept to a minimum because that surface area is spread over more than one clutch disc:

✔ If you can possibly afford a twin-disc or multi-disc clutch, buy it. The holding capacity of twin and multi-disc clutches is phenomenal. When you get used to a bit more clutch noise and a very on/off clutch feel, shifting with one of these is much like stock. Tilton, Clutchmasters, and Exedy all offer excellent twin and multi-disc clutches.

✔ If you must get a single-disc clutch, get a carbon or carbon/Kevlar blended friction disc, not the organic and street compounds. The organic materials, like what is on your stock clutch, burn and glaze in short order, whether or not you're using a heavy-duty pressure plate or ultra-light flywheel. The carbon and Kevlar blends better resist this burn-off and allow a bit of slip before showing fatigue or wear.

Flywheels

A *flywheel* is one of the components of the clutch assembly, and it can make a big difference in how your car responds to throttle inputs. A lightweight flywheel is made of aluminum or chromoly (see Figure 16-3). It reduces rotating mass by dramatically trimming weight.

This reduction in rotating mass pays big dividends in how willing the engine is to rev, and it can help or hinder launching, depending on your driving style. Because there's less inertia in a lightweight flywheel, blipping the throttle to match revs on downshifts becomes a breeze.

Figure 16-3:
A light-
weight
flywheel.

Given the disastrous consequences of flywheel failure, a purpose-engineered part by a reputable manufacturer is the clear way to go. Some builders claim that the same or substantially similar results can be achieved by machining down the stock flywheel to save some money. However, given the relatively low cost of an upgraded flywheel (expect to pay $300 to $500 for a quality flywheel from Jun, Toda, or others), the potential risk of structural failure on a lightened (machined) stock piece, and the catastrophic results of such a failure, is hardly worth the risk. Imagine a 10–15 pound circular saw blade, spinning at thousands of rotations per minute, coming apart with only a thin walled transmission case housing keeping it from intruding into the car's passenger compartment, and you can see why drag race sanctioning bodies often mandate the use of a scatter shield to prevent injury to the driver.

Lightweight flywheels usually are included in twin and multi-disc clutches, so there's no extra cost for a separate flywheel for those clutches.

If your stock flywheel ever needs to be resurfaced, consider just springing for a new one rather than risk taking off too much material.

Axles

Stock axles are meant for nearly stock power levels on street tires. Prepare to snap axles in short order if you

✔ Add substantial power to your car

✔ Install a clutch that can cope with more power

✔ Intend to launch the car hard on any kind of race or drag slicks (wrinkle wall or otherwise)

The performance aftermarket likely has an answer for you. By switching over to heavier duty axles, you greatly raise the point at which these components fail.

This isn't quite as rosy as it may seem. The stress and strain of all that power must go *somewhere*. Other weak points may include load-bearing driveline components in your car, such as

- Driveshafts
- CV (constant velocity) joints

Figure 16-4 illustrates some high-performance axles and their accessories:

- The pleated rubber boots at either end of the half shafts are the CV boots, which cover the CV joints.
- The circular parts in the middle are the axle hubs, flanked by beefy axle bolts.

Some cars take well to the extra power with little to no additional fuss, while others snap axles like twigs. When in doubt, check with your local owners' club or online message board and research what others have to say.

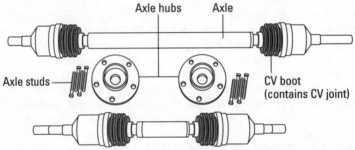

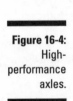

Figure 16-4: High-performance axles.

Engine and transmission mounts

As you increase the power that your engine sends to the ground, you are also increasing the engine's torque as it is channeled to the chassis through the engine mounts.

The engine mounts, which are generally metal pins surrounded by a rubber cushion, are designed to

- Shield the engine components from vibration
- Prevent stress to the car's chassis
- Stop vibration from reaching the car's cabin

The stock engine mounts become less effective as

✔ The engine generates more power

✔ The rubber mounts wear and degrade with age and use

By upgrading to stiffer rubber, polyurethane, Derlin, or aluminum engine mounts, your engine moves less under load and power delivery is more immediate, with some trade-off in vibration harshness.

Substantially stiffer engine mounts don't just shake *you* harder, they shake your car's chassis harder, which causes premature metal fatigue.

There are a couple of options for stiffening engine mounts:

✔ The cheapest method is simply to pour a two-part polyurethane solution (durometer rated between shore 80 and 90) into your factory mounts as a mild reinforcement.

✔ When you are making much more power than stock, get rid of the rubber entirely in favor of something with more movement resistance:

• For mostly street driving, polyurethane or special hard rubber formulas are best.

• Serious track junkies can use Delrin or aluminum as an extreme upgrade.

These aren't recommended for a car that's either street-driven or hasn't had its chassis reinforced.

One of the latest trends in Japan is the use of mountain bike front shock absorbers, with special brackets designed to provide resistance against fore and aft movement of the engine, by tying the cylinder head to the firewall. This allows some of the benefits normally associated with stiffer engine mounts without incurring the negative impact of vibration to the car's chassis.

Chapter 17

Thinking of Adding Boost

. . . .

In This Chapter

▶ Weighing the pros and cons

▶ Picking the right forced induction for you

▶ Supporting a boosted engine

. . . .

*B*oost is all that is both wrong, and so very, very right about the performance tuning scene all wrapped up in one snail-shaped package. Nothing else even comes close to boost for getting the biggest bang for the buck. The whistle of a blow-off valve, the roar from the wastegate, and the burst of power that makes your engine feel as though it has suddenly doubled in size are nearly impossible to resist. But the dangers are there, too. More engines have been lost to boost addiction than most enthusiasts are willing to admit. Making big power is advertised to anyone willing to listen. Losing an engine to boost addiction is quietly swept under the rug. Before embarking on the journey of adding boost to your car, or simply increasing the boost you already have, read on to make sure that you know what it is that you are after, you understand the components involved in doing it right, and you're aware of the risks before proceeding.

This chapter covers the only the special requirements for turbocharging, supercharging, or nitrous oxide. Chapter 16 covers the basic requirements for making your engine and chassis ready for more power, however you add power.

Do You Want Boost?

Boost (adding oxygen by turbocharging, supercharging, or nitrous oxide injection) is the tried and true method of adding power in ways that a naturally aspirated engine scavenging at peak efficiency can only dream of. Where a naturally aspirated engine relies on pulling in as much air volume as it can breathe at normal atmospheric conditions, a boosted engine is creating its own atmosphere. Rather than helping an intake gulp in as much air as it can get from the engine bay, boost force-feeds air into the engine.

There is an old adage among the muscle car crowd: "There ain't no replacement for displacement." Modern technology has shown us that this is partially true: "... except for boost." Boost can make a 1.8-liter four-cylinder Honda engine, properly fortified and tuned, make more power than an 8.3-liter ten-cylinder Viper engine.

Higher revs can also be considered a "replacement for displacement." The higher you can rev your engine and keep it in one piece, the more power you will make and the wider your power band. From a practical standpoint, boost is much more dramatic, and also makes power everywhere, just like adding displacement. Revs only add up top. For this reason, boost most closely replaces displacement.

Boost benefits performance enthusiasts in two key ways:

✔ Standard bolt-on modifications become a whole lot more effective.

The open element air intake that added 2–4 whp (wheel horsepower — horsepower as measured at the wheels) is now adding 4–8 whp on top of what the turbo or supercharger is already providing. The exhaust that gave 6–7 whp is now providing 12–14 whp, and so on.

✔ Without any other modifications, boost in any of its guises is nearly impossible to beat for bang-for-the-buck.

A bare-bones, low-dollar turbo system can easily provide more power (sometimes two to three times as much power) than all of the most expensive bolt-on parts combined.

If you live at a high altitude, boost is even more effective. Outside air pressure is lower at higher elevations, so normally aspirated cars gasp for air. Turbocharged and supercharged cars can create their own atmospheric pressure, so they're much less affected by high altitude.

Of course, boost isn't without its downsides:

✔ You must consider *lag* (the delay that takes place between when the throttle is applied and when the turbocharger or supercharger can pressurize the intake tract and deliver the goods).

✔ Turbochargers and superchargers, even when properly configured, add stress to the other engine parts.

✔ Properly installing a quality turbocharger or supercharger, and providing the proper tuning and other part upgrades, isn't cheap.

Prices for barebones turbocharger kits are deceptively low. The final price tag after labor and supporting hardware can easily double or triple the price of the kit itself.

Still intrigued? Read on.

Forced induction

When you add a turbocharger or a supercharger, you're making more power by forcing more air from the atmosphere into your engine.

Think of a turbocharger or supercharger as a fan that is blowing compressed air into your engine. The more air you give your engine, the more power your engine can give you (if you also add the right amount of fuel and spark). The extra air adds oxygen so you can burn more fuel. But if you want a reliable, drivable car with a turbocharger or a supercharger, you must make sure all of the parts of your entire car work together.

The decision to use nitrous oxide may depend on how long you want to use the extra power:

✔ A turbocharged or supercharged car can run on the track at full power until the gas tank is empty.

✔ A nitrous oxide system has a limited boost time before you have to return to the mother ship and refill; when you're out of nitrous oxide, your car is a 98-pound weakling again.

You must consider whether all of the engine, driveline, and chassis parts can handle big power increases. Chapter 16 covers the basics of making your car tough enough.

Some companies are known for over-engineering their designs; others are not. When your buddy with a late-model Toyota Supra tells you how easily and seamlessly his car transitioned from its stock 300 hp to 600 or 800 hp with minimal fuss, don't assume that your 100 hp Kia or Hyundai can cope as gracefully with 200 or 300 hp.

Turbochargers

The *turbocharger* is powered by the exhaust gases generated by your engine after combustion.

Generally, a bigger turbocharger takes longer to spin up to speed, but it delivers more maximum power. The time the turbo takes to spool up is seen by the driver as *lag,* or delay time. The driver may mash the throttle, but the engine won't produce "turbo" power until the turbocharger is up to speed.

How a turbo works

A turbocharger consists of two parts:

- Turbine
- Compressor

These two parts are each essentially a snail-shaped housing inside of which spins a wheel (much like a pinwheel). These wheels consist of tiny blades that are designed to efficiently move gases. Exhaust gases are routed from the exhaust manifold into the turbine, where they spin the wheel inside of the turbine like the wind turns a windmill. The turbine wheel is connected to the compressor wheel by a common shaft, so that as the exhaust gases spin the turbine wheel, this causes the compressor wheel to spin. The vacuum created by the spinning compressor wheel draws in ambient air, compressing it inside of the compressor housing before being sent on to the intake manifold. See the following figure for a schematic of this process.

Generally, the turbine wheel is smaller than the compressor wheel.

- A small turbine wheel is advantageous because it spools quickly.
- A large compressor wheel is advantageous because it can move more air.

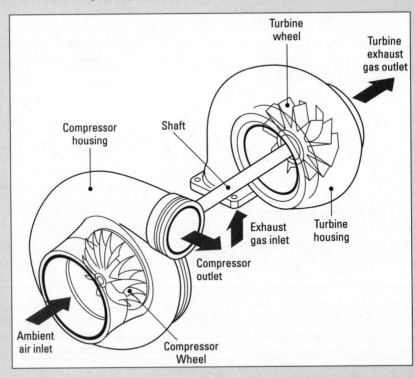

Figure 17-1 illustrates a turbo system on a two-liter Toyota 3SGTE engine:

- ✔ The four curved pipes at top are the runners of the exhaust manifold, gathering in the manifold's collector before being routed into the turbine (at the flange in the center of the image).

- ✔ The large snail shape in front is the compressor, with the air intake not yet installed at the large opening on its side, and the piping to carry away the compressed air not yet installed at the snail's head.

- ✔ The large-diameter pipe evident on the left-hand side of the image is the down-pipe, carrying exhaust gases out of the turbine and into the rest of the exhaust system.

- ✔ The cylindrical piece attached to the manifold at the rear of the image is the wastegate, which is discussed later in this chapter.

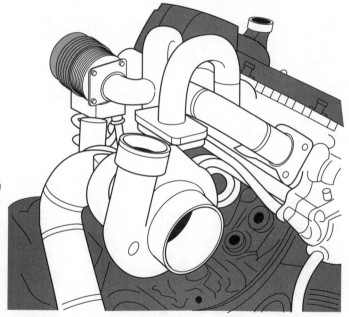

Figure 17-1:
Turbo
system on a
two-liter
Toyota
3SGTE
engine.

Turbo manufacturers have created hybrid turbos geared toward supporting big power while also minimizing lag by using innovative ball bearing cartridges and fin assemblies that help the turbo spool as quickly as possible.

A free-flowing exhaust helps allow the turbo to quickly spin up to speed because it increases exhaust flow.

Turbo durability

When you consider turbocharging your normally aspirated car, you are looking at a drivetrain that the factory engineers may never have dreamed would be force-fed with boost. Some drivetrains take to boost like a fish to water, others reject the turbo like a bad organ transplant and quickly turn terminal. Fortunately, there are ways to reach an informed decision about how well your engine can cope with the stresses of boost.

Unless you are the very first person to own a brand new model of the car, introduced to the world for the first time where you happen to live, someone, somewhere owns a car like yours and has tried to turbocharge it. Whether you own a minivan, pickup truck, or exotic thoroughbred, someone probably has already installed a turbo of some sort and written in to a magazine about it, or posted to an online discussion forum or newsgroup to express either elation with how well it turned out, or utter dismay at how quickly the engine blew to pieces.

Take the results of your research on your engine with a grain of salt. The sampling you come up with may be well short of scientifically conclusive. You may have stumbled on

- ✔ Extremely lucky enthusiasts with ticking time bombs that have yet to explode despite inherent poor planning and design.
- ✔ Blown engines that should have worked, but failed due to either poor workmanship or user error (that is, reckless use of the boost controller).

Planning your system

Use your best judgment and keep the following items in mind when evaluating whether to take the plunge. Installing a turbocharger is one of the fastest ways to turn engine parts into fragments. A couple of guidelines can help you decide whether your car can be turbocharged successfully.

Similar factory turbos

If your normally aspirated car was also offered with substantially the same engine but with a factory turbo, odds are good that adding a turbo to yours will go more smoothly than it may for another vehicle.

For example, the Toyota 3SGE engine, a kissing cousin to the turbocharged 3SGTE (the "T" standing for turbo), needs very little to accept turbocharging or supercharging.

Turbo-tough basics

You're better set up to introduce boost if your engine shares the fundamental attributes that differentiate a factory turbocharged engine from many normally aspirated variants, such as

✓ **A sturdy iron cylinder block instead of aluminum.**

✓ **A closed deck design to keep flex and deformation at a minimum.**

The *deck* is the upper part of the engine block. A closed deck features reinforcement to the upper mounting surface of the engine block, where the head mates to the bottom end. Adding boost in whatever form increases cylinder pressure, which can twist the block and the head, resulting in head gasket failure. Several companies market cylinder sleeves and block guards that are designed to reinforce an open deck into a closed or semi-closed deck. This added reinforcement isn't necessary for a properly tuned engine running cylinder pressures that are anything short of extreme, but as power levels climb to stratospheric levels, cylinder sleeves and block guards are worth considering. The choice is yours; consult with your engine builder if you intend to run significantly higher cylinder pressures on an open deck engine, as the need for these reinforcements varies from application to application.

Figure 17-2 illustrates an open deck V-6 engine block, and Figure 17-3 illustrates a closed deck V-6 engine block. Note that the difference is visible at the jacket surrounding each cylinder.

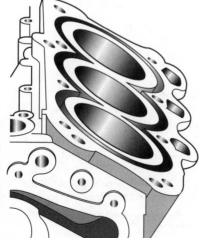

Figure 17-2:
An open deck V-6 engine block.

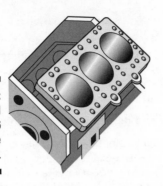

Figure 17-3:
A closed deck V-6 engine block.

✓ **A relatively low compression ratio.** *Compression ratio* is the cylinder volume above the piston at bottom-dead-center (BDC), versus the volume above the piston at top-dead-center (TDC). A higher compression ratio translates into more compression (and thus more pressure) within the cylinder. An engine running with a higher compression ratio responds better (faster) when the car's not in boost, but can handle comparatively less added cylinder pressure, thus limiting the amount of boost to which you can safely subject your engine. From a drivability standpoint, it is ideal to start with a higher compression ratio because the car will feel livelier off boost. From a reliability standpoint, in terms of the amount of flexibility you have to work with in the amount of boost you will eventually end up running, it is better to start with a low compression ratio. A typical compression ratio for a stock turbo is about 8.5:1 to 9.5:1. A typical compression ratio for a normally aspirated car is about 10:1 to 11:1. You can lower the compression ratio by choosing a different head gasket and/or different pistons.

✓ **An oil cooler.** An *oil cooler* is basically an air-cooled or water-cooled radiator through which your car's oil is routed in order to bring down the oil temperature.

It is important to keep your engine oil in the optimum temperature range because in many ways your car's oil is its lifeblood. By that I mean that the oil is used to lubricate moving parts to prevent metal surfaces from fusing together, and it's also used as a coolant for bringing down the temperature of the turbo and/or pistons. If the oil's temperature climbs too high, the engine will begin to suffer the effects of viscosity breakdown (where the oil loses its lubricating ability), and you also see a dramatic rise in your engine's operating temperature, leading to an increased risk of detonation and engine failure. Cool, clean oil is the single most effective way to ensure the long-term reliability of your turbo. Some cars come with factory oil coolers, and usually these are water-cooled. For running relatively stock boost levels on the street, these factory oil coolers are usually enough. But if you're going to be on boost all day long (for example, at the track), or if you're running substantially more boost than stock, then you are well advised to get a bigger, more efficient aftermarket oil cooler, ideally one controlled by its own thermostat. Aftermarket oil coolers are pretty much all air-cooled, and they are mounted where they can get some airflow. Figure 17-4 illustrates a GReddy air-cooled oil cooler, complete with the radiator-like core, braided steel lines, and mounting hardware.

Given the significantly higher operating temperatures seen by forced-induction cars under boost, you should use a quality synthetic motor oil of the appropriate grade for your car (such as Mobil 1 or Red Line) and frequently change the oil (no more than 5,000 miles between changes for normal street driving; 1,500 to 3,000 for track use).

One of the other benefits of adding an oil cooler is the additional oil capacity that you will gain. Typical cars will gain one or two quarts of additional oil capacity. For those serious track junkies, an even better way of addressing your engine's oiling needs, and adding even more capacity, is to change from a stock wet sump oiling system (consisting of an oil pan and a single pump) over to a dry sump oiling system (a dual-pump system using an external reservoir). Dry sump oiling systems come stock on many track-bred cars, including the Porsche 911.

✔ **Generous coolant jackets (water jackets) in the cylinder head.** Coolant jackets are a way to cool the upper cylinder head and the area around the pistons. They contain passages through which the coolant circulates. When rebuilding an engine, people tend to incorporate a larger number of water jackets, or increase the diameter of the ones they've got, to get more coolant around the cylinder heads in order to reduce the chances of localized boiling of the coolant. When coolant starts boiling, it foams, and the foam doesn't circulate (this is called *cavitation*). Cavitation can also happen at the water pump.

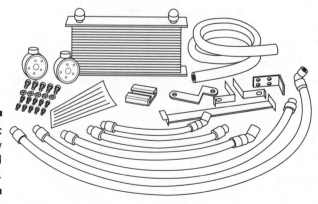

Figure 17-4: A GReddy (Trust) oil cooler.

Generally, turbocharged and supercharged cars put a greater strain on their cooling systems than normally aspirated cars due to the added heat associated with forced induction. To help keep coolant temperatures at tolerable levels, you may need either or both of these upgrades:

✔ An appropriately sized radiator (a larger radiator means more cooling)

A larger radiator with more coolant capacity means more *weight*.

✔ A different coolant

You have a couple of options for increasing your coolant's performance:

• Run Evans NPG+ Waterless Coolant. This special waterless coolant is environmentally friendly and can be run with low to no pressure. It doesn't blend with water or coolant, so the entire coolant system needs to be carefully flushed before switching to Evans NPG+. You will see an increase in coolant temperature, but that's because the coolant is doing a better job of absorbing the energy and carrying heat away from the engine. For this reason, it is often a good idea to switch to a lower temperature thermostat. Evans NPG+ is often used by WRC (World Rally Championship) teams, because rally cars are most susceptible to a puncture in the coolant system — so you can patch a ruptured hose with duct tape and finish the race with no pressure.

• Reduce the coolant-to-water ratio (70 percent water as opposed to the usual 50/50) and supplement your coolant with Water Wetter from Red Line. It's a *surfactant* that changes the slipperiness of the coolant and also has corrosion inhibitors.

You can run just water with Water Wetter on a pure race car, if you flush the system and change the fluid after every race. But if you aren't religious about the flushes, you'll get corrosion because Water Wetter doesn't prevent corrosion as well as regular coolant. Also, Water Wetter won't prevent the water from freezing and damaging your engine if the car is in freezing temperatures.

When running conventional coolant or Water Wetter, it is often a good idea to switch to a higher-pressure radiator cap. By increasing the pressure of your cooling system, you are raising the boiling point of your coolant.

Always use *distilled* water in your water/coolant mixture. You don't want mineral deposits in your cooling system. It's fine to top off your system with a hose in an emergency situation, but flush the system and refill as soon as you get the chance.

There are open-deck engines with aluminum blocks, aggressive cams, and high compression ratios that cope surprisingly well with moderate levels of boost. For example, variants of Honda's B-series engines have an astounding ability to cope with turbocharging.

Purchasing the parts

First-time turbo installers are almost always best served by going with a premade kit, at least as a starting point, when one is available.

At a minimum, a premade kit provides the essential pieces to physically bolt a turbo onto your car. This normally includes these basic parts:

- **Turbocharger**

- **Wastegate:** Regulates boost by allowing excess exhaust pressure to bleed off. Wastegates generally come in two types:

    - An *internal* wastegate (see Figure 17-5) is controlled by a wastegate actuator (which can be controlled by a boost controller) and bleeds directly into the exhaust system.

    - An *external* wastegate (see Figure 17-6) is controlled by a boost controller and can be directed to bleed either into the exhaust system or directly into the atmosphere. It is generally mounted wherever there's space for it.

        An external wastegate can generally handle more boost, but usually it's too big to fit in the space next to the turbo.

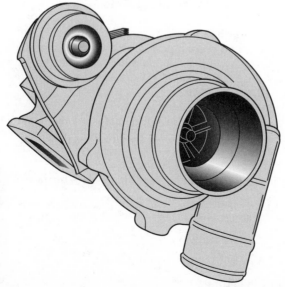

Figure 17-5:
A Garrett GT2871R turbo with an internal wastegate.

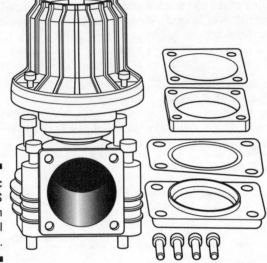

Figure 17-6:
An HKS
50mm
external
wastegate.

✔ **Intake and exhaust pipes, including**

- **Manifold or adaptor plate:** Used to bolt the turbo to the cylinder head (intake and exhaust sides).

- **Exhaust downpipe**

✔ **Oil and coolant lines**

✔ **Necessary mounting hardware and gaskets**

Is that really all it takes to run a turbo? Nope. The bare-bones kit is designed for a manufacturer to meet a certain price point. Competition in the tuner aftermarket is stiff. Being able to sell a complete turbo kit at a popular price point, whether it is $999.99 or $1,999.99 (US dollars), is where the manufacturers are looking to make their money.

Make sure you allow for the cost of the extras that you need or want in your budget. These extras usually double or triple the price of the bare-bones turbo kit:

✔ **Boost gauge:** Indicates boost and vacuum levels. The more sophisticated gauges may either

- Store peak values

- Play back a short duration of your previous run

✔ **Increased fuel flow with either or both**

- Larger fuel injectors

- Higher capacity fuel pump

✔ **Intercooler:** Think of an intercooler (also called an *after cooler*) as a radiator for your supercharger or turbo. An intercooler's job is to cool the intake charge, which has been heated up by compression in the supercharger or turbocharger, before it is fed into the intake manifold for combustion. The purpose of cooling the intake charge is to increase the density of the air so that more oxygen makes its way into the combustion chamber. There are two basic types of intercoolers (Table 17-1 compares them):

- An *air-to-air* intercooler relies on the surface area of a large, finned aluminum core that is exposed to constant airflow.

- An *air-to-water* intercooler relies instead on a pump and constantly circulating supply of cool liquid.

Table 17-1	Pros and Cons of Air-to-Air versus Air-to-Water Intercoolers		
Air-to-Air Pros	*Air-to-Air Cons*	*Air-to-Water Pros*	*Air-to-Water Cons*
Mechanically simpler	Potential for pressure drop	Resists heat soak better	Mechanically more complex
Quicker recovery from heat soak	Placement constraints	Potentially more stealth	Heavier weight
Lighter weight	High visibility	Less pressure drop	Potentially more expensive

When upgrading your intercooler, it helps to consider how you most often use your car:

- Air-to-air intercoolers usually are best if the car is kept at speed over any length of time (such as track racing).

  As long as the intercooler is seeing a constant airflow across its surface, it is resistant to heat soaking (*heat soak* is when an intercooler is no longer able to cool the intake charge because its core is taking on heat faster than it can shed it).

  Some cars, like the Subaru WRX STi, spray water on the *outside* of the air/air intercooler. This cools it quickly and gets rid of some heat soak.

- An air-to-water intercooler is a better choice for applications where the car sits between shorter runs (such as drag races).

  An air-to-water intercooler is more resistant to heat soak, but when the water has been brought up to temperature, it cools down much more slowly than an air-to-air intercooler.

✔ **Compressor bypass valve (or "blow off" valve):** Turbo systems didn't always have compressor bypass valves. Then again, turbos never used to last very long. The compressor bypass valve vents boost pressure whenever the throttle is released (when shifting, for example), which has a couple of benefits:

- It prevents a pressure wave from bouncing back into the turbo impeller (the wheel in the turbine) and causing premature fatigue failure.

- It reduces lag, because the turbo is kept spinning rather than suddenly stalling and needing to spin back up to speed.

Depending on the design, there are two methods by which the cracking pressure is released:

- A push configuration (a plunger is pushed against a spring with a specific stiffness to open it under the appropriate pressure)

- A pull configuration (a plunger is pulled down, like the HKS Super Sequential blow off valve)

Vented pressure is routed in one of two ways:

- Most stock compressor bypass valves and several aftermarket valves are routed back into the intake.

- Many aftermarket turbo systems vent it straight into atmosphere. This is a good idea only if your car is equipped with a Mass Air Pressure sensor (MAP).

If your car has an air metering device that measures the volume of incoming air in order to send the appropriate signal to the Engine control Unit (ECU), such as an air-flow meter (AFM) or Mass Airflow Sensor (MAF), don't vent your blow off valve to the atmosphere. The ECU can't account for the missing air, because it is downstream of the metering device. Your car will run overly rich with an erratic idle, backfiring, and stalling.

The number-one reason anyone wants one of these is for the dramatic "pshhht!" sound that they make when vented to atmosphere. If you've never heard a tuned turbo import, it sounds something like the air brakes on a bus. If you want to waste $150, you can buy a *sound system* that plays the sound outside your car at the press of a button. Go to www.sunamiturbo.com for a good laugh and, please, keep your credit card securely in your wallet.

✔ **Retuned factory ECU (Engine Control Unit):** Because you're dramatically changing the volume of air going into your giant air pump (engine) by adding boost, there will be a corresponding set of changes that you will need to make in everything from fuel delivery to ignition timing within your factory ECU, and you would be advised to read up on ECU tunes, including chips and reflashes, piggyback controllers, and standalone ECU systems (see Chapter 20). Failure to do so will most assuredly result in your turbo system providing the best five minutes of fun you ever had — and that's it.

✔ **Boost controller:** Boost is nothing without control. Whether you rely on a simple mechanical controller to set the amount of boost you're running, or a sophisticated and expensive electronic controller that allows an array of features inside your car's cockpit, make sure you've got this item addressed when planning a turbo system.

Upgrading the engine

Even if you have the bolt-on kit and the appropriate extras, you're still limited to running relatively low boost if you haven't taken the appropriate precautions to reinforce the engine itself for the added cylinder pressure that a factory turbo car can cope with. It isn't unusual for a factory turbo car to peak as high as 19 psi or more (the Mitsubishi Lancer Evo does just that); most aftermarket turbocharger kits for normally aspirated cars recommend running no more than 6–8 psi to prevent engine damage.

To make your engine survive while matching the higher boost levels of factory turbo cars, expect to get into a bit of work within the engine itself. This can include

✔ Lowering the compression ratio

✔ Replacing the factory cast pistons with beefier forged pistons

✔ Upgrading the head gasket

✔ Changing the cams to better utilize the airflow added by the turbo

After all the hardware has been purchased and installed, the spending continues, and you can expect to spend many hours at a reputable tuning shop tuning the car to set the appropriate

✔ Air/fuel ratio

✔ Ignition map

✔ Boost map

Superchargers

Superchargers are mechanically driven off of the crankshaft as it rotates, not driven off of exhaust gases like a turbo.

Superchargers are the preferred method for adding forced induction to a car that later will be either turned in at the end of a lease or resold because superchargers require fewer modifications to the standard car.

There are several common supercharger designs. Your choice depends on

- How you drive
- How the supercharger fits your car

Fixed displacement

Fixed-displacement superchargers deliver a set amount of boost to your engine according to how fast they turn.

Twin-screw

The twin-screw supercharger, also known as the "Whipple Charger," is a fixed-displacement supercharger. It's driven directly from the crank. Figure 17-7 illustrates a cutaway view of a twin-screw supercharger.

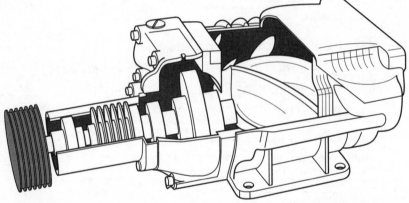

Figure 17-7: Cutaway view of a twin-screw super-charger.

The twin-screw supercharger is considered the best compromise in super-charger design because of

- High volumetric efficiency
- Lightweight, compact design
- Virtually silent operation
- A flat power curve with nearly no lag

As the name implies, the twin screw supercharger relies on two screw-type compressors (placed side-by-side) and meshing that synch the intake charge through intake, compression, and discharge phases as they spin counter to each other.

Twin-screw superchargers have a couple of advantages that make them easier to live with than some other designs:

✔ There's less internal mechanical wear than with a roots-type super-charger, because the parts inside a twin-screw supercharger never touch each other.

✔ They don't require tapping into the engine's oil supply, like centrifu-gal superchargers, because twin-screw superchargers are internally lubricated.

Twin-screw superchargers often have a couple of drawbacks:

✔ They're usually more expensive than centrifugal and roots-type superchargers

✔ They have more parasitic loss because they're constantly compressing air — even when it isn't needed.

Roots

The roots supercharger is a fixed-displacement supercharger. It relies on two counterrotating meshed lobe rotors pushing air from the inlet (connected to the air intake) to the discharge port (at the throttle body). Figure 17-8 illus-trates the basic airflow of a roots type supercharger.

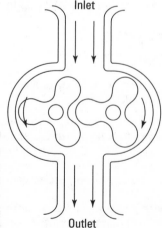

Inlet

Outlet

Figure 17-8:
Airflow of a
roots type
super-
charger.

This is the granddaddy of superchargers — it's the big box you see on top of Top Fuel dragster engines.

The roots blower is favored for smaller displacement engines (most 4-cylinder engines, 2 liters or less) because it makes boost at low rpm — the part of the power band where small engines generally need the most help.

Tuners like Jackson Racing use roots-type blowers (manufactured by Eaton) for many of their Honda, Acura, and Mazda applications.

The primary drawback of the roots supercharger design is its thermal inefficiency. It usually requires either an after cooler or water injection to maintain reasonable intake charge temperatures.

Centrifugal

A centrifugal supercharger, although mechanically driven, delivers progressively more boost as it spins up to speed — not unlike a turbo.

A centrifugal supercharger spins an impeller off a belt driven by the car's crankshaft. The easiest way to conceptualize this is as a belt-driven turbo. Centrifugal superchargers are favored by tuners to either

✔ Add power on the top end in cars that have plenty of bottom-end power

✔ Fit a supercharger in a cramped engine bay

The centrifugal supercharger is the easiest supercharger to fit because its compressor can be mounted away from the intake manifold.

Tuners like Dinan have favored these superchargers for BMW applications.

Centrifugal superchargers have a few drawbacks:

✔ They must spin quickly to make good power.

✔ They make a characteristic supercharger "whistle" which can attract unwanted attention from your local traffic officers.

✔ They require tapping into the engine's oil supply to provide lubrication and cooling to the moving components (but so do turbos and other superchargers).

Figure 17-9 is a basic schematic of a centrifugal type supercharger.

Figure 17-10 illustrates a Honda S2000 with a massive front-mounted centrifugal type supercharger. Incidentally, the two canisters mounted horizontally above the radiator are remote reservoirs for the coilover suspension.

The belt that drives a centrifugal supercharger puts a drag *(parasitic loss)* on the system when it is boosting the engine. Many systems use a clutch that disconnects the supercharger and removes the drag when the engine doesn't need boost. (It's like the clutch that disconnects the air-conditioning compressor when you don't want it.) This increases fuel economy when the car is puttering to the store or idling at a traffic light.

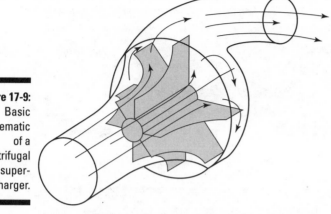

Figure 17-9:
Basic
schematic
of a
centrifugal
type super-
charger.

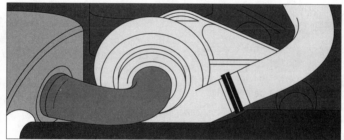

Figure 17-10:
Centrifugal
type super-
charger on
a Honda
S2000.

Nitrous oxide

It's not just for your dentist anymore. Nitrous oxide has been glamorized in entertainment and villainized by the media as the upgrade that every street racer has or wants; see Figure 17-11. In reality, nitrous really isn't a very attractive upgrade path. Few real-life tuners who can install turbo systems or superchargers rely on nitrous as a power adder.

Nitrous oxide is a gas that burns very efficiently by breaking down into a powerful mixture of nitrogen and oxygen during combustion. With this leaner burn comes power. As nitrous is plumbed into the engine in greater quantities, more fuel is needed to keep destructive detonation at bay:

- ✔ When fed into the combustion by itself, a nitrous system is known as a *dry set-up*.

- ✔ A *wet set-up* combines a mixture of nitrous with fuel to offset the lean burn that would otherwise result.

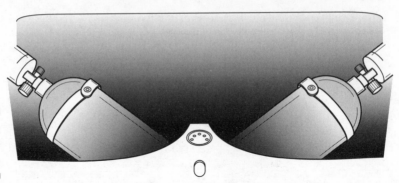

Figure 17-11:
Two bottles
of power.

Turbocharger or supercharger?

Supercharging and turbocharging suit different car builders and car designs:

✔ **Installing a supercharger (if there's space for it) is much easier than adding a turbo.** There are fewer components, and the packaging (although bulky) is less complicated. It takes less time to install, and it's also easier to remove the supercharger and return the car to factory stock condition if you want to either recertify the car for emissions or sell it.

✔ **A turbocharger is more easily tuned and altered than a supercharger.** With a simple boost controller, a turbocharger can generate anywhere from just a few psi of boost to 30 psi or more (if the compressor is physically capable of producing that much boost). Changing trim sizes (on the compressor wheel) on turbo compressors is inherently easier than on a supercharger. Many popular hybrid turbos offer easy mix-and-match, ready-to-go wheel trims and compressor size variations for common configurations. As your car is upgraded to handle more power, the turbo can be modified to deliver more power.

The only way to get dramatically different results with a supercharger is to swap the compressor unit — no small feat. An existing supercharger's boost characteristics can be altered by swapping pulleys and belts for larger and smaller diameters, respectively, to achieve the target boost. This range is a relatively narrow range of adjustment — only a few psi.

The choice between supercharging and turbocharging can come down to what you drive and how you drive:

✔ A supercharger may be an attractive solution to your cravings for more power if you are sticking with 6 to 10 psi of boost (a moderate power increase). It's especially good if you have a larger displacement engine, like a traditional American V-8

✔ A turbocharger is probably the better option if you want to add more boost as you build your engine's ability to cope with the added pressure, or if you have a smaller displacement engine that would be sapped by any parasitic loss.

Nitrous is burned at an alarming rate to get meaningful amounts of power, and it's bulky to store. A tank is usually good for only a few continuous minutes of use. For practical purposes, this means that its appeal is strictly limited to the straight-line stoplight warriors and drag race guys. Anyone needing power on a regular basis should look elsewhere. Nitrous is much cheaper than turbocharging or supercharging (and a far easier modification to install or remove), but its mythical status is largely unwarranted.

Nitrous oxide shines as a supplement to a very lag-prone turbocharger in a competitive drag racing engine. Nitrous is often used to help spool the turbo and bring the car up to speed in the lower rpms and to smooth the transition from no boost to full boost. Here, it works wonderfully. The nitrous allows the driver to transition from nitrous-assisted power to all turbo on the top end and maintain a relatively linear power curve.

With drag racing generally taking place in quarter-mile and eighth-mile increments, nitrous can be very effective for this purpose. For continuous performance, other methods are better for adding power.

Supporting a Boosted Engine

Turbocharged, supercharged, and nitrous boosted cars have a few special requirements for reliable performance.

Chapter 16 covers essential improvements and tests for reliable performance with any power increase, including turbos, superchargers, and nitrous.

Fuel systems

As the factory fuel system approaches its maximum capacity, you need to make sure that your fuel system is up to the task of providing enough fuel to match your boost level. If you don't, you risk a lean burn condition and terminal engine failure. There are a couple of options:

- ✔ **An adjustable fuel pressure regulator** can increase the fuel pressure in proportion to the boost being added.
- ✔ **A high capacity fuel pump, rail, and injectors** will ensure that you have sufficient fuel capacity for the boost you are adding.

This is always the preferred method for adding fuel, instead of simply increasing the pressure and pushing the factory components to their limits.

Timing

Even with enough fuel, your factory ignition timing curve is far too aggressive for turbocharging or supercharging. To remap the timing, you need one of the following:

- A piggyback fuel controller
- ECU reflash/chip upgrade
- Standalone ECU replacement

By retarding the timing, the air/fuel mixture is lit off at the correct time to avoid pre-ignition detonation and potential terminal engine failure.

Cooling

Both superchargers and turbochargers *heat* air as they compress it. This heat can hurt the combustion process by changing the density of air entering the intake manifold from a relatively cool, dense charge to one that is not.

A couple of tools are available to reduce the heat of the intake air:

- Intercooling (a radiator-type device that cools by either air or water)
- Water injection (spraying a water vapor into the intake tract to cool the charge)

Other upgraded cooling components can help keep the combustion, engine, and temperatures under the hood within factory tolerances:

- A larger, more efficient radiator
- An auxiliary oil cooler

As boost is added to the engine, adopt spark plug temperature ranges that are one or two heat ranges cooler. Your plug choice depends on the amount of maintenance you're prepared to perform:

- ✔ Iridium-tipped plugs combine good performance with durability.

- ✔ Copper-tipped plugs work best, but require frequent replacement.

Platinum-tipped plugs are best avoided because they've been shown to be problematic in boosted engines.

Engine internals

With boost comes a corresponding rise in cylinder pressures. Some engines can cope with these pressure increases with relative ease; others cannot. To prevent serious engine damage, it is often a good idea to install

- ✔ A stronger head gasket
- ✔ Stronger head studs or head bolts

Many tuners replace the pistons with sturdier forged units that are better able to cope with detonation than their cast factory counterparts.

With more extreme boost pressure, the engine connecting rods and crankshaft may also need to be swapped for sturdier replacements. Sturdier moving parts may be

- ✔ Shot peened (hardened on the surface)
- ✔ Cryogenically treated
- ✔ Constructed of billet or forged materials

Intake and exhaust

Both turbochargers and superchargers need to be able to pull in air easily and push it out again with little effort:

- ✔ If your turbo or supercharger kit doesn't include an upgraded air intake, be sure to install one that flows enough CFM for the engine.
- ✔ A free-flowing exhaust helps evacuate spent exhaust gases after combustion.

Exhaust improvements on turbocharged engines dramatically reduce turbo lag.

Gauges

Turbocharged engines can benefit from several gauges in addition to the common gauges for performance cars:

- ✔ At a minimum, add a boost gauge to ensure that your turbocharger or supercharger is working properly.

- ✔ Two gauges can monitor the performance of your turbo or supercharger system and provide an early warning if there is a problem:

  - An air/fuel gauge shows you whether the current ratio is safe.

  - An EGT (exhaust gas temperature) gauge shows whether current temperatures are safe.

Chapter 18

Have Boost, Need More

In This Chapter

▶ Living with a bigger turbocharger or supercharger

▶ Installing cams to get the most out of your turbo charger or supercharger

▶ Cooling your engine

▶ Installing water injection

To paraphrase urban jargon, "More boost, more problems." Just as there is no free lunch, more boost is rarely ever a simple turn of the boost control knob away. Well, actually, it is just a mere turn away . . . but if you intend to safely run more boost, you'll have many more considerations at play.

Think of this chapter as a next step beyond simply having a functioning and complete turbo or supercharger system. This chapter is for you if all of these items are true:

✔ You own a car with either a factory or aftermarket turbocharger or supercharger.

✔ You want to make more power by upgrading to a larger turbocharger or supercharger.

✔ You have taken the basic engine and chassis precautions for any power increase, as covered in Chapter 16.

✔ You've taken the basic steps for a reliable boosted engine, as outlined in Chapter 17, including

   • Engine management for fuel, timing, and boost adjustments

   • A factory or aftermarket intercooler

   • A factory or aftermarket oil cooler

   • A free-flowing intake and exhaust

✔ You have upgraded your engine parts to handle extra boost, including any necessary upgrades of

- Head gasket

- Head studs

- Pistons

- Connecting rods

- Crankshaft

Living with More Boost

Whether you are running a factory turbocharged or supercharged car, or one that has a basic bolt-on kit, if your power cravings have taken you to the limits of your current setup, and you're ready to take the plunge to a bigger turbocharger or supercharger, then read on. You have spent some time trying to run more boost on your current turbo or a smaller pulley on your supercharger, and you have come to the conclusion that you need/want more serious firepower to reach your goals.

Before you take that next step into big boost, it is important that you appreciate the drivability tradeoffs that come with a much larger turbo/ blower:

✔ Most factory turbocharging and supercharging packages, and many after-market kits, strive to be seamless. As you apply throttle, the engine begins making power and the turbo or supercharger almost instantaneously jumps into action, aiding in acceleration.

If your car is your daily driver, you'll find yourself on boost when accelerating more often than not. Boost is there, omnipresent, whether just pulling away from a light in first gear and short shifting the car at 3,000 rpm, or using ¾ throttle overtaking another car on the freeway. Carving along your favorite mountain road, you'll be able to power out of a turn using boost with relative ease. There is no planning or antici-pating. Whether you elect to take a turn at 2,000 rpm in third gear, or higher in the rev range dropping down into second, as the right foot goes down, the boost comes on.

✔ Imagine an alternate reality in which your right foot goes down and nothing happens. You short shift the car at 3,000 rpm around town, and your boost gauge never comes up from vacuum. Your car, when driven around conservatively, is much slower than it had been before. The boost is gone. In its place, your car now drives like a normally aspirated car with too low of a compression ratio and a huge exhaust obstruction (the turbo).

However, keep your foot down . . . and wait for it . . . and like a violent explosion, your car begins accelerating forward, gathering speed at a blistering rate. You prepare to shift, but you find the engine already bouncing off the rev limiter. When you do shift, the process begins again. The first few times you do it, you'll be giggling uncontrollably. It is as fun as it sounds. But is it really what you wanted?

The answer isn't the easy, "of course!" that you might believe. A gap opens in traffic . . . but you can't take it. A car revs at you in the next lane over, the light turns green, and he's off. You'll reel him in eventually, but more often than not, you'll find yourself chasing down cars and then passing rather than staying with them. The mountain road you used to love becomes a chore. Off boost, the car cannot be steered by throttle as it once could. On boost, the car either oversteers wildly or doesn't spool in time to bring the tail around.

Even when the coast is clear, and the roads are straight and empty, hitting warp speed boost is an exercise in scanning for highway patrol and planning when and where to boost, rather than just letting it happen as a matter of course.

My big fat Japanese turbo

When I first had a much larger turbo installed in my car (I had already replaced the stock turbo with a mild upgrade and decided I wanted to go big this time), the tuner and I were out on a long, straight, and desolate road with no one around for miles and no turns or bumps to worry about. Just us and a long stretch of pavement. Mounted directly in my field of vision on the steering column was a brightly lit boost gauge. My tuner turned to me and said, "Listen, David, I've got the datalogging equipment all set up, wideband and laptop are here in my lap, and I have the handheld controller for your ECU . . . I need you to do one thing: Drive in a straight line at full throttle and tell me what the peak boost reads on the boost gauge." Sounds simple enough, right? After all, I had been driving turbo cars for years. How hard could it be to drive in a straight line and tell him what the dial right in front of my face reads? Turns out I couldn't do it. Off boost, I had no problem looking at the gauge, but when boost came on, the car accelerated so violently, literally jumping sideways as the turbo came on, that for the life of me I couldn't look down at the gauge. After about the

sixth or seventh attempt, I was finally able to give him a reading — 18 psi. "Okay," he said, "Let's see how we do at 22 psi. . . ."

Boost became an *event,* not an aid in accelerating. The car felt nothing like it had before with either of the prior turbos. There was none of the seamless acceleration I had become accustomed to, making my four-cylinder engine feel like a bigger six- or eight-cylinder powerplant. Instead, it felt like I was driving a donkey cart and then got rear-ended by a Mack truck.

As time went on, I came to find myself driving 20, 30, or 40 miles without once hitting boost. I could shift the car gently, and never once wake the turbo. Rather than driving more aggressively, I found myself driving *around* the turbo when just getting from point A to point B. Where I used to hit boost 20–40 times during a longer commute, after installing the huge turbo, I would use boost once or not at all. Around town, I wouldn't hit it at all. I found it fascinatingly ironic that a ridiculous amount of power made me a much more sedate driver.

Cams and Tuning

With a well-matched set of camshafts and adjustable cam gears, a good tuner should be able to smooth the transition to boost and to play with the power delivery to allow some of the seamless acceleration to return.

Cams achieve this goal by regulating airflow through the cylinder head. The big boost supercharger or turbocharger is trying to push an enormous volume of air through the engine. Even if every restriction in the intake and exhaust path has been eliminated, the bottleneck created by stock cams impacts the power delivery and makes for a shorter and peakier powerband.

A set of performance camshafts (intake and exhaust, see Chapter 15 for further discussion) adds more valve lift and duration to your cylinder head. They allow you to run less boost with comparable results. The downsides are that they

✔ Take more labor than simply upping the boost

✔ Reduce your low-end power

✔ Mess with your idle (cams with a high duration and lift have a distinctive loping idle)

✔ May make your car's emissions illegal. Since cams are altering the way your car burns air and fuel, your tailpipe emissions may be affected.

Tuning for the real world

Many tuners spend quite a bit of time going for a perfect power curve on the Dyno. The problem with this approach is that the Dyno is an artificial environment. If no time is invested in logging data on what the car is doing in the real world, you may end up with terrific full-throttle acceleration maps and horrible part-throttle maps (where you'll likely be doing the majority of your driving).

Tuning is a science, and a good tuner works with you to ensure that your car is set up to meet your goals:

✔ If your car is nothing but a straight-line drag racer, then the only time it ever goes anywhere, the gas pedal is buried in the carpet, and part-throttle response may not matter much to you.

✔ If your tuner is accustomed to going for the gusto with wide-open throttle (WOT) tuning only, and your car is only driven at WOT a fraction of the time, then spend the extra time to ensure that the part-throttle response is tuned properly for your driving style and setup.

It's nearly impossible to hide a cammed car's idle from Johnny Law without a turbo. Many highway patrol officers are gear heads, or they have spent time around gear heads. They know what a cammed car *sounds* like.

Intake Charge Cooling

A cool intake charge is a dense intake charge. A dense intake charge means there is more oxygen available to burn in combustion. More oxygen means a bigger explosion when spark and fuel are added, and a bigger explosion means more smiles per miles. Keeping your cool is the key to big power.

Intercooler upgrades

Whether you're running a stock intercooler or one that came with your turbo or supercharger kit, a much larger turbo or supercharger requires a similar increase in intake charge cooling capacity. When your existing intercooler exceeds its ability to shed heat (a phenomenon known as *heatsoak*), your turbo pumps ultra hot air straight into your intake manifold — not a good thing. Of course, the more turbo-savvy readers are probably already saying, "Hey! Wait a minute! If I'm running a smaller turbo past its efficiency range on a compressor map, then I should be generating less, not more, hot air with a larger turbo at the same power level." This point is entirely true. However, the operative point of the statement is "at the same power level," and I assume that you're considering a bigger turbo (or supercharger) with your eyes on higher horsepower numbers in the very near future. In this sense, big power really does mean big cooling capacity.

Fundamentally, you have two options for beefing up the intercooler system on your car:

✔ Replace an existing air-to-air intercooler with a larger unit.

Most cars with a factory-installed intercooler use an air-to-air intercooler. Upgrading usually means adopting a bigger core and larger diameter pipes in the factory location. Occasionally, the core is so much larger that you have to install it in a different location. For example, the Subaru WRX often loses its top-mount intercooler for a much larger upgraded front-mounted intercooler.

✔ Convert to an air-to-water intercooler.

Bigger is almost always better from a cooling standpoint, but bigger can also be a huge negative from a drivability standpoint. The turbo is called upon to pressurize a much greater volume before the manifold has positive boost pressure. For this reason, there are several design features to consider when evaluating an intercooler upgrade:

✔ Larger intercooler cores and bigger pipes can increase pressure drop.

Pressure drop is the reduction of boost pressure in the intercooling system after leaving the supercharger or turbocharger and before entering the throttle body. A larger core and bigger pipes take more time to pressurize. For this reason, the time it takes for your turbo or supercharger to pressurize the system is time that increases turbo lag and delays full boost pressure. This inefficiency can be reduced by using

• Shorter pipes with smooth bends

• Surge-tank style end tanks at the intake manifold

• An efficient intercooler core fin design

The bar and plate design is very efficient. Apexi and ARC use a bar and plate design. GReddy, Spearco, and HKS use fin and tube design.

✔ Intercoolers for high boost must be able to cope with much more pressure than a stock intercooler ever sees.

For cheap insurance against blowing an intercooler pipe loose, use

• Quality high-pressure silicone hoses and couplers

• Either T-Bolt style or constant torque hose clamps

Air-to-air intercooler

An air-to-air intercooler, acting as a radiator, cools the intake charge by sending it through a finned aluminum core. The core is kept cool by the constant movement of air across its surface. There may be an electric fan to pull air through the fins when the car isn't at speed (for example, in bumper-to-bumper traffic). An air-to-air intercooler is lighter and mechanically simpler than an air-to-water intercooler. It's also more susceptible to heatsoak than an air-to-water intercooler, but it recovers from heatsoak faster.

If you want high boost for extended periods, such as for road racing, the benefits of shedding heat quickly with the air-to-air intercooler are hard to beat. In a road race environment, for example, the car is at speed and the intercooler gets plenty of airflow while the car is in motion. The intercooler may have heatsoak as the car slows for traffic, but it quickly recovers and works as well as before when fresh air is once again being pulled through the core.

An inexpensive mod to cool down the intercooler core on your air-to-air intercooler involves fitting a surface water sprayer, like those found as factory equipment on the Mitsubishi Lancer Evo and Subaru WRX STi. You can tap into your factory water spray reservoir and use a manual switch to trigger the water spray, or set up a more sophisticated system that sprays based on intercooler core temperature. However, the most dramatic results in dropping intake charge temperatures are still associated with injecting water vapor directly into the intercooler piping using a water injection system.

Air-to-water intercooler

An air-to-water intercooler relies on a large reservoir filled with water to cool down the intake charge. An air-to-water intercooler is much more resistant to heatsoak than a traditional air-to-air core because the water can absorb extra heat.

Air-to-water intercoolers have a couple of drawbacks:

✔ Recovery times from heatsoak are much longer. When the water is warmed up, like a hot bath (in a sealed metal box!), it takes a long time to cool down.

✔ Air-to-water intercoolers burden the car with a weight penalty of several gallons of water in a tank near the intake manifold.

Every gallon of water weighs eight pounds — you may need expensive carbon fiber parts elsewhere on the car to *save* as much weight as you *add* with a few gallons of water.

Figure 18-1 illustrates an air-to-water intercooler mounted on a turbocharged engine. In the center of the illustration is the metal tank that holds the water. In the lower-left corner, you can see the piping leading from the air intake to the turbo, and then from the turbo on to the intercooler.

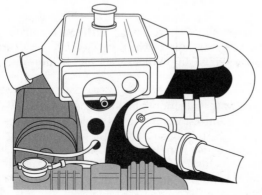

Figure 18-1:
An air-to-water intercooler installed on a turbocharged engine.

If your car is used mostly for short spurts of acceleration (such as drag racing), air-to-water intercooling is the way to go:

✔ Air-to-water heatsoak isn't a deal breaker for short races:

  • By dumping a bag of ice in the reservoir between runs, it is very simple to bring intake charge temperatures down to actual air temperature or below.

  • The intercooler has time between runs to shed heat.

✔ The air-to-water cooling is very effective at low speeds, so it's working as soon as you leave the starting line.

Water injection

Water injection cools the intake charge through the latent heat absorption of water in the evaporation process. This uses essentially the same principle as patio misters. The water vapor absorbs the heat in the intake charge and cools it down. It also cools within the cylinder itself — which no intercooler can hope to achieve. The way this works in practice is that the high-speed pump pulls water from a reservoir mounted somewhere in or near the engine compartment (often, the windshield washer reservoir can be used, with windshield solution and water mixed) and, using a high-speed valve and specialized nozzle, injects a fine mist of water into the intercooler pipes a short distance before the throttle body. By either pulsing the water on and off with the fuel injectors, or by mapping the water with a laptop or handheld controller, you can map out just how much water you need to provide enough cooling without robbing the engine of power by displacing too much oxygen.

Figure 18-2 illustrates a water injection system. The cylinder in front houses the high-speed electromagnetic pump. The atomizing jet, which physically injects the water in right before the throttle body, is located above and to the left of the pump.

Water injection isn't a new invention. Nearly all of the WRC rally teams have been running it for years. Historically, it was first used in agriculture at the turn of the century (early 1900s), in WWII aircraft, and by hot-rodders in the 1950s and 60s.

Today, the technology in water injection kits, like those offered by ERL/ Aquamist, allow for fully atomized water vapor thanks to high-pressure pumps and purpose-built jets, microprocessors that allow for 3D mapping of the water injection, and even a handheld controller that can drive extra fuel injectors! The physics behind it is fundamentally the same, but the technology in today's systems is far beyond what had ever previously existed or continues to exist in the crude DIY systems.

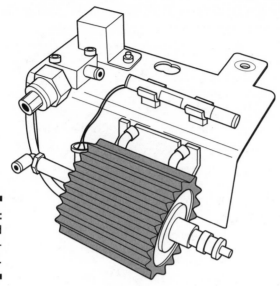

Figure 18-2:
Integrated
water injec-
tion unit.

Water injection systems displace a small amount of air volume from the combustion process by replacing it with water vapor. Water injection slightly reduces the amount of available air, but that tiny reduction in air volume is more than made up by reducing the *temperature:*

✔ A cool, dense intake charge provides for better combustion than a hot one. When the intake charge heats the water mist (turning it to steam), the water absorbs a tremendous amount of heat energy.

✔ The water mist slows down the burn rate of fuel during combustion and provides a cooling effect where it is most needed — within the cylinders themselves:

• The slower burn rate makes pump gas behave more like high octane race gas.

• The cooling in the combustion chamber both ensures a dense, even burn, and also steam-washes away carbon deposits (which are a prime culprit for pre-ignition detonation).

When either space is tight or your budget is limited, water injection may be able to match the cooling benefits of an upgraded intercooler.

Part VIII
Faster Thinking

In this part . . .

To optimize your car's performance and reliability, you will want to make sure that your car's brain is able to get the most out of all the fancy hardware you're bolting on under the hood. Whether you're looking for a mild performance increase on an otherwise stock car, or you have extensively modified your car and need to ensure that your car's brain can cope with the changes, this part walks you through the basics — and it isn't brain surgery!

Chapter 19

Scanning the Codes

....

....

*O*n-board diagnostics (OBD) can be a tremendous asset to automotive enthusiasts — in particular, if you are interested in making sure that your car's engine is in good shape before adding power, or even during the tuning process. OBD can quickly help you troubleshoot a tricky install by letting you know whether the mods are causing a drivability problem, or whether the issue lies elsewhere. By investing in an inexpensive code scanner, you can save literally hundreds, if not thousands, of dollars on troubleshooting, unneeded Dyno time, and repair fees.

On-Board Diagnostics (OBD)

Both skilled tuners and ordinary enthusiasts use OBD to monitor what is going on inside a modern car's engine.

OBD is a federally mandated standard developed by the SAE (Society of Automotive Engineers) to provide for a universal interface for the purposes of monitoring emissions equipment on cars.

While OBD was initially designed to monitor the status of your car's emissions equipment, as emissions equipment became increasingly sophisticated and connected with the car's ECU (Engine Control Unit), so too did the quantity and depth of information available through the OBD port increase.

By using a diagnostic scan tool on your car, you can

1. Figure out why the check engine light is on.

2. Identify what adjustments or repairs are needed.

3. Reset the check engine light.

For the often-small investment in a scan tool, even a non–performance oriented car owner can save dealership diagnostic and service fees. Rather than walk into the service center and tell the mechanic, "My car is making a funny noise and my gas mileage seems to have gone down," a customer can come in with a list of fault codes and what they mean — along with an idea of how much the repair bill will be. (Some OBDI cars display codes without a special tool. Check your car's factory service manual for details.)

OBDI scanners

OBDI was the first version of nationally standardized ports for downloading trouble codes. If your car was sold in the U.S. between the 1992 and 1996 model years, this is what you have.

In many respects, OBDI is the more coveted platform for performance-minded enthusiasts:

✔ OBDI allows a tuner to swap chips, the tiny circuit boards that are burned or soldered into the car's ECU, for greater performance. By tapping into the OBDI connector, the user can verify air/fuel readings and check for common trouble points like a failed oxygen sensor.

✔ OBDI scanners tend to be much less expensive than OBDII scanners.

Nearly all OBDII scanners can retrieve codes from OBDI-equipped cars.

✔ OBDI can't detect a missing catalytic converter (which may be why tuners prefer it when a catalytic converter isn't mandatory).

By purchasing the appropriate scan tool (and extension), OBDI can detect faults with

✔ EGR (exhaust gas recirculation) system

✔ Oxygen sensor

✔ ECU

✔ Fuel system

Compared to OBDII, OBDI has a couple of significant drawbacks:

✔ OBDI scanners offer nowhere near the level of standardization available from OBDII. Nearly every car needs its own adapter.

✔ OBDI can't trigger a check engine light before a system fails. By the time the light comes on, something needs to be replaced.

OBDII scanners

OBDII is designed to monitor the extra sensors that are used in modern fuel injection and emission controls. For example, newer cars have two oxygen sensors (including one downstream from the primary catalytic converter), not just one oxygen sensor. OBDII also monitors fuel pressure from a sensor inside the car's fuel tank. This is used to check the status of the car's evaporative system. (The U.S. government forbids disabling OBDII systems on street cars.)

For a performance enthusiast, OBDII has several advantages over OBDI:

✔ **OBDII allows the ECU to be reprogrammed electronically, rather than swapping chips as has been done in the past.** It also allows a greater range of altered parameters and reprogramming directly through the OBDII port.

✔ **OBDII handles problems and trouble codes according to their importance.** Depending on the importance of the problem, OBDII switches the check engine light on

  • Immediately

  • After repeated occurrences during a single drive cycle

  • Never; the code is stored without triggering the light

✔ **OBDII won't allow the check engine light to be reset (switched off) without fixing the underlying problem.**

  On an OBDI car, you can reset the light and ignore the underlying problem (much to the joy of unscrupulous used car sellers). OBDII triggers the light again if the problem persists.

OBDII doesn't allow simple chip swapping. So much for buying cheap reprogrammed chips at eBay, including the illegal and pennies-on-the-dollar hacks of top tuner chips from companies like Dinan, Mugen, and Spoon.

Enthusiasts can buy OBDII scanners from a number of sources:

✔ AutoTap and Digimoto OBDII scanners and software are available in Windows or Palm-based configurations and start for as little as $99, but can go up to $500, depending on which modules you need. AutoTap and Digimoto have similar capabilities and slightly different interfaces. They provide many of the useful features of a full factory-level scan tool at the enthusiast's fingertips for a fraction of the price.

The Digimoto's advantages are its intuitive datalogging ability and built-in accelerometer for measuring acceleration (both 0 to 60 and quarter-mile) as well as a Dyno emulator for plotting power and torque curves. On the other hand, I have seen plenty of top-level performance tuners carrying around the signature red AutoTap carrying cases on tuning sessions. Figure 19-1 illustrates the AutoTap scanner (top), the signature red carrying case (bottom right), and a complete kit (bottom left).

✔ Auterra makes a Palm-based OBDII scanner that retails for $269 to $289. While only for OBDII vehicles, it has a trick accelerometer, much like the Digimoto. Figure 19-2 illustrates the Auterra system: scanner, necessary cables, and software on CD.

✔ The CarChip by Driveright (illustrated in Figure 19-3) is designed to be left in place for 75 to 300 hours of continuous driving. The CarChip can be used to track longer-term driving habits and parameters than conventional scanners. It retails for $179 for the basic model.

The CarChip software is uniquely configured to track trip activity, store accident info, and generally play "Big Brother" in monitoring the activity of a car or fleet of cars.

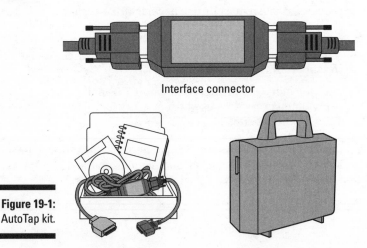

Interface connector

Figure 19-1:
AutoTap kit.

Kit with software
and manual

Carrying case

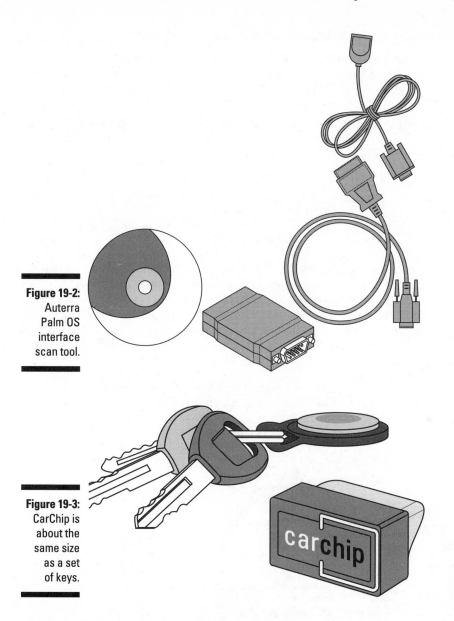

Figure 19-2:
Auterra
Palm OS
interface
scan tool.

Figure 19-3:
CarChip is
about the
same size
as a set
of keys.

Switching Generations

With the prevalence of engine swaps — in particular, from Japanese home
market donor vehicles — a cottage industry has evolved around OBD adapters
and emulators:

✔ **Adapting ODBI engines to newer cars:**

- In Japan, even late-model vehicles often use only OBDI connectors. When swapping an engine from a late-model JDM vehicle into an American car, it is often necessary to adapt the American car to previous-model specs.

- Even when it is technically viable to "update" a car to OBDII specs, you may want to use a Japanese-market ECU that is only available for OBDI.

✔ **Adapting OBDII engines to older cars:**

When a late-model engine uses an OBDII port connector, but the vehicle itself predates OBDII, it is often handy to have a means of interfacing the car's sensors — including oxygen sensors and emissions equipment — to function with the newer OBDII-based ECU. You can buy an electrical loom that adapts your under-hood connections to the new OBDII (or OBDI if you're retrograding) ECU. These are available for a number of different cars, but they are most easily available for Hondas and Acuras, since so many Honda engines can be swapped for so many different applications and models. Frog Engine Controls offers OBD swaps for many Honda-powered vehicles, with premade looms and harnesses (illustrated in Figure 19-4) to handle all aspects of engine swaps between various American and Japanese model Honda and Acuras — including the very important VTEC switchover, as well as harnesses for popular piggyback controllers such as the A'PEXi Super AFC and GReddy eManage. Expect to pay between $130 and $190 for the appropriate harness adapter for your Honda or Acura.

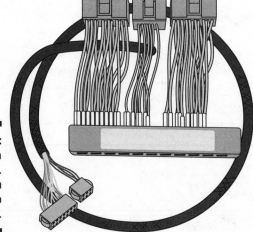

Figure 19-4:
Frog Honda
S2000 loom.
The loom
plugs into
the ECU.

Chapter 20

What's inside Your Car's Brain

*P*ut in the simplest terms, your car's ECU (Engine Control Unit) is your car's brain. Once upon a time, cars had no computer equipment to speak of — all systems from air and fuel delivery to fans and fluid temperature control were mechanically controlled. Those days are well behind us. For today's car enthusiasts, the ECU is the Holy Grail of making the bolt-on modifications under the hood work safely, reliably, and effectively.

What Is the ECU/ECM?

The *ECU,* also known as the ECM (Engine Control Module), is the central computer that gathers inputs from a number of sensors on your car, including

✔ Oxygen sensor

✔ Airflow meter (AFM/MAF) or mass air pressure sensor (MAP)

✔ Temperature sensors

✔ Knock sensors

By continually measuring and monitoring these readings in conjunction with a series of "maps" or programs, the ECU ensures that your engine is operating correctly.

Figure 20-1 illustrates the factory ECU of a Subaru WRX, with the wiring harness coming off the left side of it.

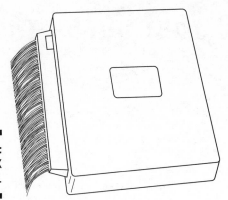

Figure 20-1: Subaru WRX factory ECU.

The ECU is responsible for continually setting and adjusting ignition timing, air/fuel ratio (where applicable), and boost, relative to such input variables as

✔ Outside air temperature

✔ Altitude

✔ Octane of fuel in your car's gas tank

The ECU/ECM performs these basic functions:

✔ Confirms that your emissions equipment is functioning correctly

✔ Sets rev and speed limits on your car

✔ Controls fuel cut and boost cut to prevent over boosting in the event of a wastegate malfunction on turbocharged engines

✔ Sets speeds for underhood radiator and intercooler fans

Your ECU interfaces with a number of on-board modules, including those that handle the operation of factory-installed

✔ Cruise control

✔ Airbags

✔ Air conditioning

✔ Traction control

✔ ABS brakes

✔ Anti-theft system

✔ Throttle-by-wire and drive-by-wire systems

Your car's ECU performs these calculations continuously — often within milliseconds — for the entire life of your car, and makes adjustments on what it has learned about your driving habits and the environment.

What kind of awesome computing power does it take to run all of these calculations quickly and reliably? Surely the auto manufacturers must be equipping cars with 8 GHz processor boards that can run laps around home computers. If only this awesome processing power could be used to run video games. . . . In reality, a modern car's ECU runs only around 30–40 MHz. Not very fast at all compared to home computer standards. The trick to the ECU's performance is a very efficient and simplified method of processing information from your engine's output devices.

Deciding to Upgrade

You should make appropriate changes to your car's ECU any time you dramatically

✔ **Change the car's ability to take in or expel air.**

Adding a cold air intake doesn't mean you need to upgrade your ECU. However, you *do* need to upgrade your car's ECU of you swap in a set of more aggressive cams or install a much bigger turbocharger (or add a turbocharger or supercharger where one didn't previously exist).

✔ **Change the car's ability to ignite the air/fuel mixture.**

To get the most out of changing over to a colder heat range spark plug and/or ignition amplifier, you need to make appropriate changes to your car's ignition timing maps.

✔ **Add or subtract fuel flow.**

Installing a larger capacity fuel pump doesn't mean you need to make ECU changes. You need to make ECU changes if you replace the injectors with larger ones or add auxiliary injectors.

✔ **Alter its internal dimensions, such as compression, displacement, or airflow.**

Putting in a new head gasket, stronger forged pistons, or heavy-duty head studs doesn't necessarily warrant changing anything in the ECU. (By themselves, stronger internal parts don't automatically increase engine performance if they're the same size as the factory-installed parts.)

You need to change the ECU, however, if your new engine parts

- Change the compression ratio

- Increase the displacement (either by stroking or boring)

- Increase airflow through the cylinder head

When in doubt, you need to consider whether you have fundamentally altered the basic variables for combustion, including available air, fuel, and spark. If the answer is "yes," there are two reasons you should clue your ECU in to those changes:

✔ Your factory engine management usually makes small adjustments for small changes, including such basic bolt-on parts as

- Intakes

- Exhausts

- Ignition amplifiers

- Underdrive pulleys

When you install bolt-on performance parts, ensure that your ECU "relearns" the new operating parameters. You can clear the memory on your factory ECU by either

- Disconnecting the battery (as simply as disconnecting the ground)

- Using a scan tool

✔ When you make dramatic changes to air, fuel, or spark characteristics, they're beyond your factory ECU's ability to adjust and compensate.

Even with minor bolt-on parts, an ECU upgrade can help optimize the ability of your engine to benefit from relatively small changes like most bolt-on tuning parts. If you want to get the most from your intake/exhaust combo, an ECU tune ensures that the components you have bolted on are giving you 100 percent of their potential. The more significant the hardware installed under the hood, the more power unleashed with an ECU tune.

Closed and Open Interface Systems

When you decide to upgrade your factory ECU, you will choose between what I call *open* and *closed* interface systems.

- ✔ A closed interface ECU upgrade, like a reflash or chip swap, is not generally user accessible.

- ✔ An open interface ECU upgrade, like a standalone ECU or piggyback controller, allows you to access and alter the maps when changing performance hardware under the hood.

Closed interface

A closed interface isn't easily accessible. As such, it's ideal if you don't often want to retune or recalibrate your ECU, and you prefer a plug-and-play solution. Examples of closed interface upgrades are

- ✔ ECU chip swaps
- ✔ Reflashes
- ✔ Pretuned ECUs

A closed interface upgrade has a couple of benefits:

- ✔ It doesn't require any guesswork or Dyno time. Once installed, the car can be started and driven hard.

- ✔ It looks and behaves much like a stock ECU, which is desirable while your car is under warranty and subject to dealer scrutiny during scheduled maintenance appointments.

The biggest disadvantage of a closed interface upgrade is that you can't easily tune or adjust it:

- ✔ If you're constantly trying new engine hardware, a closed interface makes incremental changes to the car's ECU much more difficult, time-consuming, and expensive.

- ✔ If your plans involve either leaving your car stock, or making all of the upgrades at one time and then not changing the car for a while, the lack of adjustability may not be a problem for you.

Open interface

Open-interface ECU upgrades, like standalone ECUs or piggyback controllers, allow you to modify your ECU maps to reflect hardware changes under the hood. For example, your car may have one set of engine mods at the time you first upgrade the ECU, but a week or year later, may have very different bolt-on modifications under the hood, necessitating an entirely different tune.

This flexibility has a price:

- ✔ You can spend many times the price of your open-interface hardware on such hidden costs as
  - • Dyno time
  - • Tuner fees
  - • Datalogging
- ✔ Open-interface ECU upgrades are more likely to be spotted by service technicians when you request factory warranty repairs. If this happens, you may have to dip into your own pocket for repairs.

Selecting an Upgrade

This book has four chapters that cover different kinds of upgrades. If your car needs an upgrade, the best upgrade depends on

- ✔ The car's original engine-management system
- ✔ What you expect from your car
- ✔ Your wallet

Reflashes and EPROM swaps

If you meet the following criteria, you are usually best off sticking with an EPROM swap or a reflash:

- ✔ You want to maintain the new car warranty.
- ✔ You want a plug-and-play solution you never have to tinker with.
- ✔ You don't want to spend money on installation or Dyno tuning.
- ✔ You want a stealth mod that is difficult to detect.
- ✔ You want to raise the factory rev limit and you want the faster response of a stock ECU without a junction box in between.

Chapter 21 covers reflashes and EPROM swaps.

Black boxes

Chapter 22 covers single-purpose black boxes such as speed delimiters.

Piggybacks and standalones

Piggybacks and standalones let you make changes on the fly and tune your car on the Dyno.

The best system for your car depends on

- ✔ Your budget
- ✔ Available systems for your car

Integrated piggybacks

Who is best served by a piggyback? You might be, if you meet the following criteria:

- ✔ You can't quite afford the entry price for a standalone ECU.
- ✔ You have a car for which there is no *premapped* standalone ECU.

Chapter 23 covers integrated piggybacks.

Full standalone ECUs

A full standalone ECU has its own special processor and operating system that replace the stock systems.

You may be best served by a standalone ECU if the following are true:

- ✔ You're comfortable spending extra to buy a standalone ECU.
- ✔ You're willing to spend the time and money to have it installed and Dyno tuned.
- ✔ You need the flexibility and control of being able to
  - Tune on the fly
  - Make changes at the track
  - Record performance data *(datalog)*
  - Run additional devices or features, such as water injection, traction control, or launch control

A standalone ECU gives you full control of the engine management, but that means you must map every aspect of the engine's operation. It's much more complicated than other management options:

✔ Either work with a tuner or do your homework when you're trying to establish what kinds of features you really want or need:

- If you aren't using half the features, or you don't need the capacity of a full race system in your street machine, you'll do a lot of work and spend a lot of money without much to show for it at the end.

- If you rely on a local tuner or shop to work with you on setting up your car, follow the tuner's recommendations closely.

  It doesn't help you much to have a top-of-the-line Motec if your tuner is a Haltech expert and doesn't know anything about Motec systems.

✔ Check whether the system can use the car's original engine sensors. Some standalone ECUs require *replacing* most engine sensors with custom sensors (which is neither cheap nor quick).

Chapter 24 covers full standalone ECUs.

Chapter 21

Reflashes and EPROM Swaps

In This Chapter

▶ Hacking your car's brain

▶ Stepping up to an EPROM or reflash

*F*ew power modifications deliver more bang for the buck than an ECU (Engine Control Unit) upgrade. The beauty of a reflash or EPROM swap is that you gain all of this performance without changing the stock appearance of your car.

For value and sheer stealthiness, an EPROM swap or reflash is hard to beat.

ECU Reprogramming

EPROM (Erasable Programmable Read Only Memory) is part of your car's ECU and contains such key operating parameters for your car as the fuel, ignition, and boost maps. It is the chip that you can remove and replace with a new chip that has had different maps burned onto it for increased performance.

The difference between reflashes and EPROM swaps is how the data change is installed in your car:

✔ If your car was made between 1992 and 1996, it probably has an OBDI-compatible ECU with a removable EPROM.

You can *upgrade* an OBDI car's tuning by physically swapping either the EPROM or the whole ECU.

✔ If your car was made in 1996 or later, it probably has an OBDII-compatible ECU.

You can reprogram an OBDII car's tuning by attaching a compatible computer directly to your car and *reflashing* the CPU (downloading a new tuning program to the CPU's flash memory).

Should you reprogram?

You should consider whether to reprogram your car's ECU, via reflashing or an EPROM swap, based on how you see your car as an investment.

Honda owners rejoice

If you have a 1992 to 1995 Honda or Acura, hacking your ECU is a piece of cake. With Uberdata, a freeware "crack" of the factory ECU (similar to much more expensive aftermarket solutions like those offered by Hondata), Honda owners now have an open source means of creating their own OBDI EPROMS. Your total investment can be under $150 for everything to get started.

Here's how it works:

1. **Download the freeware, most commonly known as Uberdata, from** `www.ecimulti.org/uberdata/downloads/app/`.

2. **Get some small parts from an electronics store, like Radio Shack. You need these:**

   A ¼ Watt 1.0k Ohm resistor. The colored bands on a resistor indicate its *value* and *tolerance* (accuracy). A brown band followed by an orange band indicates a value of 1.0k Ohms. A gold band indicates 5 percent tolerance; a silver band indicates 10 percent tolerance.

   Two 0.1µ Farad ceramic disc capacitors.

   One 74HC373 IC (integrated circuit), as shown in the following figure.

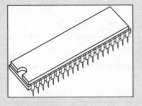

3. **Get a 28-pin 29c256 EPROM, as shown in the next figure.**

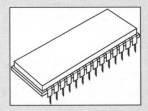

   It can be purchased online from `www.bootroms.com` or `www.moates.net`.

   This will be your custom ECU.

4. **Get an EPROM burner.**

   This can be sourced from an online site, such as `www.batronix.com/electronic/circuits/eeprommer.shtml`.

5. **Follow the online step-by-step instructions at** `www.ecimulti.org/uberdata/faq/index.html`.

You can even download and trade maps by registering for the online message board linked from the same site.

Violà! You are a certified automotive ECU hacker and can make chips for yourself and all of your OBDI Honda buddies.

Reflashes and swaps

Reflashes and EPROM swaps usually are the best solution if you

✔ Want to make a quick "plug-and-play" upgrade.

✔ Don't want to make changes while you drive.

✔ Lease your car.

✔ Have factory warranty coverage.

Even if your car's "bumper-to-bumper" warranty has expired, it may be covered by a warranty for emission compliance (it's a federal law). If you violate the emission warranty with a modification, you may have to pay the whole cost yourself to make your car's breath squeaky clean again.

✔ Want to use the factory diagnostic system.

✔ Plan to sell your car someday in factory-stock condition.

Nothing upsets buyers like seeing a hacked up wiring harness or signs of an aftermarket piggyback ECU controller install.

Cheaters often try to use reflashes and EPROM swaps in "stock" motor sports classes.

Standalone and tunable controllers

You should consider a full standalone or tunable controller instead of reflashing or an EPROM swap if you

✔ Want to make changes while you drive.

✔ Own (you don't *lease*) your car.

✔ Aren't worried about warranty coverage.

✔ Don't care about using the factory diagnostic system.

✔ Don't care about selling your car in factory-stock condition.

Chapter 20 guides you to the right kind of standalone or tunable controller for your car, and the following chapters of the book cover them in detail.

Reprogramming factory ECUs

Both reflashes and EPROM swaps are changes that take place within the confines of the stock ECU. The ECU is reprogrammed with new mapping data, including

- ✔ Fuel
- ✔ Ignition timing
- ✔ Turbo boost maps

Cars with reflashes and EPROMs often fly under the radar for routine dealer service and warranty work because the ECU case looks completely stock (at least from the outside), and dealership service technicians can retrieve OBDI diagnostic codes from the tuned ECU. However, the car manufacturers are loath to pay for warranty repairs caused by unapproved tuning. Service centers have a couple of methods to detect tuned ECUs:

- ✔ Scanning with a special diagnostic tool
- ✔ Test driving

A simple test is to run the engine to the factory rev limit. If the engine can go past the factory rev limit, the service center opens the ECU and checks whether the EPROM has been swapped.

EPROM swaps (OBDI)

OBDI cars are reprogrammed by physically swapping a reprogrammed EPROM (either by itself or in a complete ECU).

EPROM upgrades come in several forms for OBDI cars. Depending on your car and your tuner, your upgrade will be either

- ✔ A reprogrammed EPROM chip that you install in your current ECU.

  If your car uses OBDI (like most 1992 to 1996 models), it has a chip that can be physically removed from your ECU's primary circuit board and swapped with a new tuned chip.

- ✔ A complete ECU with a reprogrammed EPROM chip.

  You may not be able to easily identify and remove the EPROM (for example, when the EPROM chip is soldered to the ECU). Depending on the tuner, you may opt for either

  - **Installing an off-the-shelf pretuned ECU:** You keep your stock ECU. This is more expensive, but you can swap between your stock ECU and tuned ECU.

  - **Exchanging or reprogramming the ECU:** You give the tuner your stock ECU to reprogram. This is cheaper, but you don't have a stock ECU anymore. (You can buy a stock ECU later if you want one.)

If you have a tuned OBDI EPROM, you can sell it or move it to another car like yours.

Reflashing (OBDII)

OBDII-standard cars (mostly 1996 and newer) are flash programmable. Recalibrated mapping parameters are saved to *flash memory,* which is much like the memory used by digital cameras and MP3 players.

From the car hacker's perspective, flash data uploads are a mixed blessing:

- ✔ A reprogrammed OBDII system is harder for service technicians to identify than a swapped EPROM in an OBDI system. That means warranty coverage is less likely to be cancelled simply because of benign reprogramming.

- ✔ You can't simply swap stock and tuned chips in an OBDII car.

  Only a small fraction of flash tuners offer the necessary remote programming module for OBDII.

OBDII reflashes don't disappear if your car's battery is disconnected. Removing the battery resets the *learning parameters* back to the ECU's default, but the *tuned maps* don't disappear.

Tuners are adapting pretty well to reflashing:

- ✔ Tuners can reflash an OBDII ECU anywhere without even removing it from the car or opening the case.

  A tuner can download any of hundreds of maps to the ECU from a laptop computer with an OBDII connection cable. If the tuning isn't exactly right, a new setup is just a few clicks away.

- ✔ Tuners can remotely customize maps for common *combinations* of bolt-on modifications.

  Companies like WORKS (a leading Mitsubishi Evo tuner) have maps for nearly every conceivable combination of their bolt-on performance products, as well as for many popular third-party bolt-ons. These maps give modders some room to make more modifications without completely retuning. (Some tuners go on the road to personalize these reflashes during group Dyno sessions.)

Figure 21-1 illustrates a Mitsubishi Evo VIII ECU upgrade marketed by WORKS (the box) and the WORKS P2 Boost Tube — a mechanical modification the ECU relies on to prevent boost taper.

Figure 21-1:
ECU
upgrade for
Mitsubishi's
Lancer Evo.

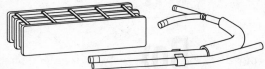

Reflashing makes a tuner's combination more difficult to copy without permission. (Unauthorized copies of tuned OBDI chips are common.)

Chapter 22

Black Boxes

*S*ingle-purpose black boxes (also called *piggyback controllers*) are a staple of car modifiers for controlling ignition mapping, fuel delivery, and/or boost. Generally speaking, the industry is moving away from single-purpose black boxes because standalone ECU (Engine Control Unit) replacements have come down in price and have become more user-friendly, and also because multifunction controllers have consolidated many of the functions once addressed by black boxes. Still, the relative low cost and simplicity of black boxes remains a compelling avenue if you're a novice car modder.

This chapter explores the functionality of the single-purpose black boxes and offers tips and guidance for how these inexpensive controllers can address specific performance needs in engine tuning.

Mixture Control

Combustion requires proportionate parts of fuel and oxygen. Too much of either isn't good for lighting off the mixture of air and fuel. Getting the ratio of fuel and oxygen just right is a key ingredient in tuning a car for maximum reliable power.

The combustion process is a series of controlled explosions in the combustion chamber. A perfectly timed spark lights a mixture of fuel and oxygen. This blend of oxygen and fuel needs an optimal ratio for a clean, powerful explosion. The goal for power is to run as *lean* (more oxygen) a mixture as possible, while running *rich* (more fuel) enough for safety. It's counter-intuitive to think of fuel as a fire *stopper,* but that's what it amounts to — if there is too much fuel in the mixture, it won't burn.

A famous drag race tuner explained the importance of mixture to me in horrifying detail by casually flicking a lit cigarette into a pan filled with gasoline that had been drained from a tank early in the day. The cigarette hit the pool of gasoline and, to my amazement and relief, was promptly extinguished. Of course, had it ignited the fumes of evaporating fuel on the way down, a spectacular explosion would have occurred — but the lit cigarette traveled with enough velocity to land in liquid fuel and be put out. Don't try this at home, kids!

Air/Fuel Controllers

An *air/fuel controller* offsets extra air being delivered to the engine by introducing more fuel into the mixture. It's a crude but effective tool that tuners have used since the early days of fuel-injected engine management. The controller changes the voltage signal that the factory air flow meter (AFM) sends to the ECU; the ECU delivers fuel in proportion to the amount of oxygen it thinks is available for combustion. These values are usually manipulated by the user in the cabin of the car through a numeric and/or graphical interface expressing a percentage of richening or leaning of the air fuel ratio. Companies like A'PEXi (AFC and S-AFC) and HKS (Super AF-R) sell air/fuel controllers for around $300 to $400 (U.S. dollars).

Air-fuel controllers are used with everything from open-element air intakes to more aggressive cams and turbo chargers/superchargers. The controllers are also used by tuners to either

✔ Lean out a factory air/fuel ratio on relatively stock cars in an attempt to gain power over the often very rich running mixture of the factory tune.

The most power usually comes from a slightly rich mixture.

✔ Tune out some fuel as the result of running larger fuel injectors coupled with a higher-flowing fuel pump.

Whether you use them to add or take away fuel from the mixture, air/fuel controllers are always employed to achieve an optimal ratio as expressed in a proportion of parts of air to fuel (12:1, 10:1, and so on). Generally, forced induction cars require more fuel (a richer mixture) than their lean-burning, normally aspirated counterparts.

A simple air/fuel controller has one dedicated task: controlling the mixture of, well, air and fuel. For tuning, it's a one-trick pony. While the air/fuel controllers currently on the market are relatively user friendly, with easy-to-navigate interfaces, they rely on feeding an altered or tweaked signal to the ECU. The ECU receives false information. These controllers have some major shortcomings as tuning tools:

- ✔ **Air/fuel controllers can't control the ignition timing maps.** The air/fuel controller can't directly pull back or move forward the point where the air/fuel mixture is ignited.

- ✔ **For forced induction, the air/fuel controller can't control how much boost the wastegate allows into the engine.**

- ✔ **Because information the ECU receives from the air/fuel controller is altered, on modern cars with sophisticated adaptive learning capability, the ECU can't alter the ignition and boost mapping with reference to a true and exact signal.** This in turn opens the door to a domino effect wherein the ECU learns to operate under a fixed percentage of fuel being added or taken away and that this fixed percentage may be significantly off when, for instance, the air becomes thinner at altitude or more dense on a cool day or less dense on a hot and humid day.

- ✔ **Whenever an intercept or junction box (like an air/fuel controller) is placed between a signal source and the ECU, there is (in theory) a delay when the interceptor box receives the signal, and makes the change, and spits the altered signal out to the ECU.** Given the speed that an engine runs (a typical four-cylinder automotive engine goes through over 50 cycles per second at high rpm), any delay can prevent a clean and safe combustion cycle.

- ✔ **Air/fuel controllers need to receive their source signal straight from the sensors.** Although this can occasionally be accomplished with a harness adapter, wire connections often must be spliced — a risky proposition if you want repairs under warranty.

Wiring and using an air/fuel controller like the A'PEXi AFC (Air/Fuel Controller, as shown in Figure 22-1), S-AFC (Super Air Fuel Controller, as shown in Figure 22-2) or HKS Super AF-R (Air/Fuel Regulator) is fairly straightforward. A novice can install one of these controllers with basic hand tools in less than two hours. Wiring steps are just

- ✔ Tapping for power and ground

- ✔ Running wires to retrieve signals for the mass airflow sensor (MAF) or manifold air pressure sensor (MAP), rpm, throttle position, and O_2.

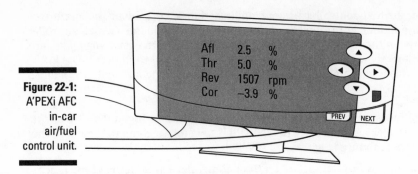

Figure 22-1:
A'PEXi AFC
in-car
air/fuel
control unit.

The display is usually mounted in the cabin so that the driver can adjust on the fly while either road or Dyno tuning. You adjust the map by adding or reducing percentage values from the base fuel map using toggle buttons on the controller's display. Some of the more sophisticated air/fuel controllers, such as the HKS Super AF-R, add Electronic Idle Stabilizer (EIDS) function, which allows built-in correction when using a blow-off valve vented atmospherically on a forced induction engine (when the metered air is vented to atmosphere on a MAF or AFM equipped car, the ECU doesn't know about the missing air and dumps too much fuel for the air in the system. This rich condition can cause stumbling on throttle lift and at idle). A'PEXi offers a similar feature, Deceleration Air Flow Correction, on its S-AFC. In addition, the S-AFC can monitor and replay intake manifold vacuum/boost pressure, air flow capacity, intake manifold pressure, Karmann frequency, engine rpm, throttle position, and air flow correction percentage in numerical, analog meter, and graph displays.

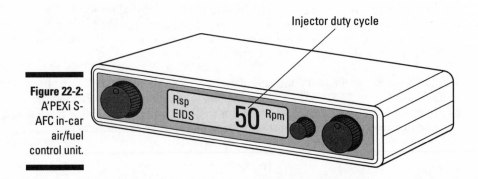

Figure 22-2:
A'PEXi S-
AFC in-car
air/fuel
control unit.

Auxiliary Injector Controllers

Auxiliary injector controllers (AICs) provide more fuel when enlarging the factory fuel injectors isn't practical and so extra injectors are installed. AICs, which retail for between $600 and $900, typically work by controlling the current to injectors, so they can drive both high- and low-impedance fuel injectors.

Most modern AICs can drive up to eight more injectors. These injectors are generally mounted in either the intake stream or the intake manifold.

A modern AIC, such as the HKS AIC-SI, uses two independent fuel curves for *boost pressure* (your turbocharger or supercharger pressure) and rpm. Each fuel curve is independent of the other, yet both can work simultaneously. As the two curves overlap, they provide the *sum* of the two enrichment values. Many AICs also allow the user to monitor injector pulse width and duty cycle for both rpm and boost. This is useful on forced-induction cars in which boost, and the corresponding need for more fuel, increases with the rising rpms.

The AIC is a piggyback junction box. While the air/fuel controller's job is to take a voltage signal from the factory AFM (or frequency for MAF) and tweak it before sending it on to the ECU, the AIC monitors the duty cycle and pulse width of the factory fuel injectors and sends this signal to drive the extra injectors according to boost and rpm. For example, a car can be tuned to run on the factory fuel injectors in their unaltered state, and then begin driving the auxiliary injectors to bring in more fuel as boost increases with higher revs.

An AIC's user interface is fairly straightforward, usually a couple of dials and a numeric LED display. An AIC can be installed with basic hand tools in an hour or two. The primary unit is mounted visibly in the cabin for easy access and monitoring.

The shortcoming of AICs as a tuning tool is their relatively high price for the simple function of delivering more fuel. Many standalone computers can drive extra injectors while controlling such variables as ignition and boost mapping. An AIC, such as the HKS AIC-SI and the GReddy Rebic IV (shown in Figure 22-3), is a must-have item for users limited to adding piggyback boxes on top of the factory ECU, but most users faced with the prospect of at least $600 for an AIC, and another several hundred for an ignition controller and electronic boost controller, generally move on to using a full standalone to address more parameters than just fuel delivery.

Figure 22-3:
The GReddy
Rebic IV.

One notable exception towards the trend moving away from AICs is the cost-effective MF2 controller introduced by ERL/Aquamist (which costs about $350). This controller has eight potentiometers capable of driving four high-impedance injectors and two low-impendence injectors. It can map the delivery of both water injection and more fuel. Tuners who use water injection to cool the intake charge on forced-induction engines are using the MF2 to provide accurate fuel and water delivery mapping from a single box.

More comprehensive controllers, like the GReddy E-Manage ($350 to $650, depending on configuration), are filling the role that the Rebic and AICs used to dominate. While the Rebic and AIC are still (in theory) the kings of the hill for driving up to eight injectors, the E-Manage's ability to drive two extra injectors is often enough to add a bit of fuel to the mixture with auxiliary injectors.

Ignition Timing Controllers

An *ignition timing controller (ITC)* is basically a corollary to the air/fuel controller. Timing when the spark lights off the air/fuel mixture is critical. Timing the ignition for complete combustion occurs by either moving forward (advancing) the point when spark is introduced, or delaying (that is, moving backward or retarding) the point at which the air/fuel mixture is ignited:

- ✔ *Advancing* timing (aggressive timing) usually makes more power.

  Too much advance causes *detonation,* which can shatter pistons.

- ✔ *Retarding* the timing is safer at the cost of some power.

  Timing must be retarded to avoid detonation when running boost on engines originally designed to run naturally aspirated.

The ITC usually is mounted in the car's cabin for easy access.

Sophisticated multifunction piggyback controllers and less expensive premapped standalone ECUs are replacing most ITCs.

A'PEXi

The A'PEXi S-ITC (Super Ignition Timing Controller) is a single-purpose black box that receives a signal from the crank angle sensor and either adds or removes a fixed percentage of timing advance (up to 15 percent).

Setting the S-ITC is a relatively straightforward affair. Five dials on controller box represent points in the rpm range; the S-ITC extrapolates between these five points to create a spark curve.

MSD

MSD offers timing control boxes for most cars, trucks, and SUVs. Prices range from $130 to $300. The simplest models pull out fixed percentages of timing to compensate for bolt-on modifications. High-end models provide sophisticated boost-referenced ignition mapping for drag racing.

Turbo Boost Controllers

A *boost controller* adjusts the amount of boost (the *intake manifold pressure*) allowed in a turbo engine.

The boost controller is in the vacuum circuit that goes from turbocharger to the wastegate actuator:

✔ The *wastegate* is a bypass for the *turbine* (hot exhaust) side of the turbo.

   When the boost pressure gets to a designated level, the wastegate door opens to limit the boost to that level. Allowing exhaust gas to bypass the turbo prevents the turbo from overboosting and damaging the engine and/or over-spinning the turbo to the point of failure.

✔ The *wastegate actuator* is a pressure-operated diaphragm that moves the flapper door of the wastegate. As boost pressure increases, that pressure builds against the wastegate actuator.

 With the exception of hybrid mechanical boost controllers, the easiest way to conceptualize the practical difference between a mechanical or electronic controller is the ability to change the amount of boost from inside the cabin. More specifically, an electronic boost controller operates a solenoid that acts on the wastegate, thereby allowing the control box for the solenoid to be mounted in the cabin. On the other hand, a mechanical boost controller is a simple bleed or relief valve mounted under the hood.

✔ A mechanical controller is a set-it-and-forget-it affair.

✔ Electronic controllers allow adjustments on the fly from inside the car's cabin, stored boost settings, and gimmicky features such as scramble boost, ghost map tracing, and self-learning.

Mechanical controllers

The two primary types of mechanical boost controllers are the bleed valve and the relief valve. A couple of interesting hybrids employ variations on these two themes.

A simple mechanical boost controller can be made for less than $20 in parts from a hardware store.

Bleed valve

A *bleed valve* leaks (bleeds) some boost pressure from the wastegate actuator to the atmosphere. Adjusting the manual boost controller controls the size of the leak. As the boost rises, the wastegate actuator senses less pressure because some pressure escapes from the feedback line before reaching the wastegate actuator. The boost therefore rises as some pressure is vented and a new equilibrium is created at a higher boost level — this is sensed by the wastegate, which opens.

The primary disadvantage of a bleed valve is that the boost increases more slowly. There is a constant leak until the designated peak boost level is reached. The wastegate allows some exhaust gas to bypass the turbo that would otherwise spool the turbo faster.

Relief valve

A *relief valve* (also known as a *ball and spring* type controller) is a mechanical air pressure switch. A small ball bearing in the relief valve is held under pressure onto a seat by a spring. Air pressure lifts the ball off its seat at a preset *cracking pressure* (which is set by the spring's tension pressing against the ball). The cracking pressure is adjusted by changing the spring's tension.

When the ball is off its seat, air flows through the valve. As the air pressure falls, the tension in the spring becomes the greater force, causing the ball to close off the valve, which prevents air from flowing through the relief valve.

No air passes through the valve until the spring's cracking pressure is reached.

Hybrid controller

The mechanical hybrids include the following:

- **TurboXS Dual Stage boost controller:** This controller, which costs about $240, uses two mechanical valves stuck together with an electric solenoid that switches between them.

- **Hallman controller:** This controller, which costs about $105, is basically a relief valve type controller. A cable running into the car's cabin allows the tension to be adjusted on the go.

Electronic controllers

An electronic boost controller uses a solenoid to vent some of the pressure signal from the compressor before it reaches the actuator.

Electronic controllers offer several benefits:

✔ The fast-acting solenoid can quickly and precisely control the wastegate actuator, so the wastegate can be held shut longer. The turbocharger (in theory, if not in practice) spools faster than with mechanical control.

✔ Different boost settings can be stored for selection on the fly — like when the car in the next lane revs at the light.

✔ Boost can be mapped directly to engine rpm.

In fact, the HKS EVC Pro ($1,400) allows boost mapping for throttle position, engine rpm, and vehicle speed.

✔ Nearly all modern electronic boost controllers have graphic electroluminescent displays and some method of playing back the boost in either a numeric and/or graphic format.

Of course, with a price approaching that of a well-specified standalone ECU, even a trick boost controller like the EVC Pro loses most of its appeal.

That said, when a standalone ECU isn't being employed to map boost, as between an electronic and mechanical boost controller, the functionality and flexibility of an electronic boost controller generally justifies the higher cost of entry over mechanical counterparts.

An electronic boost controller can be wired and mounted without much trouble using basic hand tools. Generally, installation requires

✔ Providing power to the unit

✔ Installing the solenoid valve

✔ Installing the pressure sensor

✔ Installing wiring for the rpm pickup

When peak boost is dialed in, you set the primary boost modes by using the display's graphic interface. Most users find that the extras — self-learning, scramble boost, and rpm mapping — take more time to understand and master.

Manifold Air Pressure Sensors (Speed Density Systems)

A *manifold air pressure sensor (MAP)* replaces a factory air flow meter (AFM) or mass airflow sensor (MAF). There are a couple of reasons to make this switch:

✔ **Airflow:** A MAP sensor doesn't restrict airflow by pulling it through a measuring device.

An AFM or MAF sensor flows only as much air as its housing allows. While it's possible in some cases to upgrade to a larger AFM or MAF from another vehicle, usually from the same manufacturer, often either a larger unit isn't available or the calibration settings on a larger AFM or MAF aren't suited to your application.

✔ **Turbo engine performance:** On turbo engines, an MAP system can vent a blow-off valve to atmosphere to avoid stumbling at idle or running extremely rich on throttle lift.

The blow-off valve produces the ever-important *pssssssshhhh* sound that characterizes modern turbo street machines.

To understand the nature of the restriction, it helps to understand how MAFs and AFMs tell the ECU how much air is in the system. An MAF (or a Karmann Vortex airflow sensor) is hindered by a flow restriction. The inlet of the sensor has an obstruction in the airflow path that generates a constant stream of vortices (mini tornadoes) directly behind it. The velocity of the incoming airflow determines rate that these vortices spin off. An ultrasonic speaker and microphone placed across the stream of vortices measures their rate (the vortices spin off in alternating directions, which produces an alternating FM shift of the received signal from the speaker). The mass airflow sensor measures outside air temperature, outside barometric pressure, and incoming airflow velocity to provide the ECU comprehensive data for determining the total mass of the air that the engine is taking in. On the other hand, mass airflow measurement is more precise than the speed-density system insofar as the MAF calibration isn't affected when modifications are installed to change the engine's volumetric efficiency.

The two types of air flow meters are

✔ **Vane (also called flap or flapper door):** This meter sends two signals to the ECU:

• A *flapper door* is pushed open by the incoming air. The position of this flap (which restricts the air entering the engine) is synced to a potentiometer that sends a voltage signal to the ECU.

Another vane in a closed chamber behind the main vane damps the movement of the main vane for more accurate measurement. This vane doesn't send its own signal to the ECU.

• An *air-temperature* sensor in the AFM tells the ECU the temperature of the incoming air. The ECU uses this to calculate *air density*.

Warm air is less dense than cool air, so warm air can't burn as much fuel.

✔ **Hot wire:** This meter uses a series of wires in the air stream. The resistance of the wire at normal operating temperature is a known constant and allows a set voltage through it. As the air passes over the hot wire, the wire cools and its resistance decreases, so more voltage passes through it. The ECU receives this voltage signal to set the appropriate fuel delivery. Here, the resistance is manifested by the physical bore of the wire's housing.

Historically, the speed density system conversion was accomplished by installing an HKS VPC (vein pressure converter). Although recently discontinued, the VPC still circulates in the market. The VPC uses a 16-bit processor reading its own intake air temperature sensor and absolute pressure transducer (B-MAP sensor) signals. This processor allows the VPC replace the factory airflow-metering device and eliminates the need for a fuel cut defencer (discussed in the following section).

Wiring a VPC can be time-consuming. Car-specific harnesses make it easier if there's a wiring harness for your car.

The VPC is a victim of its cost (up to $1,250) and lack of versatility. Declining prices for standalone ECUs make the VPC less attractive.

Fuel and Speed Defencers

Fuel and speed cut defencers are simple boxes that respectively overcome factory fuel and speed cut-off points.

Auto manufacturers have technical reasons for employing both fuel cut and speed cut:

✔ Fuel cut prevents engine damage in such cases as when a wastegate on a forced induction engine fails and can allow a massive boost spike that would damage the engine. However, the fuel cut threshold may be set so low that it prevents engine modifications for higher safe boost levels.

✔ Speed cut may keep the vehicle from exceeding a maximum allowable speed for legislative or safety reasons. This maximum allowable speed may be attributed to

- Regulations in countries where the car is sold (for example, cars produced in Japan for home market use are restricted to approximately 112 mph)

- Insurance brackets

- Tires on the car when new were rated to a lower speed than the vehicle is otherwise capable

Check the speed rating on your car's tires. Chapter 5 explains how.

Fuel cut defencers

A *fuel cut defencer (FCD)* prevents fuel cut-off. The FCD tells the ECU that mass airflow never exceeds the factory limit setting. The output from the FCD is the same as the input until it reaches the limit. The type of FCD output depends on whether the car is running an AFM- (Air Flow Meter), MAF- (Mass Air Flow), or MAP- (Manifold Air Pressure) based system.

- ✔ AFM-equipped cars limit *voltage.* The FCD receives the airflow meter's sensor output.

- ✔ MAF-equipped cars limit *frequency.* The FCD receives the mass air flow sensor's output.

Fooling the ECU into believing the engine is consuming less air than it really is results in a *leaned-out mixture* — a dangerous effect that requires more fuel tuning for a safe air/fuel ratio.

Installing the FCD requires splicing into the factory harness. Model-specific instructions must identify the appropriate wires to splice.

Speed cut defencers

A *speed cut defencer* is a device that effectively raises a car's top speed by eliminating the factory engine cut that would prevent a car from exceeding a preset maximum speed.

The Vehicle Speed Sensor (VSS) limits a car's maximum speed under the governed limit. On the transmission, the VSS measures the car's speed by tracking the number of wheel revolutions. When the engine ECU decides that the car is traveling at its speed limit, the ECU either stops at least two injectors or cuts the ignition.

Two popular products can defeat speed cut:

- ✔ **The HKS Speed Limit Defencer (SLD), which lists for $125 to $700, depending on the model of car**

    The HKS SLD intercepts the VSS signal and sends a slower speed signal to the ECU. Because the engine ECU only limits normal engine operation if it knows maximum allowable speed is reached, this disables the factory speed limit.

> ✔ **A'PEXi RSM (Rev Speed Meter), which lists for $289**
>
> It features a variety of vehicle monitoring and performance display modes. The user can defeat or enable the factory speed cut by pressing a button.

SLDs are vehicle-specific. Wiring usually involves little more than plugging the unit into the factory harness. The appropriate SLD for a car depends on whether the car is equipped with a *CAN (Controller Area Network)* — a vehicle communication network first appearing in 2003 models:

> ✔ HKS SLD (Type I-II) for non-CAN equipped cars (various pre-CAN models). These retail between $125 and $500.
>
> ✔ HKS SLD (Type III) works with CAN. It retails between $600 and $700.

Although marketed primarily as a performance and engine function monitoring display, the A'PEXi RSM also features a speed cut elimination option for vehicles equipped with a factory speed cut. The RSM measures and monitors data such as vehicle speed, engine RPM, and elapsed times. Although wiring the RSM is a bit more involved than the plug-and-play SLD because of the extra signals needed for its greater functionality, it can be installed with basic hand tools by even a novice/intermediate installer.

Chapter 23

Integrated Piggybacks

*I*ntegrated piggybacks combine the functionality of several single-purpose standalones in an integrated unit that allows you to interface with the factory ECU. Because the ECU remains in place and continues to handle many, if not all, of the engine's functions, these all-in-one boxes are still piggybacks and still rely on a tweaked signal to trick the ECU into doing what the performance-minded enthusiast asks of it.

Piggyback Controller Functions

Piggyback controllers are used to tweak factory fuel and ignition maps. However, piggybacks can't control certain parameters — including the factory rev limit.

Piggyback controllers are relatively easy to wire — especially if a plug-and-play harness is available for your vehicle. But piggybacks aren't for everyone and exist in a funny middle ground between an EPROM swap or reflash and a full standalone. Chapter 20 can guide you to the *right* kind of ECU upgrade. Other chapters cover those upgrades in detail.

Controller Models

Piggyback controllers are available with a variety of prices and capabilities. The following sections describe the three most popular piggyback controllers.

GReddy e-Manage

The e-Manage by GReddy (see Figure 23-1) is essentially a piggyback air/fuel computer, not unlike the single-purpose controllers described in Chapter 20. However, the e-Manage supports extra tuning parameters for a more integrated approach to tuning your car's ECU.

The e-Manage can increase or decrease air/fuel as much as 20 percent by intercepting and altering the signal coming from the factory MAP or MAF sensor. Because the e-Manage doesn't have its own display screen, like the A'PEXi S-AFC, the tuning is accomplished through a Windows-based laptop.

Figure 23-1:
The GReddy
e-Manage.

The extra features that take the e-Manage out of the league of the S-AFC are its ability to

- ✔ Act as a VTEC controller for Honda and Acuras
- ✔ Control ignition timing (through an optional harness)
- ✔ Drive one or two extra fuel injectors
- ✔ Log data on your engine's performance via laptop (with optional hardware)

e-Manage can't handle boost mapping on turbocharged cars (a separate boost controller is required to raise or lower boost).

The e-Manage can be used on many Asian and European car models, and it isn't model-specific. Expect to pay around $300 to $400 for an e-Manage and to spend up to three hours installing it with basic hand tools.

Chip Torque Xede

The Xede by Chip Torque is preconfigured for specific models, including several popular Japanese car models. The Xede is a more comprehensive, and certainly more cost effective, method of tuning than an array of single-purpose piggyback controllers. The Xede is fully capable of mapping ignition, fuel, and boost. Figure 23-2 illustrates an Xede installed on a Mitsubishi Lancer EVO — it's the small box on the right side with two sets of wires coming out of it.

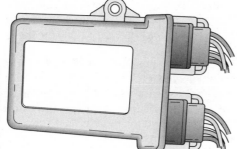

You can buy a more capable full-standalone ECU (such as an AEM engine management system or the A'PEXi Power FC) for about the same $900 you can expect to pay for the Xede piggyback controller.

The primary reason for choosing the Xede over a Power FC or AEM system would be solely because your local tuner is more familiar with that unit and can save you time and money on the Dyno. From a technical standpoint, the Power FC and AEM are both far more advanced.

TurboXS UTEC

The UTEC (User Tunable Engine Computer) by TurboXS is a modified and pretuned board that slides right into your factory ECU case and connects to the factory harness.

The best way to think of the UTEC is as a hybrid piggyback controller:

✔ Common tuning parameters are fully independent. The UTEC takes control of such parameters as ignition timing and boost. In these cases, the UTEC is acting as a full standalone.

✔ Some signals are tweaked before they reach the factory ECU.

✔ Some parameters remain untouched. The factory ECU remains in charge for

• Air/fuel

• Cold start

- Hot start

- Acceleration fueling

- Closed loop fuel control

The UTEC is preloaded with maps so you can get started quickly — you can install it in less than 20 minutes by simply sliding it into the factory ECU case and connecting the harness. Expect to pay around $1,000 for the UTEC.

The TurboXS Tuner is a wideband oxygen sensor (useful when tuning with or without the UTEC). This $700 device lets you build maps from the UTEC, in conjunction with the more accurate wideband oxygen sensor, and then access the maps through a graphic interface on a laptop, PDA, or even a Nintendo GameBoy Advance SP, as shown in Figure 23-3. (Now you have a legitimate reason to keep a GameBoy in your car!)

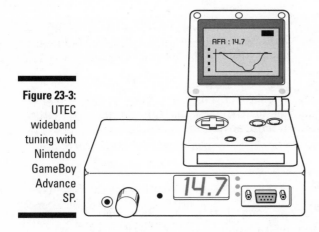

Figure 23-3:
UTEC
wideband
tuning with
Nintendo
GameBoy
Advance
SP.

Chapter 24

Full Standalone ECUs

As the price of full standalone ECUs continues to come down toward the budget of most performance-minded enthusiasts, the tuning parameters once available strictly to big-budget race teams are now finding their way into a much wider range of cars.

Before delving into the implications of this "standalone revolution," it helps to define what a standalone entails. Unlike a piggyback, reflash, or EPROM, a standalone replaces the entire ECU. The ECU is removed and put on a shelf to collect dust. The standalone takes over all the functionality of the factory ECU.

Because the standalone uses its own microprocessor, its own user interface, and its own method of running everything that the factory ECU once handled, it's the fastest, most direct, and most comprehensive method of manipulating engine management.

With great capability comes a steep learning curve, along with the potential for major engine damage. The sky's the limit not only for performance, but also for disaster. If you aren't sure you need the expense, complication, and risk of a full standalone ECU, Chapter 20 compares it to other types of ECUs (which are explained in other chapters).

If you're considering a full standalone system, check whether it's designed to work with your car's stock sensors:

> ✔ The new crop of plug-and-play standalones dramatically reduces installation time and expense by working with the factory sensors. These systems also allow you to swap quickly and easily between the factory and standalone ECU. You can put the factory ECU back in place when you
>
> • Sell the car

- Service the car

- Want the factory diagnostic codes

✔ Some standalone ECUs require wiring in new sensors for everything from the crank angle sensor to oxygen sensors, temperature sensors, and pressure sensors. This is neither easy nor cheap.

Deciding on a Full Standalone ECU

When making the decision about whether to take the plunge into full standalone, budget roughly twice the actual price of the unit for premapped plug-and-play systems, and three times the unit's price for systems that aren't premapped and require wiring.

This means that a $1,000 standalone can easily cost you $3,000 or more after installation, Dyno time, and a tuner's expertise have all been accounted for. Still, if you want the ability to tune your car periodically for different mods or simply wish to avoid sinking a small fortune into piggyback controllers (each of which also needs to be tuned), let alone rely on a piggyback to send tweaked signals to the factory ECU when a more direct approach is available, a standalone ECU may be the only way to go.

Keep in mind that a standalone renders your car no longer street legal from an emissions standpoint. Because a standalone can't control factory emissions equipment, let alone retrieve factory diagnostic codes, unless the factory ECU can quickly be swapped back into place, don't even think about upgrading to a standalone on a leased car, a car that needs to go in for emissions testing, or a car that you anticipate might need warranty work at some point in its life.

When you're considering which standalone to purchase, you should take into account the installation and tuning features of various standalones. Some of the differentiation points for the installation and tuning among standalones include the following:

✔ **Plug-and-play harness:** Some systems rely on the factory sensors and come with a plug-and-play harness, thus greatly reducing the installation and initial tuning time. Others require extensive rewiring and more sensors.

✔ **Premapped software:** Another time saver, the premapped systems allow you to immediately start and drive your car to your local Dyno. Others do not.

✔ **Number of cylinders:** Some systems can run more cylinders than others.

✔ **Ability to drive peak and hold (low impedance) injectors:** A must-have if you are even considering running this style of fuel injector in your engine.

✔ **Knock control:** Some systems have user-tunable knock control; others do not.

✔ **Boost control:** Some systems can map boost; others require the use of a separate boost controller.

✔ **Ability to run distributorless ignition coils:** Some units can, some can't.

✔ **Crankshaft position referencing accuracy:** Either relies on the factory signal or generates its own.

✔ **Extra outputs:** Useful for running auxiliary systems like water injection or nitrous.

✔ **Resolution:** The number of load points at a given rpm. The higher the load point, the better the resolution and the better able the system is of making incremental changes.

✔ **Ignition correction maps for air and coolant temperatures:** Useful when tuning a car to the ragged edge, and when the car is pushed hard in a wide range of conditions.

✔ **Ability to work off of a wideband oxygen sensor:** This may not be an issue if you're doing all of your tuning in open loop under WOT (Wide Open Throttle). On the other hand, if you tune for closed loop (part-throttle) transitions, a wideband can be much more accurate than the factory oxygen sensor.

✔ **Datalogging:** The ability to record, store, and play back data, including peak temperatures, knock readings, and performance numbers. This is very useful when road-tuning a car.

✔ **Autotune:** At least one standalone, Autronic, can save you some money on the Dyno by incorporating an autotune feature to help develop its own base maps.

✔ **User interface:** Slick but less stable Windows, or more stable but clunky DOS.

✔ **Ability to access full parameters:** Surprisingly, some systems, like the Power FC, lock the user out of parts of the tuning process because these are reserved for authorized Power Excel tuners. Never to fret . . . there is a workaround (see the "Plug and Play" section, later in this chapter).

✔ **Clock Speed:** Not all ECUs are created equal, and as with home computers, the processor speed may differ between models. This is more of an issue as auxiliary devices are added that require input from the ECU — for example, traction control, water injection, or data telemetry systems that might otherwise take a toll on the factory ECU's processor.

Other considerations you should take into account when you're deciding which standalone to purchase concern the driving and performance features of various standalones. Some of the features to investigate for performance and driving include the following:

- ✔ **Anti-lag:** The same technology used by the WRC teams to keep their turbos spooled can be used through some of the standalone systems on the market. Of course, the extra wear and tear on your turbo is another matter!

- ✔ **Traction control:** The ability to integrate with your car's ABS sensors to detect and prevent a spin by modulating the brakes at each individual corner of the car.

- ✔ **Launch control:** The ability to adjust boost and throttle inputs to prevent wheel spin under hard launching.

- ✔ **Flat shift:** The ability to allow foot-to-the-floor shifts without the need for lifting.

Plug and Play

Perhaps the most exciting recent development in the world of standalone ECU replacements is the new breed of plug-and-play ECUs that come preloaded with base maps.

Buy the least expensive system that meets your needs. If there's a plug-and-play solution for your car (they don't exist for every model), go with it. It drastically reduces the cost and time of installation and tuning.

The Power FC and the AEM are basically competing products that do the same thing. Their technical specs might be slightly different, but they have roughly the same functionality at the same price point:

- ✔ **Base maps.** The AEM starts as a more open interface because you don't have the locked-out sections that the Power FC has. The Power FC base maps, in my experience, tend to be more reliable.

- ✔ **Handheld controller.** The Power FC has from the very beginning come bundled with a commander unit. A company called Gauge Ware now offers a Commander-style display for the AEM EMS.

- ✔ **Professional tuners.** Both Power FC and AEM have dedicated tuners available to help with Dyno tuning the car.

- ✔ **Factory ECU compatibility.** Both the Power FC and the AEM unit can be swapped with the stock ECU in minutes for troubleshooting or quick trips into the local dealership's service department for warranty work.

The Power FC allows the factory ECU to remain in place, so you can get diagnostic codes by just reconnecting the factory ECU. This is helpful when troubleshooting mechanical problems that may arise during the tuning process, such as vacuum leaks and failed oxygen sensors.

A'PEXi Power FC

The Power FC was certainly one of the first, and perhaps remains the best, plug-and-play engine management solutions for the limited roster of vehicles that it's available for.

For the money and ease of installation, let alone the smooth interface and inherent appeal of the Commander, the Power FC is hard to beat — even in comparison to much more expensive wired-in standalones, such as the Motec or Autronic.

The Power FC mounts in less than five minutes. Essentially, the harness from the factory ECU is removed and plugged into the Power FX box. The car can be driven immediately. With the optional Commander unit, you can both monitor and set many of the engine tuning parameters without a laptop. A'PEXi offers a boost control kit based on the fast-acting solenoid used in its renowned AVC-R boost controller to allow the Commander to monitor, set, and store multiple boost settings.

While the Power FC is inexpensive (by standalone standards) to buy, install, and map, it has its drawbacks:

✔ The Power FC's base maps are just that — base maps. They're relied on as a guideline for getting started; you'll need to bring the car to the Dyno for further tuning. These aren't the end-all-be-all performance maps that hopeful enthusiasts want them to be.

✔ The Power FC doesn't include datalogging.

You can datalog from the Power FC with a third-party box offered by FC-Datalogit. It hacks the Power FC interface so that you can log from the Power FC through the serial port of your laptop.

✔ You can't access the device's full functionality. Some higher-level processes (certain correction factors) are intended to be accessed only by A'PEXi Power Excel–certified dealers using a special laptop interface to tune the car.

The FC-Datalogit provides a workaround to get to these hidden features, but this workaround isn't supported by A'PEXi.

✔ Even with the FC-Datalogit, the Power FC lacks some of the more advanced functionality of the other systems, such as

- The ability to drive auxiliary devices like water injection

- Integrated launch control

- Traction control

AEM EMS

The AEM EMS follows the Power FC model, in some ways improves on it, and in other ways falls a bit short. By way of improvement, the EMS system works with more vehicles than the Power FC, offers more on-board capabilities, including launch control and traction control, and isn't as limited as the Power FC without the FC-Datalogit.

The AEM EMS has its downsides:

✔ The wider range of vehicles has done little to ensure that the preloaded base maps are a good starting point for tuning a car.

✔ The AEM isn't offered with an integrated boost control kit or viewer/ setting unit. To tune the EMS, you must provide both boost controller and laptop.

Some Assembly Required

Some traditional standalone systems have car-specific wiring harnesses, and some come with self-tuning ability, but they remaining systems aren't plug and play to the same extent as the AEM and A'PEXi units.

You need the greater flexibility of the bet race-dedicated standalone you can afford if you're

✔ Racing

✔ Willing to spend the time to wire everything in

✔ Willing to spend the money up front

✔ Using an array of ECU-driven devices

Motec

Widely considered the end-all-be-all of engine management systems, and with a price to match, Motec offers several flavors of its renowned stand-alone ECUs.

Starting with the entry-level M4, the model range also includes the M4 Clubman, M4 Pro, M48 Clubman, M48Pro, and M8. Each system is based on the same processor, and the distinction between the garden variety ECUs and the "Club-man" and "Pro" variants are features than can be enabled but are otherwise inaccessible to the end user. The functionality is sufficiently different on each of these models that it would be best to consult with a Motec dealer/reseller to determine which model best suits your needs.

While each of the systems has a host of features, usually you need the more expensive models if you want

✔ High resolution mapping for fuel and ignition

✔ The ability to cope with more cylinders

✔ Extra performance features, such as launch control and flat shifting

✔ More auxiliary inputs

Haltech

The granddaddy of engine management systems, the Haltech E6X has both key advantages and disadvantages:

✔ Many tuners are familiar with its interface and setup.

✔ It's a very capable system.

✔ Its stable DOS interface is often called archaic.

A lot of the old school, seasoned tuners are adept and comfortable work-ing in a DOS environment. A lot of younger tuners are more comfortable using a Windows environment. Newer interfaces (such as Windows) are more user friendly, which is why they've caught on, but DOS is generally more *stable* (has fewer glitches and crashes less often).

✔ It requires the installation of its own coolant and air temperature sensors in many import vehicles.

Autronic

The Autronic slots somewhere between a Haltech and Motec, providing much of the cutting edge technology of the Motec, along with the modern interface, but at a price point closer to that of the Haltech.

The primary points of distinction with the Autronic, at least from an end user's standpoint, are its optional autotune feature that, along with its adaptive learning, can give you greater flexibility in road-tuning the car. Obviously, this keeps down Dyno fees and does a better job of setting the car for the real-world environment where it's driven.

Electromotive

The TEC II and TEC III offered by Electromotive are perhaps more in line with the Motecs of the world — long on features, but perhaps overkill for most entry-level enthusiasts. Electromotive's claim to fame was being one of the first manufacturers to embrace direct-fire ignitions and develop a crank angle sensor in conjunction with its standalone ECU. Of course, while this pays dividends in ignition accuracy, it's one more piece to the puzzle that must be installed by the end user along with the usual array of sensors to replace the factory counterparts.

Although the TEC II received mixed reviews on its user interface, the TEC III seems to have been more widely accepted, both as a result of the extra functionality in the TEC III, and by the fact that more people have had a chance to play with these units and understand how they work relative to the Haltechs and Motecs of the world.

MegaSquirt

If wiring in a piggyback fuel controller isn't challenging enough for you, and you'd like to save some money, the MegaSquirt electronic fuel controller may be right up your alley. MegaSquirt is not as much a finished product as it is the essential elements of a DIY standalone ECU kit, rivaling many high-dollar standalones with ignition timing control and auxiliary drivers for nitrous systems, traction control and water injection. Since the MegaSquirt is powered by its own processor — faster in fact than many factory ECUs — it is much more than a traditional delay reaction interceptor box. With the proper coolant and air temperature sensors (Negative Temperature Coefficient (NTC) thermistors) it can take over most if not all of your essential ECU functions.

To get the functionality of a MegaSquirt system from a ready-made system, you could spend $1,000 or more. MegaSquirt offers the key ingredients and instructions for under $200. You provide the rest.

Part IX
The Part of Tens

"Frankly sir, issuing you reasonably priced auto insurance isn't going to be easy given the number of crashes you've been involved in."

In this part . . .

Here you find the best online resources to use for inspiration, research, and good advice about modifying your car. You also find ten common problems that you may face when you're modifying your car, along with solutions to those problems.

Chapter 25

Ten Online Resources

In This Chapter

▶ Finding your car's online community

▶ Utilizing general automotive sites

▶ Taking advantage of motorsport sites

▶ Finding aftermarket parts and support online

*B*efore the advent of the Internet and online message boards, the hobby of modding or hacking your car was highly regionalized. Generally, your best source of information came from a narrow cross-section of people from your local community. As a result, the breadth and scope of car modding resources were considerably narrower. Trends also migrated nationally and globally at a slower rate, resulting in a more fragmented and localized perspective on what it meant to mod a car. In other words, chances were good that if you were situated in Detroit, you'd have no problem finding informed people with hands-on experience pertaining to American muscle cars, but it might be a bit of a struggle to find an equivalent level of insight into your foreign import. Obviously, if you were a Mustang owner in Tokyo, the reverse was likely the case.

Nowadays, you have the Internet and online car communities to thank for the instant access to information, both archived and in real time, available for nearly every make and model of car in existence. There is, however, something to be said for the quality of information that one can glean from a hands-on expert in a garage environment as opposed to an anonymous voice typing in cyberspace. Quantity and 24-hour convenience doesn't always trump quality.

But by no means should this caveat deter anyone from relying on the Internet as the single most valuable resource for discovering both beginner and more advanced car hacking and modding techniques. Online car message boards and communities will continue to be your primary tool in car modification projects, second only in significance to what you yourself experience working on your car.

Enthusiast Sites

The single best place to discover more about what works and doesn't work on *your* car is the enthusiast message boards and forums for your car's make and model. Whether you own a Dodge truck, Alfa Romeo roadster, or Mitsubishi Lancer Evo, there's a cyberspace community of like-minded people who live, breathe, and fixate on the car that you are looking to hack or mod.

There are few mods that haven't already been tried by someone, somewhere in the world, for whatever car you have. From putting a turbo on a Yugo to installing a lift kit and mud tires on a Cadillac, someone has done it with either good or bad results.

To get the most out of your online information-seeking endeavors, it helps to keep a couple of fundamental guidelines in mind. Adhering to these will greatly increase the chances of your finding useful information quickly, efficiently, and reliably, without alienating those who participate in what is oftentimes a structured information exchange:

✔ **Take everything you read with a grain of salt.** The advice you get online is worth what you paid for it. It's free advice, and while you should welcome it and use it as a starting point for thinking critically about your project, don't instantly take it as gospel without investigating a bit into the backgrounds of the people giving the advice — even if there appears to be a clear consensus.

A skilled writer may not be a technical expert. The very articulate, professional-sounding person that is so helpful answering your questions promptly — even at 3 a.m. — may be a 14-year-old kid. The person of few words with all the spelling mistakes may be a seasoned veteran who has rebuilt more engines and rewired more electrical systems than all of the mechanics at your local dealership put together.

One pitfall of enthusiast message boards is the tyranny of the vocal minority. If you understand this dynamic going in, you can think critically about who is telling you what online:

• The seasoned veterans have seen it all before. They sit back and read, rarely posting unless something really captures their interest.

• The newer crowd (who could stand to learn a thing or two from the old guys) has opinions — very strong opinions — on everything and anything from what wax you should use on your car to what turbocharger to choose. Question whether these strong opinions are gospel truth, subversive guerilla marketing tactics, or self-justifications for overpriced/under-performing products.

✔ **The search function is your friend.** It's part of proper netiquette. When I have a question, I typically proceed by seeking an answer in the following way:

- Spend a few minutes (in some cases, a few hours) using the search feature on message boards to see whether my question has been asked and answered previously.

- Check whether an FAQ section answers common questions (usually a separate forum or "sticky" thread). Only after I have exhausted these avenues do I register an account and post to the board/forum.

✔ **When you register, let people know about you.** You will be less faceless (and will receive many more helpful responses) if your profile lists such basic information as your geographic location, Web or club affiliations, hobbies, and interests.

Never, ever, type in all caps or alternating caps or engage in flame-baiting tactics likely to upset the community. There is a hierarchy to these forums, established over time, and people do spend a lot of their time there. People are proud (and sometimes sensitive) about their cars and their automotive accomplishments, and being disrespectful of others in the forums won't net you any friends, and such behavior may even get you banned.

Treat these virtual communities as though they're a real community in which you are the newcomer, and you're more likely to be well received.

You might see me browsing in these sites. My handle is "DavidV" or "BoostedMR2."

Asian brands

Perhaps more than any other grouping of cars, the leading Asian platforms for car modders, which include Honda, Toyota, Nissan, Mazda, Mitsubishi, and Subaru, have the largest and most active Internet message boards and car communities in cyberspace. If you're at all interested in hacking or modding one of these cars, you should have no problem finding more than adequate resources online. To get you started, I've listed a few of my personal favorites below. But this, of course, only represents the tip of the iceberg.

Toyota products

Despite the undeniable global popularity of Honda vehicles as the tuner platform of choice for car modding enthusiasts, Toyota has among its current and past offerings several notable enthusiast-oriented cars, including the near limitless power of the Supra, the exotic mid-engine MR2, and, within its Lexus line, the Altezza/IS200/IS300 and the Soarer/SC300, not to mention its quirky Scion offerings.

✔ **Toyota MR2:** `www.mr2oc.com`

As an owner of an MR2, I read this board almost every day. It's a terrific spot to exchange information on all three generations of Toyota's mid-engine sports car.

This is a great place to get some insight into turbocharger and super-charger tuning theory because these cars came equipped with both devices at various points.

✔ **Toyota Supra:** `www.mkiv.com`

Right off the bat, these guys can be opinionated, to put it politely, and while you may not share their belief that the mighty MKIV Supra is infal-lible, or that the BPU++++ is the most meaningful way to categorize per-formance modifications, you can't get away from the fact that if monster horsepower imports strike your fancy, this is where to read about them. Discussions on 700, 800, or 900+ hp cars are no big deal here. If big turbo power is what you are after, look no further.

✔ **Lexus IS300:** `www.is300.net`

This is not yet a hugely established board, but the turbocharged IS300s out there are a fun read. Talk about a sleeper. I expect big things for this board after the next generation IS300 is released.

✔ **Scion:** `www.scionlife.com/forums/`

If these cool-looking little cars are where it's at for you, this is where you want to be. Perhaps more so than any other board, on this one, you know that Big Brother is watching closely.

Honda products

Possibly more than any manufacturer, Honda/Acura has made significant inroads in the enthusiast community, with easy adaptability within its various engine and vehicle offerings and a terrific mix of both front-wheel and rear-wheel drive platforms, ranging from the humble Civic to the S2000, and ulti-mately the NSX:

✔ **Honda Civic:** `www.clubsi.com`

Although named after the Si model of Honda's ubiquitous Civic, the high-est designation sold in the U.S. (U.S. buyers were never offered the Type R variants), Club Si is an excellent all-around Civic performance resource. In fact, because of the great similarity across the entire Honda/Acura model range, this site represents a good starting point for anyone getting started in the world of Honda performance.

✔ **Honda performance:** `www.superhonda.net`

This site is a bit broader in scope than Club Si, and often covers more technical subjects. SuperHonda.com represents another great resource, whether you're seeking information on basic bolt-on performance upgrades, or higher-level ECU hacks and custom forced induction applications.

✔ **Honda/Acura performance:** www.templeofvtec.net

The granddaddy of Honda/Acura performance sites, the Temple of VTEC has fallen off significantly since its heyday in activity, as new Honda and Acura performance sites have cropped up to pull away discussions from what was once the central online meeting point for Honda/Acura enthusiasts. Nonetheless, the Temple of VTEC still represents a solid resource for learning about upgrading your Honda/Acura.

✔ **Acura NSX:** www.nsxprime.com

This board isn't as active as some others, but if the archetype of Japanese super cars intrigues you, this is the place to find out more about it.

✔ **Honda S2000:** www.s2ki.com

More active than the NSX board, and with a great general-interest car forum to top it off, s2ki is a fun site for S2000 and general car enthusiasts alike.

s2ki.com seems to get all the good car-related videos first.

Mazda

Nowhere near the size of Honda/Acura and Toyota, Mazda nonetheless is responsible for bringing some innovative and highly capable performance vehicles to the arena of car modders around the world, including the MX5/Miata and the rotary-powered RX7 and RX8:

✔ **Miata:** www.miata.net

Not only a great Mazda site, but you would be hard pressed to find a better resource for intelligent discussions on handling and suspension setup.

✔ **RX-7:** www.rx7club.com

If Wankel engines are your thing, or you just want the absolute most detail-oriented discussion on detonation control, this is your destination. This is a very active board with some very creative minds.

Mitsubishi products

The following sites are great sources of information on Mitsubishis and similar Chrysler products:

✔ **Mitsubishi Lancer:** www.evolutionm.net

Whether it's the base model Lancer, Ralliart, Evo, MR, or other Lancer-platform-based car, this is where to talk shop.

✔ **Diamond Star Motors:** www.dsmtalk.com

This is the site to check out if you are interested in the offerings of Diamond Star Motors, whether it's the Eclipse/Talon or the 3000GT/Stealth.

Other Asian brands

Whether you drive the technological tour de force known as the Skyline GTR, or one of the 300ZX or 350Z variants, let alone cult classics like the Sentra SE-R, there's no doubt that Nissan has its own modification-friendly and highly capable vehicles:

✔ **Nissan:** www.freshalloy.com and www.nissanforums.com

These sites are terrific places to find out more about Nissan cars and trucks.

Terry Heick, contributing editor to this book, has written some wonderful articles on Fresh Alloy. Mike Kojima is the renowned engineering guru behind Nissanforums.com.

✔ **Subaru:** www.i-club.com and www.clubwrx.net

These sites are the places for discussion. Whether you are worried about the "glass transmission" or just want to gloat about how the STi trumps the Evo (or does it?), this is the place for you.

European brands

Whether you drive one of the original Volkswagen "hot hatches" (the Golf/GTI), or you're a *roundel* fan and dream of a track-prepared E30 or E46 BMW M3, the European cars of both yesterday and today offer compelling platforms for modification, from mild to wild, encompassing nearly any budget and experience level. Aftermarket support for European cars has historically been as strong as those from Asia, and there is no limit to the breadth and scope of projects available to the Euro car tuner:

✔ **BMW:** www.roadfly.org/bmw/forums

This forum is a great resource for fans of the Roundel. This board can be agonizing to navigate when doing research, thanks to its archaic layout, but it's still one of the leading BMW discussion sites on the Net.

✔ **Lotus Elise:** www.elisetalk.com/forums

Colin Chapman's vision lives on in the ultimate case for power/weight ratio. The Elise has been a long time coming to the United States, and this board has one of the most rabid and devoted followings around.

✔ **Volkswagen/Audi:** www.vwvortex.com

   This site is a terrific place to find out more about Volkswagen and Audi cars. Also happens to have one of the best car lounges around with great posts on all types of cars.

American brands

From their heyday of hot-rodding in the 1950s and 1960s, through the oil crisis lean years of the 1970s and 1980s, and the current renaissance from the 1990s and beyond, American muscle in all of its guises has proven to be among the most durable, lasting, and consistent performers for automotive performance enthusiasts. Whether your idea of American performance conjures images of a '55 Chevy or a Dodge SRT-4, the global aftermarket industry has never neglected automotive performance coming from Detroit.

✔ **Mustang:** www.stangnet.com

   Catering to all generations of pony car owners, including the 5.0 Fox Body crowd through to Ford's innovative 2005 iteration of the classic Mustang model, StangNet offers a world of performance discussions and insights for the classic "little car with a big engine" crowd.

✔ **Corvette:** www.corvetteforum.com

   Yes, I read up on Corvettes occasionally. Shocking, but these guys first turned me onto the wonderful line of Zaino waxes, so I have to at least give them credit for that. They also happen to know a thing or two about big displacement late model horsepower — mostly of the normally aspirated variety.

✔ **Camaros/Firebirds:** www.ls1.com

   Even more shocking, yes, I lurk here too. Again, this site is a surprisingly fun-to-read board and another Zaino-fueled haven for detailing fanatics. The LS1 engine has a devoted following, and this is a terrific place to discover more about those engines — if only to know what you are up against at the traffic lights.

The list goes on and on. You'll soon find you have your own list of favorites that may or may not have anything to do with the particular car you drive. Some are for detailing tips, others for technical innovations, and still others for the sheer humor of reading about people who know less than you — whatever your level of knowledge might be. Add to this list the regional forums for car clubs and events in your area, and you have a virtually infinite wealth of knowledge at your fingertips. Thanks to the Internet, you can hang out in all the right places (and the wrong ones too) to find out what works (and what doesn't work) when modifying or hacking your car.

General Information

Some of the best automotive sites on the Internet have no make or model affiliation whatsoever, but are invaluable resources regardless of what is parked in your garage or driveway. Each of these sites will provide plenty of food for thought and innovative problem-solving approaches in your car hacking and modding endeavors.

Autospeed

www.autospeed.com

Putting aside the fact that you'll smirk when a car hood is called a *bonnet* and that some of the people being interviewed are completely unfamiliar to you, Autospeed is probably the single best resource for intelligent discussions on technical-minded subjects pertaining to modifying your car.

A subscription-based news site that also features an online store, Autospeed becomes the perfect next step for further exploration of subjects introduced in this book. For example, whether you are interested in building your own intercooler water sprayer or simply want to find out a bit more about the engine management systems discussed in this book, you'll find that Autospeed has well-written, technical-minded content that is well worth the price of the subscription.

The fact that Autospeed also has new car reviews on models not available elsewhere in the world, feature articles on tuner cars from down under, and a store front that carries a number of interesting items (yes, they ship internationally) gives you have all the makings for hours of entertaining and informative Web browsing.

How Stuff Works

www.howstuffworks.com

As a reference for understanding how common automotive systems work, How Stuff Works is a goldmine of information. How Stuff Works is (as the name implies) an encyclopedic catchall for looking up difficult-to-understand concepts. For example, you may be familiar with the performance advantages of a limited-slip differential, but may not know how one operates internally (what *differentiates the differentials,* you might say).

How Stuff Works supplements its clear and concisely written text with excellent illustrative material (sometimes animated) and links to further reading on the subject. How Stuff Works is a perfect companion piece to the subjects addressed within the pages of this book.

Autopia

www.autopia.org

Autopia is a comprehensive resource for automotive detailing information on line. If you're a pro-level detailer looking for tips on ordering in bulk and billing your services, or if you've never washed a car before in your life and want to find out whether it's okay to use steel wool to remove bird droppings from your hood (drop the steel wool — *now*), Autopia has the information you crave.

The best part about Autopia is that it presents a large cross-section of voices. There are the folks who are looking for the quickest and most efficient regimen for keeping their cars basically clean and presentable, and there are the guys and gals who are up at 3 a.m. applying their 120th coat of Zaino, scrubbing the wheel wells, and obsessing over whether the license plate bolts are oriented the same way (you know who you are!).

When doing research on Autopia, it's easy to get caught up in seemingly endless debates on the merits of product X versus product Y (each has its advocates and detractors), but as a rule

✔ Your finish only looks as good as your prep work allows.

✔ Technique counts for at least as much as the products being used.

Babel Fish and Google

http://world.altavista.com

www.google.com

When it comes time to take your car to the next level, and you have become bored of what you can find out from local enthusiasts, consider broadening your horizons. If you have a German car, consider looking at what the Germans are doing to tune your make and model. If you car is Japanese, chances are that the guys in Japan are at least a year ahead of the curve compared to what is being done in the United States or elsewhere.

The best way to go about it is to use Google just as you normally might, but to limit your search to the language used in the countries in which you are interested. One great way to get started is to search by engine or chassis code. I have found a number of great MR2-related sites, for example, by searching for the chassis "SW20" or engine "3SGTE" as used in Japanese language sites. From there, I can usually quickly eliminate the commercial sites that hold little interest and skip straight to the enthusiast sites for MR2 owners and racers in Japan.

Of course, once there, it all looks like gibberish unless you happen to speak and read Japanese (I don't). This is where Alta Vista's Babel Fish comes into play. Using Babel Fish, an online translator, you can either enter the URL and have Babel Fish do the rest, translating the entire site into the language of your choice (several are offered), or for complex Flash sites that don't readily allow for this URL-based translation, simply copy and past the text into Babel Fish and translate it that way.

What you end up with after doing this is a very rough, and often funny, translation of the original (I had no idea that "urchins" were such a dominant part of the MR2), but the gist is all there and readily understandable.

Grassroots Motorsports

www.grmotorsports.com

One of the best online resources for practical car mods is the Web site for Grassroots Motorsports, a magazine for people who enjoy making their cars go faster without spending a whole lot of money.

Motorsport Sites

Ultimately, a majority of car modding enthusiasts end up wanting to test the enhancements and alterations that they make to their cars. Even if your initial goals don't include competitive motor sports, the following Web sites will help guide you to the only safe and reliable means of pushing yourself and your car to its limits: a controlled environment off of public roadways.

SCCA

www.scca.org

The SCCA (Sports Car Club of America) is a terrific starting point for hacking and modding cars — especially if you intend to compete with your car at either a weekend autocross or rallycross or a sanctioned track race.

The SCCA site allows you to become familiar with not only the SCCA events available in your region, but also the classing guidelines that allow you to know going in what types of modifications and changes can be made to your car to allow you to remain competitive in your class, without immediately getting yourself bumped into a class dominated by highly modified, big-budget cars.

The safety guidelines used by the SCCA for its events are a great checklist for ensuring that your car is safe and sound for serious use — whether at an SCCA event or elsewhere.

For you "all show, no go" folks, the SCCA also offers links and information for classic car events and resources — so now there is no excuse for not getting started on reviving that old rusty Fiat you have stashed away behind your tool shed.

NHRA

www.nhra.org

The National Hot Rod Association (NHRA) is aimed more at the classic and muscle car crowd, including hot rods and street rods, as well as the straight-line drag crowd.

Like the SCCA, the NHRA has its own set of safety and classing guidelines that are a terrific resource — whether or not you intend on ever entering an NHRA sanctioned event. Also, like the SCCA, the NHRA site is a portal to finding out more about regional shows, clubs, and events.

Drifting.com

www.drifting.com

Drifting, the newest form of motor sports, likened by some as the figure skating of the automotive racing world, is growing by leaps and bounds both in the U.S. and elsewhere around the world. Started by Japanese automotive enthusiasts interested in displaying how far sideways they could slide their cars on winding mountain roads in Japan, the sport/art of drifting has caught hold and become one of the most hyped, if not enjoyed, forms of performance tuning and driving in recent times.

As with nearly any form of motor sports, drifting has its own preferred platforms (AE86 Toyota Corollas, known as *Hachi-Rokus,* and Nissan 240SX Silvia conversions are the current most popular drift cars) as well as set-up techniques (it isn't unusual to find $900 cars with $5,000 or more in LSD and suspension upgrades). Beyond the car itself, you must master at least half a dozen different drift techniques to be competitive in the drift arena.

Drifting.com is one of the more comprehensive drift-oriented databases, full of useful and up-to-date information and links for both new and seasoned drifters alike. Even if you have never thought of drifting your car before, Drifting.com makes for an interesting read on this dynamic form of automotive performance.

Aftermarket Parts

For those who crave the latest rare Japan-market parts, but are not fortunate enough to have a Super Autobacs down the street, sites like Taka Kaira provide not only a means of buying these much coveted parts and having them delivered straight to your door, but also give you an insight into the emerging trends and technologies in Japan. Likewise, SEMA, which represents the interests of all specialty equipment automotive manufacturers, and hosts annual trade shows in the U.S. showcasing emerging automotive technology, also provides an invaluable insight into industry trends and developments.

Taka Kaira

www.takakaira.com

More than just a virtual storefront for westerners to get their hands on Japanese import performance goodies, Taka Kaira is sufficiently up-to-date in a wide arena of automotive tuning bits, from body kits to exhausts and everything in between, for such a wide range of Japanese cars that it makes for wonderful window shopping — even if you don't have so much as a penny to spare.

If you're from Japan or Southern California, you're already familiar with the brick-and-mortar automotive chain known as Super Autobacs, catering to Japanese performance enthusiasts. For everyone else, Taka Kaira is as close as you can come to having access to a Super Autobacs. While Taka Kaira's prices tend to be on the high side of "it costs *how* much?!?" the shipping is fast and reliable and customer support is better than most.

SEMA

www.sema.org

SEMA (Specialty Equipment Market Association) is a useful online resource for several reasons:

✔ It lists the dates and times for the annual trade shows hosted by SEMA, including the SEMA show in Las Vegas and the International Auto Salon in Los Angeles, both of which are fascinating glimpses into up-and-coming aftermarket performance industry developments.

✔ SEMA has a host of useful legislative and economic development concerns focusing on the performance aftermarket arena:

- If you've ever had a dealership deny warranty coverage on your car because it has been modified, SEMA has information on the Magnuson-Moss Warranty Act, an important piece of legislation that it helped pass, which protects you against such a blanket denial of coverage.

- SEMA lists useful legislative links (including those exhaust noise regulations).

- Non-SEMA members can access a variety of research tools on the performance aftermarket industry plus the SEMA classified ads for everything from general employment at SEMA-member companies to industry rep positions.

- SEMA members can access up-to-date, comprehensive databases to further help in their online research.

Chapter 26

Ten Car Modding Problems

*T*his chapter covers ten common problems that you may encounter in the course of modding your car. Of course, just listing a bunch of problems isn't very helpful, so I also cover the fixes, workarounds, or advice on making the best of the problems.

Budgeting Time

You might think it's obvious that things often take much longer to finish than you expect them to at first blush. This applies to small and big projects alike. For those of you used to working with automotive shop manuals, you already know that basic maintenance times not only assume some familiarity with the systems involved, and the availability of special service tools where applicable, but also assume that the car being worked on is in good serviceable order. A bolt can take ten seconds to remove . . . or six hours if the bolt is rusted, seized, breaks off, and/or requires the threads to be retapped. Now, add to this the fact that many, if not most, aftermarket performance and cosmetic parts come with woefully inadequate instructions, often poorly translated or missing altogether, and the parts themselves have less R&D time invested in assuring their standardization (meaning they might not fit properly), and it becomes clear that installing an aftermarket "upgrade" can double or triple the amount of time that installing a factory part might take.

Now, this assumes that the parts and tools are in hand and ready to go. However, what happens when you have put in for time off of work to complete a project and, lo and behold, the parts don't arrive on schedule? Seasoned car modders know that you never, ever begin prep work unless you have the parts needed in hand and ready to go. It doesn't matter if you have a tracking number in hand and the friendly neighborhood FedEx or UPS delivery driver assures you that the parts are on his truck and ready to be delivered — without the parts in hand, nothing should come off the car. The reason for this is simple enough: Oftentimes, the wrong parts are shipped, the parts arrive damaged or do not fit, or some other glitch stalls the project. It's far more prudent to leave everything as it is rather than to risk putting the car back together while all of the hiccups are sorted out.

Time, as the old adage goes, is money. Remember not to waste it. If a part is going to need to be cryogenically frozen, shot peened, chrome plated, or powder coated prior to installation, make sure that the appointment to have this work done is ready to go and confirmed. If you need to set aside time to test fit the parts before sending them back out for these processes, be sure to do so (incidentally, this is always a good idea — there is nothing quite as disappointing as a beautifully chromed intercooler pipe that doesn't fit and can't be returned because it has been modified). If specialty fluids are needed, including high-dollar synthetic lubricants or gear oils (special note to you folks buying limited-slip differentials), make sure that you have sourced these fluids before starting a job or risk days or weeks of delays. If there is even the remote chance that you might need access to a welder, and you happen to be starting a job on a weekend, make sure that you know someone who can help on his or her day off. The same goes if you get stalled on a project and need a lift or hydraulic press. Make sure that you know ahead of time who will be around to help bail you out when your project runs overtime, it's 3 a.m. on a Saturday morning, and you have half a clutch job completed.

Budgeting Finances

So . . . you're thinking of picking up a turbo kit for your Honda Civic. Less than $900 buys you a "kit" at eBay or from your local performance shop. Sounds tempting, doesn't it? Would you still be so quick to click the Buy It Now! button if you knew that the fuel injectors, pump, piggyback controller, intercooler, hoses, clamps, and assorted supporting modifications totaled $1,500 or more? What about the fact that your local performance shop is going to estimate eight hours to install the kit for you at $95 per hour, and that eventually you'll get a call letting you know that the actual install time with custom fabrication was closer to 12 hours. The local powder coaters and polishers will charge another $200 to provide their services, and the local Dyno tuner will take another $700 or more to properly tune the kit. The clutch will give up the ghost within 500 miles after installation of the turbo kit ($900 parts plus $500 installation), and the local police will have written you up for an illegally modified car and/or some other moving violation while you are enjoying your new turbo, putting another $300 or more into the hands of your local municipality.

The $900 turbo kit doesn't seem like such a great deal in hindsight, does it? The performance aftermarket is brimming with stories of projects quickly ballooning out of proportion. If your gut tells you that you might be stretched short on money or, as discussed in the preceding section, for time, then flag the project and revisit it later. It takes enormous willpower to resist the siren song of a promising modification, but those of us who have been down this scenic and often ugly road one too many times can tell you from experience that sometimes (often) the smartest move is doing nothing. If you do decide to take the plunge, have cash reserves ready to go to help grease the hands of all the people that will be helping you along the way. If your car must be running for you to get to work on Monday, and someone needs to open their shop to you late on Sunday night to help you complete your project, chances are, a bribe of a six pack of beer with a bow on it is not going to cut it.

Legal Concerns

Some modifications are illegal. Some modifications are, for all intents and purposes, irreversible. Some modifications are both illegal and irreversible.

When performing modifications to your car, keep in mind that not only do illegal modifications end up costing you money and time when being cited for vehicle code infractions, but they also seriously compromise your use and enjoyment of the car. Let's face it: Any modification that knocks a few tenths off your quarter mile time is bound to be fun. However, how much fun is it in the real world when those few tenths cause your heart to skip a beat every time you spot a patrol car? It's no fun feeling like a criminal because your exhaust is too loud or your car is too low.

In my immediate group of friends, we always have the guys that show up to a track event between 2 and 3 a.m., exhausted and bleary eyed. While the vast majority of the track regulars have had a chance to drive up together during the day, enjoy a nice dinner and drinks, and turn in early the night before a track day, the twilight-hours crowd is unable to enjoy such a leisurely journey to the track. By virtue of their illegally modified cars, and general paranoia of being cited on the way to the track, they drive their cars in at the dead of night, coasting in to the parking lot as everyone else is sleeping. Are their cars faster and more fun? Sure. But unless you have a truck and trailer to tow them, these modified street machines are also a serious lifestyle compromise.

Warranty Concerns

Modifications that are easily reversible and undetectable are also of paramount importance when it comes to maintaining your new car's warranty. Let's face it: Cars break. They are mechanical objects consisting of highly complex systems, some of which fail prematurely. If a new car dealer can find a way to void your warranty — even if in outright violation of the Magnuson-Moss Warranty Act — you better believe that it will.

If a number of cars are suffering from, for example, a main bearing failure which would otherwise be covered under the manufacturer's powertrain warranty, and your car happens to have a modified air intake — something that has nothing to do with the longevity of the main bearing — you better believe that your local dealership service center is not only going to deny the warranty coverage that would otherwise have applied to fixing your car, but is going to log a note in your file accessible by all dealers in your region (some can even do this on a national level) informing them that your powertrain warranty is now null and void, regardless of what ailments your car may have.

This activity can and should be fought when it happens. However, if you don't have the fighting spirit, and your modifications are not easily reversible, prepare for the worst. Some cars rarely require warranty work and are a safer bet to modify than others. However, if your make and model is known to have a glitch or two that might need to be addressed sometime during its warranty period, you might be better off either staying with less invasive modifications or forgoing modifications altogether until the warranty period has expired.

Resale Value

Modified cars are generally worth less on the secondary market than unmodified cars. Mind you, the previous sentence said "worth less" not "worthless," so they *do* have value — both to the owner and to those car aficionados who can appreciate a properly modified car. However, to the general public, a performance modification to a car — no matter how benign or well executed — triggers a red flag that the car has been raced or otherwise abused. Even those buyers who don't believe this to be true will nonetheless make the argument in order to hammer down the asking price. New car dealers are loath to accept modified cars as trade-ins because it both restricts their appeal and because they need to vouch for the safety, legality, and emissions compliance of the vehicles they sell. Don't expect top dollar for your modified car as a trade-in. In the world of private-party sales, you will find yourself banking on the fact that someone else agrees with your cosmetic and/or performance ideals when looking for a car to buy. Even those that do like what you have done will likely have wanted the satisfaction of saving a bit of cash and having carried out the mods themselves.

Bottom line: Modify your car to your heart's content, but don't be surprised when the $15,000 you spent modifying your car nets you a $6,000 loss off the value of your car when it comes time for resale, compared to an equivalent unmodified car.

Free Advice

As the old adage goes, free advice is worth what you pay for it. People educate themselves and train to carry out expert modifications, and when they have become competent and recognized in this arena, tend to charge for their services either as tuners, crew chiefs, or build consultants. If someone offers you their advice on how to create the perfect fuel map, properly set up your suspension, or take out a stain on your hood with a Brillo pad and a jar of mayonnaise, they may know what they are talking about, or they may be certifiably insane — but one thing remains clear: They will not take liability for any harm you cause to your car or yourself.

This point may seem fairly obvious, but too many people rely on free advice because it is free and available everywhere. Your mailman, your mom's friend, and your local priest probably all have opinions on what would look/work great on your car. Are you going to listen to them? The funny thing is, if you are getting your input online, you probably are listening to them because they are the people putting in their two cents on the Internet forums.

As a rule, people who are paid to know what they are talking about, with rare exceptions, do not give free advice on message boards. Or if they do, they have a commercial interest or other agenda prompting the "help" that they are offering. Just like a doctor, lawyer, or other professional, experts in the automotive arena will tell you that there is no free lunch. If you value the advice of the town people of Anytown, U.S.A., you will find it for free in great abundance. If you are after the leading industry experts' opinions on how to carry out a modification plan for your car, expect to pay for it.

Knowing When to Stop

Perhaps the most important mistake novice enthusiasts make in modifying their cars is not recognizing when to step back and leave it alone. Modifications are a tricky business. They can bring out the very best in your car, and set it apart from the crowd in a good way, or they can bring out the very worst and make you the subject of ridicule. Even the best and most experienced car modders strike out once in a while, so if your last few mods have been home runs knocked straight out of the park, don't feel pressure to swing and miss.

Experience teaches that, with rare exceptions, the most impressive cars from both a performance and cosmetic standpoint came together over a long stretch of time. The 1992 E30 BMW M3 that looks so terrific today may have been in the works for over 12 years. Odds are that it did not come together in a flurry of activity in a couple months. Cars that are built quickly fail to provide a sense of perspective on the overall project. They often have stronger elements thrown together with weaker elements in an overall project that carries a tinge of mediocrity.

Time is your friend. So is experience. Know that it's okay to step back and take a breather. You'll both enjoy your mods more, having seen what each brings to the table before adding the next, and you'll better be able to get a clear picture of where you are ultimately headed. Best of all, the prospect of a suddenly bankrupted project can be kept at bay by stretching out the process over a longer period of time. When someone buys a new car, there is no taking a break from the sting of monthly car payments. Of course, the beauty of car mods is that you can and should take a break. Let a month go by without spending anything. Let a few months slide. Wait and see if you feel as strongly about your next mod after sleeping on it for a while as you did when you were first ready to pick up the phone and charge it to plastic. Fighting the urge to mod is one of the most difficult battles of all, but if you learn to savor the wait and enjoy what you have now without getting ahead of yourself, you'll come to enjoy years of modding more than by getting ahead of yourself and trying to build Rome in a day.

Selling Parts

Another common mistake made by novice modders is knowing which parts to sell and when. In general, if you might need a part to pass emissions testing, make your car street legal, or maintain your warranty, you have no business selling it. These parts should remain carefully protected and preserved in your garage. Other parts can be let go, albeit with some care. Perhaps you just ordered a new carbon fiber hood and would like to make room in your garage and pay off the credit card by selling your factory hood. This may not be a bad idea. But what if the fitment on the new hood is horrible? And even if you love the new hood for the first week, what if fashion changes and that hood now makes your car look completely out of date?

The best recent example of this, and overall the best arena to see what happens to people when they are too hasty to follow fashion and sell old parts, is in the wonderful and wondrous world of wheels. There must have been a period in the early 1990s when three spoke rims were the thing to have. Even today, you can see used cars up for sale still wearing these goofy-looking and dated wheels, with all kinds of snide remarks being made on message boards all over the Internet every time a picture is posted of such a car for sale. If the owner had the original factory rims, the car would sell for far more, and make for a respectable purchase. However, wearing the equivalent of the leisure suit (which also must have seemed like a good idea in the 1970s), the car becomes a parody of itself. The same can be said of chrome fender trim, rear window louvers, and Baby on Board stickers.

Bottom line: You have little control over whether your mods are going to be regarded as timeless or will quickly fade into objects of ridicule. Beyond the practical concerns of legality/warranty/reliability, bear in mind that what seems like a good idea today may quickly sour into a regret tomorrow. Even worse, the factory wheels/seats/body panels that you sell today may be worth a small fortune as time passes, while the "upgrades" become worthless.

Buying out of Desperation

This could almost fall under the "Knowing When to Stop" section as the corollary concept of knowing when to start. If you undertake a project before you know that you have all the bits and pieces needed to carry it out successfully, you have effectively painted yourself into a corner. This means that, rather than having the luxury of shopping around for the best deal on everything from small nuts and bolts to larger items that might have been overlooked, you are forced to spend now, spend freely, and ship expedited. Negotiating power is not on your side. Lest you think this only applies to parts, buying out of desperation applies equally well to paying top dollar for shops to accommodate you after hours, bump other customers to make room for your car, and/or tune your car in the dead of night. These perks don't come cheaply, and begging and groveling will only get you so far. Grandstanding about how important your project is to the magazines/sponsors/current presidential cabinet will do even less for you. When time has run out and the project must be completed quickly, money talks, and sellers can and will demand top dollar for their goods and/or services.

To avoid paying double or triple what you would otherwise need to spend, know when to start a project (that is, when you have everything), and know to budget plenty of extra time beyond what you think it could possibly take to get the job done. These few precautions could save you a small fortune and will no doubt bring your blood pressure way down from where it might otherwise be.

Selling a Failed/Incomplete Project

Perhaps you have ignored all of the preceding advice in this chapter, or life has just thrown you a curveball and you now have sextuplets on the way. If the project simply cannot, will not, or should not be completed — an often painful realization for car enthusiasts — then the next question becomes how to bow out gracefully and cut your losses.

A close friend of mine had a Toyota MR2 with nearly $70,000 (that's not a typo) invested in mods. After a botched rebuild, the motor was blowing massive amounts of oil past the piston rings. His options were as follows:

1. Place ad for sale: "$70,000 MR2 for sale. A bit smoky. $15,000 obo."

   However, this was unpalatable given that the car would amount to a more than $50,000 loss. You can expect to lose money on modified cars, but no sane person wants to lose $50,000 on one. You might question the sanity of anyone willing to put $50,000 into an MR2 in the first place, but there had to be a sane way to preserve as much of his investment as possible.

2. Spend $5,000 to $10,000 making it right. In his case, this would have been either a competent rebuild, or importing a Japanese spec rear clip and swapping over the core mechanical parts.

   Of course, if someone is tapped out of time, money, patience, or all three, this is not much help. Further, there was no assurance that he would not be throwing good money after bad. If he could not find a competent shop to do the rebuild in his area (it was a bit of a crap shoot, given his lack of success with three prior rebuilds) or if the used parts came in from Japan needing rebuilding, he would be even worse off than he already was. When the stakes have been raised, one can't blame him for being averse to taking the risk.

3. Part the car out and start all over when the time is right.

   I'm happy to report that this option worked out well. My friend was able to recoup over $35,000 by selling off parts, a tremendous amount more than the car would have sold for with an engine on its last legs. He still lost a fair bit of money, granted, but less than he might otherwise have with the first two scenarios. This was no easy decision for him, and I spent many long nights listening to him moan about ripping his car apart piece by piece and selling it off, but in the end, the $35,000 allowed him to start fresh and acquire another MR2 that has won him accolades all over the country, including several big magazine features. He still misses his original "cursed" MR2, but he's happy with the decision to get out when he did. He is also well regarded in the MR2 community for helping a number of people source parts that they needed to complete their own projects cars, thanks to the sacrifice of his beloved but needy car.

The moral of this story is that it's okay, and often wise, to swallow your pride and bail out on a project car. However, when the time comes, weigh your options and strongly consider selling your car by individual parts rather than selling the whole thing as "90 percent complete," or "in need of TLC." One of the most effective ways to make this work is by setting up a Web page with a list of the parts you want to sell, including pictures, and provide tracking numbers as parts are sold off. eBay can also be a great resource for selling used parts, as can local online classified ad pages like www.craigslist.org.

Index

• **C** •

• F •

• L •

• **X** •

FOR DUMMIES®

The easy way to get more done and have more fun

PERSONAL FINANCE

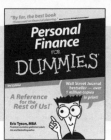

0-7645-5231-7

0-7645-2431-3

0-7645-5331-3

Also available:

Estate Planning For Dummies
(0-7645-5501-4)
401(k)s For Dummies
(0-7645-5468-9)
Frugal Living For Dummies
(0-7645-5403-4)
Microsoft Money "X" For
Dummies
(0-7645-1689-2)
Mutual Funds For Dummies
(0-7645-5329-1)

Personal Bankruptcy For
Dummies
(0-7645-5498-0)
Quicken "X" For Dummies
(0-7645-1666-3)
Stock Investing For Dummies
(0-7645-5411-5)
Taxes For Dummies 2003
(0-7645-5475-1)

BUSINESS & CAREERS

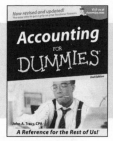

0-7645-5314-3

0-7645-5307-0

0-7645-5471-9

Also available:

Business Plans Kit For
Dummies
(0-7645-5365-8)
Consulting For Dummies
(0-7645-5034-9)
Cool Careers For Dummies
(0-7645-5345-3)
Human Resources Kit For
Dummies
(0-7645-5131-0)
Managing For Dummies
(1-5688-4858-7)

QuickBooks All-in-One Desk
Reference For Dummies
(0-7645-1963-8)
Selling For Dummies
(0-7645-5363-1)
Small Business Kit For
Dummies
(0-7645-5093-4)
Starting an eBay Business For
Dummies
(0-7645-1547-0)

HEALTH, SPORTS & FITNESS

0-7645-5167-1

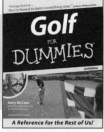

0-7645-5146-9

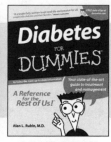

0-7645-5154-X

Also available:

Controlling Cholesterol For
Dummies
(0-7645-5440-9)
Dieting For Dummies
(0-7645-5126-4)
High Blood Pressure For
Dummies
(0-7645-5424-7)
Martial Arts For Dummies
(0-7645-5358-5)
Menopause For Dummies
(0-7645-5458-1)

Nutrition For Dummies
(0-7645-5180-9)
Power Yoga For Dummies
(0-7645-5342-9)
Thyroid For Dummies
(0-7645-5385-2)
Weight Training For Dummies
(0-7645-5168-X)
Yoga For Dummies
(0-7645-5117-5)

Available wherever books are sold.
Go to www.dummies.com or call 1-877-762-2974 to order direct.

FOR DUMMIES®

A world of resources to help you grow

HOME, GARDEN & HOBBIES

Feng Shui For Dummies
0-7645-5295-3

Gardening For Dummies
0-7645-5130-2

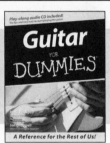
Guitar For Dummies
0-7645-5106-X

Also available:

Auto Repair For Dummies
(0-7645-5089-6)

Chess For Dummies
(0-7645-5003-9)

Home Maintenance For Dummies
(0-7645-5215-5)

Organizing For Dummies
(0-7645-5300-3)

Piano For Dummies
(0-7645-5105-1)

Poker For Dummies
(0-7645-5232-5)

Quilting For Dummies
(0-7645-5118-3)

Rock Guitar For Dummies
(0-7645-5356-9)

Roses For Dummies
(0-7645-5202-3)

Sewing For Dummies
(0-7645-5137-X)

FOOD & WINE

Cooking For Dummies
0-7645-5250-3

Cookies For Dummies
0-7645-5390-9

Wine For Dummies
0-7645-5114-0

Also available:

Bartending For Dummies
(0-7645-5051-9)

Chinese Cooking For Dummies
(0-7645-5247-3)

Christmas Cooking For Dummies
(0-7645-5407-7)

Diabetes Cookbook For Dummies
(0-7645-5230-9)

Grilling For Dummies
(0-7645-5076-4)

Low-Fat Cooking For Dummies
(0-7645-5035-7)

Slow Cookers For Dummies
(0-7645-5240-6)

TRAVEL

Italy For Dummies
0-7645-5453-0

Hawaii For Dummies
0-7645-5438-7

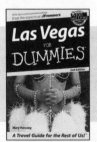
Las Vegas For Dummies
0-7645-5448-4

Also available:

America's National Parks For Dummies
(0-7645-6204-5)

Caribbean For Dummies
(0-7645-5445-X)

Cruise Vacations For Dummies 2003
(0-7645-5459-X)

Europe For Dummies
(0-7645-5456-5)

Ireland For Dummies
(0-7645-6199-5)

France For Dummies
(0-7645-6292-4)

London For Dummies
(0-7645-5416-6)

Mexico's Beach Resorts For Dummies
(0-7645-6262-2)

Paris For Dummies
(0-7645-5494-8)

RV Vacations For Dummies
(0-7645-5443-3)

Walt Disney World & Orlando For Dummies
(0-7645-5444-1)

Available wherever books are sold. Go to www.dummies.com or call 1-877-762-2974 to order direct.

FOR DUMMIES®

Plain-English solutions for everyday challenges

COMPUTER BASICS

0-7645-0838-5   **0-7645-1663-9**   **0-7645-1548-9**

Also available:

PCs All-in-One Desk Reference For Dummies
(0-7645-0791-5)

Pocket PC For Dummies
(0-7645-1640-X)

Treo and Visor For Dummies
(0-7645-1673-6)

Troubleshooting Your PC For Dummies
(0-7645-1669-8)

Upgrading & Fixing PCs For Dummies
(0-7645-1665-5)

Windows XP For Dummies
(0-7645-0893-8)

Windows XP For Dummies Quick Reference
(0-7645-0897-0)

BUSINESS SOFTWARE

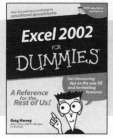  

0-7645-0822-9   **0-7645-0839-3**   **0-7645-0819-9**

Also available:

Excel Data Analysis For Dummies
(0-7645-1661-2)

Excel 2002 All-in-One Desk Reference For Dummies
(0-7645-1794-5)

Excel 2002 For Dummies Quick Reference
(0-7645-0829-6)

GoldMine "X" For Dummies
(0-7645-0845-8)

Microsoft CRM For Dummies
(0-7645-1698-1)

Microsoft Project 2002 For Dummies
(0-7645-1628-0)

Office XP For Dummies
(0-7645-0830-X)

Outlook 2002 For Dummies
(0-7645-0828-8)

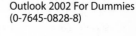

Get smart! Visit www.dummies.com

- **Find listings of even more *For Dummies* titles**

- **Browse online articles**

- **Sign up for Dummies eTips™**

- **Check out *For Dummies* fitness videos and other products**

- **Order from our online bookstore**

FOR DUMMIES®

Helping you expand your horizons and realize your potential

INTERNET

0-7645-0894-6

0-7645-1659-0

0-7645-1642-6

Also available:

America Online 7.0 For Dummies
(0-7645-1624-8)

Genealogy Online For Dummies
(0-7645-0807-5)

The Internet All-in-One Desk Reference For Dummies
(0-7645-1659-0)

Internet Explorer 6 For Dummies
(0-7645-1344-3)

The Internet For Dummies Quick Reference
(0-7645-1645-0)

Internet Privacy For Dummies
(0-7645-0846-6)

Researching Online For Dummies
(0-7645-0546-7)

Starting an Online Business For Dummies
(0-7645-1655-8)

DIGITAL MEDIA

0-7645-1664-7

0-7645-1675-2

0-7645-0806-7

Also available:

CD and DVD Recording For Dummies
(0-7645-1627-2)

Digital Photography All-in-One Desk Reference For Dummies
(0-7645-1800-3)

Digital Photography For Dummies Quick Reference
(0-7645-0750-8)

Home Recording for Musicians For Dummies
(0-7645-1634-5)

MP3 For Dummies
(0-7645-0858-X)

Paint Shop Pro "X" For Dummies
(0-7645-2440-2)

Photo Retouching & Restoration For Dummies
(0-7645-1662-0)

Scanners For Dummies
(0-7645-0783-4)

GRAPHICS

0-7645-0817-2

0-7645-1651-5

0-7645-0895-4

Also available:

Adobe Acrobat 5 PDF For Dummies
(0-7645-1652-3)

Fireworks 4 For Dummies
(0-7645-0804-0)

Illustrator 10 For Dummies
(0-7645-3636-2)

QuarkXPress 5 For Dummies
(0-7645-0643-9)

Visio 2000 For Dummies
(0-7645-0635-8)

Available wherever books are sold. Go to www.dummies.com or call 1-877-762-2974 to order direct.

FOR DUMMIES®

The advice and explanations you need to succeed

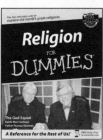

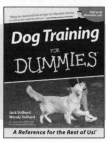

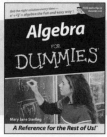

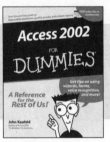